Chrystal Macmillan
1872–1937

Scottish Women Making History

Books in the series retell history through exploring the lives of Scottish women whose endeavours challenged the status quo and led to change and innovation in a male-dominated world. They were campaigners for equality, fighters for justice, artists, political leaders, authors, explorers, folklorists and more. Drawing on primary sources, each book tells the story of the woman's life in context, highlighting her contribution to history in Scotland and beyond. The series aims to bring Scottish women out of the shadows, relating their biographies to wider debates to focus on larger-frame connections and conclusions.

Published
Chrystal Macmillan, 1872–1937: Campaigner for Equality, Justice and Peace
Helen Kay and Rose Pipes

Forthcoming
Helen Crawfurd: Suffragette, Communist, Internationalist
Lesley Orr

Esther Inglis: Franco-Scottish Creative Woman
Georgianna Ziegler

edinburghuniversitypress.com/series/swmh

Chrystal Macmillan
1872–1937

Campaigner for Equality, Justice and Peace

Helen Kay and Rose Pipes

EDINBURGH
University Press

Edinburgh University Press is one of the leading university presses in the UK. We publish academic books and journals in our selected subject areas across the humanities and social sciences, combining cutting-edge scholarship with high editorial and production values to produce academic works of lasting importance. For more information visit our website: edinburghuniversitypress.com

© Helen Kay and Rose Pipes, 2024, 2025

Edinburgh University Press Ltd
13 Infirmary Street
Edinburgh EH1 1LT

First published in hardback by Edinburgh University Press 2024

Typeset in 10.5/13pt Sabon by
Manila Typesetting Company

A CIP record for this book is available from the British Library

ISBN 978 1 3995 1452 1 (hardback)
ISBN 978 1 3995 1453 8 (paperback)
ISBN 978 1 3995 1454 5 (webready PDF)
ISBN 978 1 3995 1455 2 (epub)

The right of Helen Kay and Rose Pipes to be identified as authors of this work has been asserted in accordance with the Copyright, Designs and Patents Act 1988 and the Copyright and Related Rights Regulations 2003 (SI No. 2498).

Published with the support of the University of Edinburgh Scholarly Publishing Initiatives Fund.

Contents

List of Figures	vi
Acknowledgements	vii
Abbreviations	ix
Introduction	1
1 The Edinburgh Years: Family, School, University and Beyond	6
2 Chrystal Macmillan and the Scottish Women Graduates' Case	21
3 Women, Suffrage and Parliament	37
4 Working for World Peace	65
5 Working with National Issues and British Organisations	87
6 Working with International Organisations	101
7 Entering the Legal Profession and Life at the Bar	125
8 The Nationality of Married Women	147
9 Death, Memorials and Recollections	177
10 Review and Conclusion	186
Appendix 1: Chrystal Macmillan's Membership of Committees, and Select Committees to which she gave evidence	194
Appendix 2: Twenty Resolutions from the International Women's Congress 1915	197
Appendix 3: List of visits undertaken by Women Envoys in 1915	199
Bibliography	201
Index	213

Figures

I.1	Chrystal Macmillan Building, Edinburgh University	4
1.1	Macmillan family in Corstorphine Hill House, c.1890	8
1.2	Young Chrystal Macmillan on her pony	9
1.3	Chrystal Macmillan and Form VI pupils with Miss Dove	12
1.4	Chrystal Macmillan, graduate	15
1.5	Funeral, John Macmillan, Edinburgh, 1901	16
2.1	Graduates at the House of Lords, 1908	27
3.1	Frances Simson, unknown, Chrystal Macmillan, NUWSS march, London, 1909	44
3.2	Scottish Federation of Women's Suffrage Societies, Glasgow, October 1913	51
3.3	NUWSS Scottish Summer School, St Andrews, 1913	58
4.1	International Women's Congress, 1915, platform party	72
4.2	IWC envoys waiting to meet King of Norway, 1915	76
4.3	IWC delegates with graduating class, Nursing School, Petrograd, 1915	77
4.4	Chrystal Macmillan and Jane Addams, WILPF Congress, Zurich, 1919	80
6.1	IWSA Board, Budapest, 1913	105
6.2	Meeting of the International Committee at the IWSA Congress, 1920	110
6.3	Chrystal Macmillan speaking, IWSA Congress, Rome, 1923	112
6.4	Chrystal Macmillan, President ODI, leads delegation, ILO, 1931	115
7.1	Chrystal Macmillan, barrister, 1924	132
8.1	Joint Demonstration on the Nationality of Married Women, The Hague, 1930	161
8.2	Women's Consultative Committee on Nationality of Married Women at the League of Nations, 1931	164
10.1	Portrait, Chrystal Macmillan, ODI Conference, Prague, 1933	189

Acknowledgements

We are very grateful to all the following people for providing encouragement, comments, information and support in the Chrystal Macmillan project and the writing of this book: Rosemary Auchmuty, Erika Rackley and Judith Bourne for their stimulating workshops on women and the law; Dorothy Page for her wonderful thesis, her hospitality and friendship, and her encouragement and advice on issues around the nationality of married women; Esther Breitenbach, Viv Cree, Elizabeth Ewan, Jane Grant and Siân Reynolds for comments and help with the text.

The archivists who helped guide us to appropriate files: Anna Towlson and Gillian Murphy, Women's Library, LSE, London; David Hays and postgraduate students in the WILPF archive at the University of Colorado, Boulder Libraries, Boulder, Colorado; Grant Buttars, University of Edinburgh Special Collections; Angela Tawse, Librarian, Queen Mary's Library, St Leonards School, St Andrews; Lesley Whitelaw and Barnaby Bryan, Middle Temple, London; Jacques Rodriguez, ILO, Geneva; Jacques Oberson, League of Nations Archive, UN, Geneva; George Watson's School, and Mary Erskine School, Edinburgh; Institute of Advanced Legal Studies, London.

The Macmillan family who have all been enthusiastic and supportive of the project: Ian Macmillan for sharing the treasures from Chrystal Macmillan's trunk; Hugh Macmillan for sharing data and photos from his unpublished manuscript on Chrystal and the Macmillan family; John Herdman for sharing photographs of Chrystal Macmillan; Chrystal Hart who holds Chrystal Macmillan's barrister wig; the late Ialeen Gibson Cowan who talked about meeting her great aunt, Chrys.

Janet Fenton and Elspeth King who initiated the research for the Gude Cause Project, and thereby an interest in the life of Chrystal Macmillan; Jenni Calder who made the initial connection to the Macmillan family;

Fiona Mackay, Professor of Politics at the University of Edinburgh who promoted the Chrystal Macmillan exhibition in 2015 and has always given us encouragement; Charlie Jeffery, now Vice Chancellor of York University, who, as Professor of Politics at the University of Edinburgh, supported the Chrystal Macmillan projects; Women's History Network, whose members have given criticism and encouragement on papers given by Helen Kay at conferences between 2012 and 2019.

Ersev Ersoy at Edinburgh University Press for commissioning the project, and to other EUP staff for their help at later stages.

Special thanks to our long-suffering partners, Kath Davies and the late Stefan Kay, who lived with us throughout our trials and triumphs in the research and the writing of this book.

Finally, if it is possible posthumously to thank someone whom one has never met, we want to acknowledge Chrystal Macmillan (1872–1937), politician, barrister, mathematician, writer and activist whose remarkable dedication to the goal of women's citizenship equality should be better known,[1] and we hope will be, following the publication of this monograph.

Note

1. With acknowledgement to Helen Irving, in whose book this tribute appeared. Helen Irving, *Citizenship, Alienage, and the Modern Constitutional State: A Gendered History* (Cambridge: Cambridge University Press, 2016), vi.

Abbreviations

AACW	All-Asian Conference of Women
AFL	Actresses Franchise League
AMSH	Association of Moral and Social Hygiene
BFUW	British Federation of University Women
COLPW	Committee for the Opening of the Legal Profession to Women
DORA	Defence of the Realm Act
EAUEW	Edinburgh Association for the University Education of Women
EC	Executive Committee
EFF	Electoral Fighting Fund
ELEA	Edinburgh Ladies Education Association
ENSWS	Edinburgh National Society for Women's Suffrage
ERI	Equal Rights International
EUWSS	Edinburgh University Women's Suffrage Society
GWSAWS	Glasgow and West of Scotland Association for Women's Suffrage
IACW	Inter-American Commission of Women
IAWSEC	International Alliance of Women for Suffrage and Equal Citizenship
ICW	International Council of Women
ICWPP	International Committee of Women for Permanent Peace
IFUW	International Federation of University Women
ILA	International Law Association
ILO	International Labour Organisation
IWC	International Women's Congress

IWSA	International Women Suffrage Alliance (after 1926 known as International Alliance of Women for Suffrage and Equal Citizenship)
LSE	London School of Economics
MP	Member of Parliament
NCCVD	National Council for Combatting Venereal Diseases
NCUMC	National Council for the Unmarried Mother and Her Child
NCW	National Council of Women (formerly known as NUWW)
NEC	National Executive Committee
NMWPBC	Nationality of Married Women Pass the Bill Committee
NUSEC	National Union of Societies for Equal Citizenship (formerly NUWSS)
NUWSS	National Union of Women's Suffrage Societies (later NUSEC)
NUWW	National Union of Women Workers
ODC	Open Door Council
ODI	Open Door International for the Emancipation of the Woman Worker
SFWSS	Scottish Federation of Women's Suffrage Societies
SNP	Scottish National Party
SUWSU	Scottish University Women's Suffrage Union
The League	League of Nations
WCC	Consultative Committee of Constitutional Women's Suffrage Societies (known as Women's Consultative Committee)
WCCN	Women's Consultative Committee on Nationality
WFL	Women's Freedom League
WILPF	Women's International League for Peace and Freedom
WIO	Women's International Organisation
WSPU	Women's Social and Political Union
WUWIC	World Union of Women for International Concord
YWCA	Young Women's Christian Association

Introduction

In this, the first of a series of monographs on 'overlooked Scottish women', the subject is Jessie Chrystal Macmillan, a Scotswoman, born in Edinburgh in 1872, whose remarkable achievements have until relatively recently been under-recorded; indeed, by the 1990s, even her family had little knowledge of the part she played during the early to mid-1900s as a vigorous campaigner for women's equality, a barrister and a much-admired and respected figure in the women's movement, both in the UK and internationally.

Unlike some of her contemporaries in the women's movement, such as Christobel Pankhurst, Flora Drummond, Eleanor Rathbone and Helena Normanton, Chrystal Macmillan (as she was always known) was neither flamboyant nor militant, and apart from her one moment in the headlines when she appeared in the House of Lords (see Chapter 2), her achievements received little press publicity. But while 'fame' eluded her, she was nevertheless a striking figure, very well known in feminist circles, both at home and internationally, and highly regarded by her colleagues for her persistence, strategic thinking, composure and reliability – all qualities that meant she was sought after as a leader and spokeswoman for many women's causes, and as a 'safe pair of hands' on committees. It was also due to these qualities that she was invited to speak in place of the Lord Advocate for Scotland at a dinner held to celebrate the passing of the Sex Disqualification (Removal) Act 1919, and that she was chosen to contribute an article on the legal position of women to the fourteenth edition of the *Encyclopaedia Britannica*.

To be 'overlooked' is not unusual for women of her generation: writing in the early 1990s, the Scottish women's historians Leah Leneman[1] and Elspeth King[2] both noted that, at that time, many historical studies ignored or only briefly mentioned the women's suffrage movement.

Also, as Elspeth King observed, the lack of women's history had resulted in little awareness of the struggles and political successes of previous generations of women.[3]

One reason why women such as Chrystal Macmillan have been largely absent from the historical record is that, until the mid-twentieth century, they were denied roles in those spheres of public life that would have brought them to public attention, and much of what they achieved was first forged behind the closed doors of committee rooms. As Vera Brittain wrote in 1929:

> The young professional woman should realize that her own happy situation would never have come about if, for over half a century, women had not been prepared to spend, without remuneration, the greater part of their lives in committee rooms and on public platforms.[4]

Chrystal Macmillan was very definitely one such woman; she belonged to that group of middle-class, highly educated and determined women of her generation (1872–1937) whose endeavours made possible so much of what women now consider to be their unquestionable rights, such as the right to vote, admission to the legal and other professions, and the right to retain their nationality on marriage. She was a member of the executive committees of several women's organisations and appeared on many platforms in all corners of her native Scotland, in the campaign for women's suffrage. It was a cause she continued to support after her move to London in 1913 – the city that became her home for the rest of her life, and where she trained to become a member of the English Bar.

What first brought Chrystal Macmillan's name to prominence was as a claimant for the right of Scottish women graduates to vote in elections for an MP to represent the Scottish universities. After the case was dismissed by the Scottish courts, she became the main appellant when the appeal was taken in the House of Lords. The press, beguiled and impressed by her youth, composure and striking hat, immediately dubbed her the 'Scottish Portia', but it was her brilliant advocacy, the thoroughness of her research and her impressive personal style that most impressed her compatriots, and made her a prime candidate for a leading role in the women's movement.

What is known of her contribution to women's organisations comes mainly from committee meeting minutes and press reports, which though inevitably limited, do provide valuable evidence on which the content of Chapters 2, 3, 4, 5, 6 and 8 is largely based. Organised thematically and broadly chronologically, these chapters focus on the causes and organisations to which Chrystal Macmillan devoted most of her time and energy, beginning with the Scottish women graduates' case in Chapter 2, then moving on to her role in the women's suffrage movement (Chapter 3).

Not long after her arrival in London, Chrystal Macmillan broadened the scope of her engagement with women's issues, becoming an active member of the executive committees of several women's national and international organisations. Prominent among them were the International Woman Suffrage Alliance (IWSA) and the International Council of Women (ICW). As secretary of the IWSA, Chrystal Macmillan became one of the chief architects and an organiser of the International Women's Congress, held in The Hague in April 1915 (Chapter 4). Attended by around 1,200 women from twelve countries, the highly ambitious aim of the Congress was to bring peace to warring countries through mediation, and would eventually lead to the establishment of the Women's International League for Peace and Freedom (WILPF).

After her move to London in 1913, Chrystal Macmillan continued her involvement with the National Union of Women Workers (NUWW), which had begun while she was resident in Scotland (see Chapter 5). In 1917, she joined the EC of the Association for Moral and Social Hygiene (AMSH), applying her legal knowledge and campaigning skills to the reform of legislative provisions that adversely affected women. She continued to be involved with the women's suffrage movement, and after some women were granted limited rights to the vote in 1918, she worked with Eleanor Rathbone[5] in the National Union of Societies for Equal Citizenship (NUSEC) to campaign for full and equal franchise, which was achieved in 1928.

She was a founding member of the Committee for the Opening of the Legal Profession to Women (COLPW), whose aim was not realised until the passing of the Sex Disqualification (Removal) Act in 1919: this legislation enabled her to embark on what was to be her first and only professional career, as a barrister at the English Bar (Chapter 7).

Her call to the Bar in 1924 followed four years as a pupil at Middle Temple, one of the Inns of Court in London's legal district. By then in her early 50s, she was already an established and highly respected figure, well acquainted with the workings of the law, which in her new role as a barrister enabled her to challenge with even greater authority. She became a member of the Western Circuit and of the London Sessions and Central Criminal Court, taking cases of all kinds and acting mostly for poor prisoners, which meant she was paid little if anything for her work.

Although her court work continued until her final years, she never ceased to challenge the status quo where it adversely affected women. One cause to which she devoted a good deal of her time was that of the nationality of married women, the subject of Chapter 8. Women's organisations had been campaigning on the issue for many years to stop women being deprived of their nationality on marriage to a foreign man. Chrystal Macmillan campaigned from 1914 till her death in 1937, both in Britain and internationally at the League of Nations for a woman to have the independent and indisputable right to her own nationality.

In Chapters 1 and 9 the focus is mostly on Chrystal Macmillan's personal life, starting with her years at home, school and university in Edinburgh (Chapter 1), and ending in Chapter 9 with her death and recollections of her life from friends, family and colleagues. The source materials for constructing a narrative of her personal history are lamentably few, but what there is leaves an impression of a woman capable of mischievous fun among her friends and family, of camaraderie, and above all of unfaltering loyalty and commitment to the cause of women's equality.

Hers is a remarkable legacy, and one that, thanks to lobbying by feminist academics at the University of Edinburgh, was finally acknowledged in 2008 when 'Chrystal Macmillan Building' was chosen as the name for the School of Social and Political Science – the first building in the university to be named after a woman.

Figure I.1 Chrystal Macmillan Building, Edinburgh University (courtesy Kath Davies)

Notes

1. Leah Leneman, *A Guid Cause: The Women's Suffrage Movement in Scotland* (Aberdeen: Aberdeen University Press, 1991).
2. Elspeth King, 'The Scottish Women's Suffrage Movement', in Esther Breitenbach and Eleanor Gordon (eds), *Out of Bounds: Women in Scottish Society 1800–1945* (Edinburgh: Edinburgh University Press, 1992), pp. 121–50.
3. Women's history is now much more widely studied and has been promoted by feminist historians and others, particularly though networks such as Women's History Scotland and the Women's History Network. The publication of E. Ewan, S. Innes, R. Pipes and S. Reynolds, *The Biographical Dictionary of Scottish Women* (Edinburgh: Edinburgh University Press, 2006); E. Ewan, R. Pipes, J. Rendall and S. Reynolds, *The New Biographical Dictionary of Scottish Women* (Edinburgh: Edinburgh University Press, 2018); and the Mapping Memorials of Women in Scotland project, based at Glasgow Women's Library, have also helped to raise awareness of and provide evidence for women's achievements over many centuries.
4. Vera Brittain, 'Committees versus Professions' (1929), in Paul Berry and Alan Bishop (eds), *Testament of a Generation: The Journalism of Vera Brittain and Winifred Holtby* (London: Virago, 1985), pp. 105–8.
5. Eleanor Rathbone was same age as Chrystal Macmillan, born in Liverpool 1872, member of NUWSS EC and president of NUSEC, elected to Parliament 1929–46. For more details see Sybil Oldfield, *Women Humanitarians: A Biographical Dictionary of British Women Active between 1900 and 1950* (London: Continuum, 2001), pp. 186–92; also Susan Pedersen, *Eleanor Rathbone and the Politics of Conscience* (New Haven and London: Yale University Press, 2004).

1

The Edinburgh Years: Family, School, University and Beyond

THE MACMILLAN FAMILY

Chrystal Macmillan's early family life was one of comfortable prosperity, most of it spent in the company of her eight siblings – all brothers – of which she was the second eldest, born on 13 June 1872. By that time, her 29-year-old father John, the son of a butcher and cattle salesman, was already a rising star in the Melrose Tea Company, where he had begun as an apprentice in 1859. Her mother, Jessie Chrystal Finlayson, also then aged 29, was one of the six children of Rev. Dr Thomas Finlayson, one-time Minister of Rose Street United Presbyterian Church in Edinburgh, and an honorary Doctor of Divinity at Edinburgh University. Jessie's mother, Janet Carrick Chrystal, was also known as Jessie, so the tradition of using the two names, Jessie and Chrystal, continued through three generations.

John and Jessie had married when both were aged 26, and moved to 41 Heriot Row in Edinburgh's New Town, where their first son, George, was born in 1870. They were to make three more moves, first to 8 Duke Street, Leith, where Jessie gave birth to Chrystal and to her second son, Tom, then to 2 Belford Park where six more sons were born – John (1876), William (1879), Cameron (1880), Norman (1882), Robert (1884) and Colin (1886). To have given birth to nine children, two of them when she was aged over 40, must have been a strain for Chrystal's mother, and may have been responsible for her later ill health and early death at the age of only 51.

By 1886, when Chrystal Macmillan was 14, and her eighth brother was born, John Macmillan decided it was time to buy a larger property, Corstorphine Hill House, which would not only provide more spacious accommodation for his growing children and the servants, but would also reflect his rising status in the city's business community. He was by then a distinguished and wealthy member of Edinburgh society, and principal partner of Melrose Tea Company. Tea was still a highly prized and fashionable commodity in the late nineteenth century, and as traders, the Company became highly successful. With his meteoric rise within the Company, John Macmillan was able to buy Hill House and to have what was a relatively plain building remodelled by the architect Alexander Macnaughtan in the Scots Baronial style, with turrets, spires, over thirty windows and sufficient accommodation for his large family and five indoor servants.[1] Other, outdoor servants, lived in separate accommodation and tended the extensive 74-acre grounds.

In the absence of any family papers, other than a few letters and photographs, it is only possible to surmise what family life was like for the young daughter in the family. By the time they moved to Corstorphine Hill House, George had already left home to become a boarder at Blair Lodge School, an academy for boys in Polmont, Stirlingshire, but the rest of her brothers were still living at home, and her mother must have been much preoccupied with the care of the youngest children, one of whom, Colin, was only a few months old. In his letters to George, her brother Tom referred only occasionally to his sister, mentioning in one of them that he had accompanied his sister and their father on a ride to Ravelrig, close to the Pentland Hills near Balerno, in October 1867, which must have been before the Hill House refurbishment was complete. Tom also mentions the family pets, which included two ponies, a dog, hens, pheasants and canaries. The family spent some holidays on her maternal grandparents' farm in Dumfriesshire, which Chrystal enjoyed. Speaking at a suffrage meeting in Dumfries in 1906, she recalled visiting the farm as a child, and regarded the county 'as the highest of gates of Paradise' because she passed through it 'to spend holidays at a farm'.[2]

It is not known if Chrystal was educated at home when very young, or which school she attended in her early years. It has been assumed that since her father was a member and one-time Master of the Edinburgh Merchants Company, and a supporter of girls' education, that he would have chosen one of the Company schools for his daughter, but no record of her attendance at either of the two main girls' schools in the city has been found to-date. However, according to the Matriculation Record in the University of Edinburgh's Archives, she attended Miss Matthew's School in Edinburgh for two years, and three years at St Leonards School in St Andrews (see below). What kind of school Miss Matthew's was, or when she went there, is not recorded.

Figure 1.1 Macmillan Family in Corstorphine Hill House, c.1890
From left to right: William Robert, Cameron, John (father), Angus, Jessie Chrystal, Jessie (mother), George, Colin Hugh, John Melrose, Thomas Finlayson, Norman (courtesy Iain Macmillan)

Figure 1.2 Young Chrystal Macmillan on her pony (courtesy Hugh Macmillan)

For Chrystal Macmillan, life in the opulent surroundings of Hill House was soon to come to an end because, in 1888, when aged 16, she left home to become a boarder at St Leonards School in St Andrews. To be educated at home was not unusual for girls in well-off families, but to be sent to board at an expensive and radical school like St Leonards was very much out of the ordinary. The school, founded in 1877, had a broad curriculum and a reputation for encouraging young women to earn their own living and to become active citizens. As Chrystal Macmillan's home life had been spent in a male-dominated household, to be transported to live in an all-female environment, among bright young women of similar outlook, must have been an exhilarating change.

ST LEONARDS SCHOOL

St Leonards School was exceptional in many ways, educating young women who, like Chrystal Macmillan, often went on to become actively involved in the suffrage and other movements for women's rights. Among them were Helen Archdale (née Russel, 1876–1949), who became one of the first female graduates from St Andrews University, a journalist and prominent member of the Women's Social and Political Union, and the three Murray sisters – Dorothy (b. 1873), Sylvia (b. 1875) and

Eunice (b. 1878) – all of whom were friends of Chrystal Macmillan.[3] Both Sylvia and Eunice corresponded with her in later years, and Eunice Murray's diary is one of the few publicly available sources for personal information about Chrystal Macmillan's early life.[4]

The founding headmistress of the school was Louisa Lumsden, a Scot from Aberdeen, who was educated at what later became Girton College Cambridge, and took up the headship of St Leonards after serving as Classical Tutor for a year at Cheltenham Ladies College. She had strong views and a radical philosophy about how to provide an education to encourage girls to become full citizens in society.

> Miss Lumsden had quietly and firmly carried out ideas which were then wholly new in girls' schools. Classics for girls, mathematics, proper physical training, organised games; above all trust in the girls and the responsibility given them for each other; the wise but difficult combination of freedom and watchful care. All these are accepted as principles today. In 1877 they were new and dangerous.[5]

Even more 'dangerous' were her views on women's entitlement to paid work and a profession:

> The mistake is to regard paid work as derogatory to the dignity of a lady. Why should it be less honourable for her to live by her own labour, than by that of her father, not to speak of being dependent on a brother or other relation? . . . It should be an everyday thing to enter a profession, and that to be capable of entering it should be considered honourable and desirable.[6]

For young women at that time, however liberal their home lives may have been, such sentiments would have been transformative: they were being actively encouraged to break the mould and to enter society as independent young people, capable of earning a living and being proud to do so.

Louisa Lumsden resigned from the headship of St Leonards in 1882, six years before Chrystal Macmillan arrived there. Louisa Lumsden became much involved with the suffrage movement in Scotland, becoming president of the Aberdeen Women's Suffrage Society from 1908, and later a member of the EC of the Scottish Federation of Women's Suffrage Societies, where she probably encountered Chrystal. Following her resignation from the school her regime at St Leonards continued under the headship of her colleague Miss Frances Dove, also a former student of Girton College, and the school chemistry teacher. Frances Dove was of the same mind as her predecessor; she believed that girls should be taught the importance of cooperation and empathy, and to become active citizens:

> Men acquire corporate virtues, not only at school and at college, but almost in every walk of life: whereas comparatively few women ever find themselves members of an organised profession, and the proportion even of those who have the advantage of a college life, is exceedingly small. It remains therefore for the school to teach them almost all that they will ever have the opportunity of acquiring of the power of working with others, and sinking their own individuality for the common good.[7]

> It is true that the family is the unit which lies at the base of all national existence, and which forms the foundation stone for all teaching, moral and spiritual, but it is essential to remember that it is only a unit, and that an aggregation of such families or units forms a community, a nation, and that the members of a family are likewise citizens of kingdoms, political and spiritual. To be a good citizen, it is essential that she should have wide interests, a sense of discipline and organisation, *esprit de corps*, a power of corporate action.[8]

Frances Dove also believed that young women should be treated with respect and trust: 'Make them trustworthy by trusting them, open and straightforward by taking it for granted that they have nothing to hide', and that 'The most important conditions for health are first of all a wholesome environment; secondly wholesome occupation of the mind; and thirdly proper exercise for the body.'[9]

Chrystal Macmillan was among forty-four new girls to join the school in 1888, bringing the total to 136 that year. She lived first in 'The Cottage', the boarding house known as 'Tullochs' after its founder and housemistress, Miss A. A. Tulloch, then in 3 & 4 Queen's Terrace: she was later joined there by friends Dorothy and Sylvia Murray, with their younger sister Eunice arriving a few years after.

School records attest that Chrystal Macmillan excelled in most of her school undertakings. She clearly impressed her teachers with her leadership skills, being made Head of House and captain of the House Games Team the year after her arrival, and Head of School in 1891. Pupils were encouraged to compete in sports, including cricket and gymnastics, as well as lacrosse, which was introduced for the first time in 1888, with Chrystal Macmillan appointed captain of her House team. She also took part in school plays, on one occasion playing the Duke in Twelfth Night, with her friend Sylvia Murray as Malvolio, both bedecked in magnificent garments they had made themselves – another skill in which Chrystal excelled.[10]

Figure 1.3 Chrystal Macmillan and Form VI pupils with Miss Dove (headmistress) Front row from left: Hilda Sharpe, Mary Simson, Miss Dove, Mary Grierson; back row from left: Noel Ramsay, Mary Dunn, Chrystal Macmillan, Isabel Dickson, Maud Saunders (Chrystal Macmillan's photo album, courtesy Iain Macmillan)

Such was her academic excellence that in 1890 she became School Scholar. It was clear that her path was set for higher education, and, with support from the school, in that year she sat the Girton College Entrance Examination and Oxford and Cambridge Higher Certificate Examinations, obtaining a distinction in additional mathematics in the latter, and a Scholarship to Girton. However, she was unable to take up the scholarship because her parents could not spare her from home due to her mother's failing health; as the only daughter it fell to her to return home to help out with the family.

Later in life Chrystal Macmillan acknowledged that the ethos of St Leonards had a profound influence on her. It was from the school that she acquired her life-long belief in women's right to equality of citizenship and the importance of liberty and justice. As she later wrote, 'When I was at school, years were spent in instilling into me an admiration for [the] defence of the principles of liberty.'[11]

FROM SCHOOL TO UNIVERSITY

Chrystal Macmillan left St Leonards in 1891, aged 19, and returned to Edinburgh to live with her family in Corstorphine Hill House. Fortuitously for her, only a year later, in 1892, the University of Edinburgh opened its doors to women who had not previously been permitted to matriculate at the university.

Campaigns to compel the university to admit women as undergraduates had been mounted early in the century, most notably by Sophia Jex-Blake (1840–1912), a medical student who won the right to take classes in medicine in a separate Extra-Mural School, but who fought unsuccessfully for women to be admitted to the university's medical school on an equal footing with men. It was not until 1889, with the passing of the Universities (Scotland) Act, that regulations were drawn up that allowed for women to be taught in, and obtain degrees from, the Scottish universities. Even then, women medical students were taught in separate classes and it was not until 1916, with an increasing demand for their skills, that women and men were taught together.

For other women aspiring to be graduates who were denied university entrance until 1889, classes in a wide range of subjects were offered by the Edinburgh Ladies Education Association (which later became The Edinburgh Association for the University Education of Women) (EAUEW), founded by Mary Crudelius (1839–77) and Sarah Siddons Mair (1846–1941)[12] in 1867. The Association provided classes in subjects including mathematics and moral philosophy, and in 1874 introduced a University Certificate in Arts. Eight of the women who took EAUEW courses went on to become students at the university and were the first women to graduate, in 1893. One of these women was Frances Simson (1854–1938),[13] who later became a key figure, along with Chrystal Macmillan, in what became known as the Scottish women graduates' case (see below, and Chapter 2).

Taking advantage of the 1889 Act, Chrystal Macmillan began preparing for preliminary exams in English, mathematics, French, dynamics and science, all of which she passed, and matriculated in October 1892. The courses she took at the university were in mathematics and natural philosophy and in 1894 she won a prize and first-class certificate in astronomy. That was the year her mother died, leaving her to cope with a grieving father and brothers, as well as her own loss, and household management duties. Despite these burdens, she continued to study for her finals, which she took in 1896 and gained a BSc degree with first-class honours, passing with special distinction in mathematics and natural philosophy to become the first woman to graduate in science from the university. Fittingly, it is at King's Buildings, the science campus of the university, that a millennial plaque was sited in her honour.

By now a mature student, Chrystal Macmillan chose to continue her life in academia after graduating in 1896, extending her range of subjects to include moral philosophy and mental philosophy, political economy and Greek. The following year brought a major change to family life in Corstorphine Hill house – her father married for a second time. His bride was Alwine Amtsberg, who had been the German governess of the younger Macmillan sons. The couple were married in Balerno Presbyterian Church, with Chrystal as a bridesmaid, and after one wedding reception at Malleny House, the home of Alwine's sister, Paula Law, another very grand one followed, at Corstorphine Hill House. The marriage meant that Chrystal was able to step back from her household duties, and to devote more of her time to studying for her degree. Three years later, she graduated for the second time with an honours degree in moral philosophy and logic.

It was a formative and politically active time for these early women undergraduates who, having been prevented from matriculating for so long, were now determined to assert their right to be treated as equals with their fellow male students. On 6 February 1895, the women undergraduates formed the Women's Representative Committee representing the interests of women students. Chrystal Macmillan was among the first to join, becoming chair in 1897. She coordinated their work to challenge, successfully, the injustice in the allocation of scholarships and bursaries solely to male students. The committee was dissolved in 1899 when it was decided that its business could be dealt with by a Women's Committee of the Student's Representative Council.[14]

Following her second graduation from the university in 1900, Chrystal Macmillan left Edinburgh and travelled to Berlin. According to family memory, she intended to enrol as a student there, but it isn't known what she planned to study, or why she chose Berlin. The only record of her time in the city is in the diary of her friend Eunice Murray, in which an entry for 1 January 1901 notes that Chrystal and Dorothy, Eunice's sister, were enjoying themselves there. However, their enjoyment soon turned to sorrow when Chrystal heard of her father's sudden death only one week later, and so returned home at once, leaving Berlin for good.

Figure 1.4 Chrystal Macmillan, graduate (courtesy Iain Macmillan)

POST-UNIVERSITY YEARS IN EDINBURGH

Some time before his death, John Macmillan had had several warnings that his heart was not strong, but his sudden death in 1901, after giving the toast to Queen Victoria before an illustrious gathering at the annual dinner of the Merchant Company, was a huge shock to his family, and to the city's business and wider community. His funeral was described as 'one of the largest and most impressive that has taken place in Edinburgh within recent years'[15] and photographs of the event attest to this description. The parade from Corstorphine was reputed to be a mile long, and included representatives from the City Council, the Merchant Company, Merchant schools, business colleagues and hundreds of others.

On Census night, 31 March 1901, only three months after John Macmillan's death, fourteen people were living at Corstorphine Hill House, including Chrystal Macmillan. She and her youngest brothers Colin (14) and Robert (17) were all listed in the Census as scholars; Norman (18), William (22) and Cameron (20) as apprentices; and George, the eldest (30), as a tea merchant. Also resident in the house were a nurse, two housemaids, a cook, laundry maid, table maid and kitchen maid.

Figure 1.5 Funeral, John Macmillan, Edinburgh, 1901 (courtesy Iain Macmillan)

There is no mention of Tom or John, or of the children's stepmother who, on that night, was staying with her sister Paula and family at Malleny House, Balerno. It isn't known exactly when Alwine Amtsberg moved out of Hill House but by 1905 she was living at 2 Darnaway Street in the city, and given that relations between her and the family were apparently somewhat strained, it is likely that she moved there very soon after John Macmillan died. After Alwine's departure, Chrystal presumably resumed her role as mistress of the household, living with her brothers, the eldest of whom were to marry before long.

Chrystal Macmillan's friend Eunice Murray was a frequent visitor to Hill House and according to an entry in her diary for January 1904, the mood at the dinner table there was anything but jovial. She wrote that 'a duller set of brothers never can have existed. Good looking, tall and dull. "Pass the butter Col", "Miss Murray wants jam, Bill." That is about their finest efforts.' In an entry for October that year, she referred to the brothers as 'dull as ditch water', and clearly had a low opinion of their conversational skills.[16]

Despite the demands and constraints of her life in Hill House, Chrystal Macmillan became engaged in a range of activities in the city, including the Women's Debating Society, established by Sarah Siddons Mair in 1865, which she joined in 1902, going on to become its vice-president.[17] It seems that by this time she was already being recognised as 'a safe pair of hands' for steering committee meetings, and her membership of the Debating Society would certainly have helped her to develop the public-speaking and advocacy skills for which she was later to become so celebrated (see Chapter 2). As a forum for debate on topics such as 'Has free education been a real boon to the people?', and 'Is it desirable to give uncontributary old age pensions?',[18] both of which Chrystal took part in, the society would also have introduced her to matters of general social concern, as well as many like-minded, intellectually curious women in the city.

It was during these post-university years, while still living at the family home, that she joined and became deeply involved with the NUWW, which was a branch of the ICW (see Chapters 5 and 6), the Scottish Federation of Women's Suffrage Societies, and the Scottish University Women's Suffrage Union. She also remained involved with university politics, becoming secretary and treasurer of the Women Graduates' Committee which notably, in 1906, argued for the right of women graduates to choose a parliamentary candidate to represent the combined constituency of Edinburgh and St Andrews Universities in the election of that year. It was to be a highly significant moment in her career, leading in 1908 to her acting as the main appellant in the Scottish women graduates' case (see Chapter 2).

These were very busy years for her, as will be seen from the following chapters. As well as her committee work, she spoke at public meetings all over Scotland, travelled to London to attend EC meetings of the NUWW and ICW, and in 1909 to Toronto to attend the ICW Quinquennial Congress (see Chapter 6). Not all her travels were work-related, however. She took holidays in Ireland and Iceland in 1890, and to Greece with Frances Murray, the mother of her friends Eunice, Sylvia and Dorothy, in April 1909. Having been introduced to the motorcar when still living at Hill House, she eventually bought her own, a 'baby Austin', and according to her great nephew Hugh, drove it to France on a holiday.

Towards the end of 1913, when in her early 40s, she finally left Scotland to live in London. While she and Eunice Murray were on holiday in Skye in September that year, Eunice recorded the following in her diary:

> I have promised Chrystal to go and stay a couple of months with her in London where she is going to start life. She thinks it will be advisable and I dare say a regular breaking away from her relatives will be good, and no doubt she will find more to occupy her in London than in Edinburgh.[19]

Chrystal's decision to move that year was probably in part precipitated by the sale of the Corstorphine Hill House estate which she helped to negotiate in May 1913,[20] leaving her with no family home to live in. It may also have been due to her increasing involvement in London-centred organisations and activities. She must have arrived in London in October that year because Eunice Murray's diary records that she and Chrystal 'Have settled down at 46 Cranley Gardens and like it very much. Chris means to stay on and she likes it, and so far, Mrs Grant seems very pleasant.'

From that year until close to the time of her death in 1937, when she moved back to Edinburgh, she remained in London, moving eventually to live in what was to be her final residence there, 4 Pump Court, Middle Temple, in the law district of the city.

CONCLUSION

Among young women of her generation, Chrystal Macmillan was fortunate to have had a privileged upbringing, with parents who, exceptionally for the times, believed in education for girls. Her education at a boarding school that was committed to preparing young women for active citizenship undoubtedly laid a strong foundation for her later activism, and brought her into contact with women who became friends and colleagues engaged in similar causes. She also benefited from coming of age at a time when the drive to extend higher education to women was bearing fruit, notably the admission of women to degree courses at Scottish universities.

Nevertheless, she had to face many obstacles, both institutional and private. In private life, as an unmarried daughter with brothers but no sisters, she was expected to take on the responsibility of managing a large household following the death, first of her mother in 1894, then of her father in 1901. In her institutional life she had to contend with barriers preventing women from participating in various spheres of activity, including at university, but it was perhaps the confronting and challenging of such barriers that contributed to the development of her confidence, and the determination to put to best effect what her friend Eunice Murray described as her 'first rate head'.

Notes

1. John Macmillan had a stained-glass window installed in the house, which included panes showing his and his wife Jessie's initials, and the Clan Macmillan motto, *miseris succurrere disco* (I learn to succour the unfortunate). The house, now called Mansion House, still stands, at the centre of Edinburgh Zoo, and is a venue for social and business functions.
2. *Dumfries and Galloway Standard*, 27 Mar. 1909, p. 88.
3. For entries on Louisa Lumsden, Helen Archdale, Eunice and Sylvia Murray and their mother, Frances, see Ewan et al., *The New Biographical Dictionary*, s.v.
4. Eunice Murray, *Diary (1895–1918)* (London: Women's Library, LSE, 7EGM/1).
5. G. M. N. Ramsay, 'Foundation and Government', in Julia Grant et al. (eds), *St Leonards School 1877–1927* (London: Oxford University Press, 1927), p. 13.
6. Louisa Lumsden, *On Higher Education of Women in Great Britain and Ireland* (Aberdeen: J. & J. P. Edmond & Spark, 1884), p. 14.
7. Dorothea Beale, Lucy H. M. Soulsby and Jane Frances Dove (eds), *Work & Play in Girls' Schools by Three Headmistresses* (London: Longmans Green, 1898), p. 400.
8. Jane Frances Dove, 'Cultivation of the Body', in Beale et al., *Work & Play*, p. 401.
9. Ibid., p. 397.
10. Julia Grant et al. (eds), *St Leonards School 1877–1927* (London: Oxford University Press, n.d.).

11. Chrystal Macmillan, *The Struggle for Political Liberty* (London: WSPU, 1909), p. 5.
12. See entries in Ewan et al., *The New Biographical Dictionary*, s.v.
13. Ibid.
14. *Minute and Executive Report Book of Women's Representative Committee 1895–1899* (University of Edinburgh Special Collections).
15. Company of Merchants Edinburgh, *Annual Report*, 1901.
16. Murray, *Diary (1895–1918)*.
17. Lettice Milne Rae, *Ladies in Debate: Being a History of the Ladies Edinburgh Debating Society* (Edinburgh: Oliver & Boyd, 1936).
18. Ibid., p. 99.
19. Murray, *Diary (1895–1918)*.
20. The estate was sold for £17,000 to Edinburgh City Council who later gifted it to the Royal Zoological Society.

2

Chrystal Macmillan and the Scottish Women Graduates' Case

Of the four ancient universities of Scotland, three of them – St Andrews, Glasgow and Aberdeen – were founded in the fifteenth century, and later, the University of Edinburgh was founded in the sixteenth century. But these centres of learning were for men only: it wasn't until the late nineteenth century that, after much public debate and campaigning by groups of women, legislation was passed that enabled all the Scottish universities to admit women.

The first steps towards improved education for girls was taken by Edinburgh University in 1865 when a local examination scheme was set up which encouraged the development of secondary education for girls. Three years later, in 1868, a group of Edinburgh ladies supported by a few Edinburgh University professors (in particular, Professor Masson) founded the Edinburgh Ladies Education Association (ELEA) which aimed for the general improvement of women's intellectual capability through higher education classes. This influential group encouraged women to attend the regular Association classes given by university professors and lecturers. By the 1880s their efforts were beginning to show the possibility of change: 'the women of the ELEA had shown that they were capable intellectually, physically and emotionally of studying to University standards'.[1]

The campaigning by women and their participation in public debate[2] led to the passing of the Universities (Scotland) Act in 1889, which enabled universities to admit women, should they wish to do so. So, in 1892, when women were allowed to enrol at Edinburgh University for the first time, Chrystal Macmillan was able to matriculate, and to graduate four years later with a degree in science followed by a second degree in philosophy in 1900 (see Chapter 1).

In 1906, six years after her second graduation, Chrystal Macmillan and four other Edinburgh University graduates, Elsie Inglis,[3] Frances Melville,[4] Margaret Nairn[5] and Frances Simson,[6] decided to issue a challenge to the universities of St Andrews and Edinburgh by asking for voting papers for the forthcoming election of two university candidates as MPs.

The Representation of the People (Scotland) Act of 1868 had extended voting rights to the university electorate, which comprised members on the register of the General Councils of the Universities.

> The Chancellor, the Members of the University Court, and the Professors for the Time being of each of the Universities of *Scotland*, and also every Person whose Name is for the Time being on the Register, made up in Terms of the Provisions herein-after set forth, of the General Council of such University, shall, if of full Age, and not subject to any legal Incapacity, be entitled to vote in the Election of a Member to serve in any future Parliament for such University in Terms of this Act.[7]

As the membership included staff and all registered graduates, the women graduates argued that as members of Council they had a right to exercise a vote under the terms of the 1868 Act, which specified that 'every person whose name is on the register' was eligible.

There had been no need for an election until 1906 as hitherto the Member had been returned unopposed. Thus, the opportunity to vote for a university representative arose for the first time in 1906, when there were two candidates. It was also the first opportunity for women graduates to vote since the passing of The Universities (Scotland) Act 1889 which led to the drawing up of Regulations for the Graduation of Women, in 1892, and for their instruction in Scottish universities.[8] The issue was first raised by women students in 1894 when the student newspaper noted that 'Some lady students are exercising themselves over a point abut Woman's suffrage. In the event of an election coming on now, would the ladies who have graduated be entitled to vote for the University MP? And if not, why not?'[9]

Chrystal Macmillan, along with many of her Scottish colleagues, realised that women graduates experienced an anomaly in their situation as graduates. Despite their education and work in the community, they were still denied the vote in Parliamentary elections. Helen Waddell, an Edinburgh graduate, expressed their frustration in a letter to the press:

> Edinburgh women have taken such prominent and valuable part in public life that one wonders what their present attitude to Parliamentary candidates

like Mr Strachey and Lord Dalmeny is. A candidate for Edinburgh and St Andrews Universities 'opposed to woman's suffrage!' What of the women graduates who have gone out and are going out now from these Universities to share in the work of the national life, to add to its intellectual, social and moral wealth?[10]

The legal case of the Scottish women graduates which was to become a cause célèbre in the period from 1906 to 1908, first came to the notice of the press in January 1906 when 'a large and representative meeting of women graduates of the four Universities of Scotland was held in Edinburgh: it was unanimously resolved to protest against the refusal to allow women graduates to vote in the election of University Parliamentary representatives'.[11] At this meeting, 24-year-old Chrystal Macmillan was elected secretary and treasurer of the Committee of Women Graduates of the Scottish Universities.

On 1 February 1906, Chrystal Macmillan wrote a letter to *The Scotsman*, laying out the aims of the Women Graduates' Committee:

> We are aware that the question of the electoral disabilities of women graduates has been already discussed, but this is the first time that it has arisen in connection with the Universities of Scotland. The enactments which regulate the election of Scottish University representatives are different from those which regulate any other Parliamentary election, so that our case is not identical with any previous case in which a woman has laid claim to be a Parliamentary voter.[12]

Later that month, the women's expectations of failure were realised when their request for voting papers was refused by the Registrar of the University of Edinburgh. The University Court confirmed the Principal's defence of the Registrar's decision and, on behalf of all the Scottish universities, Edinburgh University took the lead in appointing legal advisers and barristers to defend vigorously their decision, despite the Court having noted that:

> ... the women have been admitted to graduation in several of the faculties of the universities and their names have been placed on the Register of the General Council. They have attended and voted at the meetings of the General Council, and they have hitherto enjoyed and exercised all the privileges possessed by male graduates of the universities.[13]

Knowing that the refusal of ballot papers was the likely outcome, the women graduates had already prepared for the next step in their campaign, which was to take their request as a test case to the Court of

Session in Edinburgh. They understood that their challenge would be unlikely to succeed, but as Chrystal Macmillan observed in a letter to Millicent Fawcett, 'We are of the opinion that even if it were hopeless, the political effect of raising the question is worth the effort.'[14]

They had much financial help and support for their cause from within Scotland and further afield. For instance, writing from her home in Congleton to a friend, the suffragist Elizabeth Wolstenholme Elmy said that:

> I have sent the Scottish Women Graduates a good list of people able and probably willing to help and given them full information as to *Chorlton vs Lings*, etc., etc. They are pretty sure to fail in the Scottish Law Courts, but their action will help us immensely in Parliament.[15]

The women launched an appeal to raise £1,000 to fund the legal fees for their campaign, and a syndicated article appeared on the women's pages of more than fifteen regional newspapers during the first week of March 1906. Many papers were sympathetic to the women's cause, and the *Midlothian Journal* made specific mention of Chrystal Macmillan,[16] noting that her 'well-known organising faculties are placed at the service of the movement'. However, not all newspapers took a positive line. For example, *The Dundee Courier* observed that not all women supported the women graduates' cause, and that the women's suffrage campaign, started in the 1860s, was trying to move with 'unseemly haste'.[17]

In order to present a convincing argument in the Court of Session, the women graduates needed to do a good deal of research and preparatory work, which included background reading. As part of her research, Chrystal Macmillan wrote to the suffragist Helen McIlquham asking for a copy of her pamphlet 'The Enfranchisement of Women', and for any 'information with respect to women who have voted both in modern times, either being registered by mistake, or in ancient times as their just right'. She also asked for the names of any books that would be helpful to their cause, noting that 'the lawyers are absolutely ignorant of the literature or rather the facts of the subject'.[18]

THE COURT OF SESSION IN EDINBURGH

In the presence of a large number of women graduates, in the Court of Session, Lord Salvesen heard the legal arguments for the women's case on 27 June 1906. The women graduates were represented by Mr Clyde, KC, assisted by Mr Kennedy and Mr Munro, while the Dean of the

Faculty, Mr Campbell, KC, and Mr Macmillan (no relation to Chrystal) represented the University.[19] In opening the case, the women's lawyers argued that the university franchise was unlike other franchises in that it did not depend on property qualifications but on the intellectual ability of the person to become a graduate and thereby a member of the General Council. They asked two questions: did the term 'person' include women? Were women excluded when the phrase 'not subject to any legal incapacity' was used to describe those entitled to vote? They objected to women graduates being classed with 'aliens, lunatics and minors', thereby excluding them from a vote on the ground of legal incapacity.

Mr Macmillan, for the University, argued that 'it had been universally determined that women had no right to exercise the Parliamentary franchise or, indeed, any public function, unless they were expressly authorised to do so'. Two weeks later, on 5 July 2006, Lord Salvesen delivered judgement, noting that this case raised an important question. He opined that the case 'hinged on the interpretation of the word "person" in Section 27 of the 1868 Act',[20] and argued that in any ordinary statute the word would be presumed to include individuals of both sexes, but given the context it must be construed as meaning the 'male person'. He thought that as in 1868 and 1881 women were not admitted to the universities, it would not have been thought necessary to explicitly limit the university franchise to 'male persons'.

Moreover, he affirmed that women were legally incapacitated at Common Law from voting at the election of Members of Parliament, quoting decisions in the case in Scotland of *Brown* v. *Ingram*[21] and in England of *Chorlton* v. *Lings*.[22]

In finding against the women graduates, he suggested that it might be some consolation for them to know that his judgement

> . . . is not an underrating of the sex in point of intellect or worth but as an exemption, founded on motives of decorum and is a privilege of the sex (*honestatis privilegium*) . . . and chiefly out of respect to women and a sense of decorum, they have been excused from taking any share in the department of public affairs.[23]

This wording, supporting as it did the idea that it was natural for women to be excluded from sharing in civic affairs, was unlikely to be any 'consolation' to Chrystal Macmillan, who had always strongly believed that women should share responsibility with men in the management and operation of public affairs; an idea that recurs regularly in her work.

Lord Salvesen's comments provoked an angry response from a writer in *Women's Suffrage Record*:

> ... to tell them that it was a privilege for the larger half of the nation to have no voice in the making of the laws by which they are governed – that it is a privilege to be classed with paupers, lunatics, and criminals, a privilege to be entirely dependent on the casual benevolence of male legislators, a privilege to be so superior that even the most noble of all aspirations, namely, to become a full citizen of your own country, is of no account. We pity the women graduates who had to listen to such words, and we admire their patience and self-control. Such speeches ought only to be delivered to the diplodocus in the Natural History Museum.[24]

Appeal in Court of Session, 1907

The women appealed the decision, and the case was heard in October 1907 by Lords McLaren, Pearson and Ardwall in the Court of Session in Edinburgh. One report suggested that as Lord McLaren was the stepson of the late Mrs Priscilla Bright McLaren, who was President of the Edinburgh Society for Women's Suffrage, he might be 'well acquainted with arguments for and against the granting of the franchise to women'.[25] And, indeed, the report of the appeal in the *Aberdeen Press & Journal* revealed that the Lords were not totally unsympathetic to the women's case, with Lord McLaren questioning the competency of the Registrar to refuse to issue voting papers.[26] However, the Lords adhered to the judgement given by Lord Salvesen. Lord McLaren, who delivered the opinion to a court room 'thronged with ladies',[27] said:

> It is an incontestable fact that women never have enjoyed the Parliamentary franchise of the United Kingdom ... In view of these facts, we must conclude that it was a principle of the unwritten constitutional law of the country that men only were entitled to take part in the election of representatives to Parliament ... All ambiguous expressions in modern Acts of parliament must be construed in the light of this general principle ... It is difficult to conceive that the Legislature should have conferred the power of extending or withholding the franchise by devolution, a power which it has always kept in its own hands.[28]

In response to the judgement, Chrystal Macmillan wrote an article for the suffrage press in December 1907, summarising the legal grounds for the Scottish women graduates' case and details of the Court's judgement. She noted that the Women Graduates' Committee should decide whether or not to take a further appeal to the House of Lords, but in the meantime, she gave notice that £1,000 would need to be raised to make such an appeal.[29]

APPEAL TO THE HOUSE OF LORDS

The committee decided that to appeal to the House of Lords was the only way of arriving at a decision which would be legally conclusive, and they set up a funding appeal for this purpose.[30] By March 1908 they had sufficient funds to proceed, and Chrystal Macmillan and Frances Simson were delegated to undertake the task.[31]

In the four weeks before the case was heard, in the autumn of 1908, Chrystal Macmillan chose to stay in London with Edith Hooper, a colleague from Edinburgh University, who was very helpful to her in preparing for the case. As she wrote to her friend Eunice Murray, 'Edith Hooper[32] helped me to great purpose in understudying the Lord Chancellor'.[33] She was aware that her lack of legal training put her at a disadvantage, but as she said in an interview for the *Daily Chronicle*,

Figure 2.1 Graduates at the House of Lords, 1908
From left: Frances Melville, Frances Simson, Chrystal Macmillan (courtesy Edinburgh University)

'of course I have made a careful study of the subject and of the arguments used in the previous actions. Our appeal does not depend on any view of the general justice of admitting women to the franchise: it is a question of the proper interpretation of the particular statute.'[34] She had grasped the necessary grounds for arguing that the case had to be considered under Statute Law and not Common Law. 'In raising the action, the graduates' committee was particular to have it done in such a way that it was possible ultimately to appeal to the House of Lords, because only there can a final legal decision be reached.'[35]

On 11 November 1908, Chrystal Macmillan started to present the women graduates' case in front of the Lord Chancellor, Lord Loreburn, and three Law Lords – Lords Collins, Robertson and Ashbourne: it was a short hearing on that first day. The gallery was filled with graduates and many others with an interest in the case, including some prominent members of the judiciary, MPs and some of their wives, and even members of the Edinburgh School Board.[36] It was a highly significant and widely publicised moment in the history of the suffragist cause, and one which established Chrystal Macmillan's reputation as an outstanding advocate at a time when women litigants were extremely rare.

In opening her pleading, she noted that, in 1869, the first and only other woman to appeal a judgement of the Scottish courts in the House of Lords, spoke for twenty-three days! She then described the background to the women graduates' case and the reasons for their Appeal to the House of Lords. She referred their Lordships to the Acts dealing with the franchises of the Universities of Scotland which were different from those dealing with any other Parliamentary franchise, and distinct from those regulating the university elections in England. She made the point that it was a 'newly established franchise and based on different qualifications from other franchises': it had no connection with property or geographical limits but required an intellectual test. Referring in detail to the 1889 University of Scotland Act which, in turn, had led to Ordinance 18 in 1892 which permitted universities to admit women to graduation, she pointed out that all graduates, including women graduates, must become Members of the University General Council. As members, their names would be duly entered on the Register which was used as the Parliamentary Voting Register for the Scottish Universities. She dealt in detail with the women's claim that the University Registrar did not have the right to refuse them voting papers: by his action he had claimed a power that rightfully belonged to the Vice-Chancellor as Returning Officer.

On the second day's hearing, on 12 November, Chrystal Macmillan started by giving more detailed grounds for challenging the Registrar's right to refuse to issue voting papers but then proceeded to state the main point of her argument, which was 'that we are "persons" and that we are "not subject to any legal incapacity" within the meaning of this section of the Act'.[37] She went on to show how the word 'person' included women in several other Acts, including the right of women to vote in School Board elections after 1872. She also compared it with the use of the words 'male person' in other Franchise Acts. She noted that the Municipal Act of 1835 gave the franchise to 'male persons' but when the Act was amended in 1869 the word 'male' was dropped, and it was taken to mean that women thereby acquired the right to vote.

She proceeded to discuss the phrase 'not subject to any legal incapacity', pointing out that its meaning was not defined within the University Act. She also cited examples of various Acts in which use of the term 'legal capacity' did not refer to sex. Therefore, the exclusion of women graduates from voting solely because of their sex should not have been allowed. She suggested that the respondents (i.e. the University's legal representatives) were incorrect to use an argument under Common Law as Common Law could not apply to a newly created franchise.

She continued with an analysis and interpretation of various laws and judgements but just before adjourning for lunch the Lord Chancellor asked if she could show that women had a vote at any time in the past. After lunch, she continued her historical analysis, but the Lord Chancellor interrupted: 'The fact of women not being allowed the vote in Parliament within living memory is a fact that would not be altered in this place by saying that some corner of an Act of Parliament might be interpreted to mean that some women did.'[38] Not put off by his comments, she continued with her presentation, apparently unperturbed. With regard to the judgements of the Scottish Courts, she referred to Lord Salvesen's judgement and claimed that 'it is not possible to say "person" means "male person" and at the same time "subject to any legal incapacity" refers to women'.[39] 'We contend that the word [person] is not open to construction; it is a definite word, and if we do not give the definite interpretation to it, we are landed in a number of absurdities.'[40]

Referring to the Appeal Hearing in the Scottish Court of Session, Chrystal Macmillan contended that Lord McLaren's judgement was 'unsound' insofar as he claimed that 'if Parliament had intended to subvert an existing Constitutional law in favour of women graduates, the intention would naturally be expressed in plain language, and therefore if ambiguous language is used it must be construed in accordance with the general Constitutional rule'. She argued that 'the ambiguity is introduced by the assumption; it is not in the Statute itself'.[41]

She concluded her presentation by saying, 'It has not been easy to know if I have been making myself clear, as you kindly let me go on without asking questions. But if I have failed to make myself clear on any points I should like to be told before I sit down.'[42] The Lord Chancellor assured her that their Lordships had clearly understood her contention. Then Frances Simson took up the argument, making a shorter presentation to reinforce the case on behalf of the women graduates. When she appealed to the Law Lords more on the grounds of a sense of justice for the women's case she was interrupted by the Lord Chancellor and reminded that 'we are a judicial body, and what we have to discuss is the Act of Parliament and the real interpretation of the law'.[43]

Chrystal Macmillan did not make the same mistake; she knew she was speaking to people with authority within the legal system, and others of influence who were present in the Court.

> Earl Russell sat through the second day and above a dozen real peers dropped in during the day. Sir Charles Dilke and Sir John Batty Zuke – the Edinburgh University Member – stayed a considerable time. The Scottish Solicitor General heard me open and Dankwertz, one of the biggest of the K.C.s who sniffed and made impertinent remarks at the opening of the first day, listened the second, and to someone who repeated the remark to me, said it was an ably put case.[44]

For whatever reason, whether due to her compelling argument, convincing delivery or out of courtesy, the Lord Chancellor only interrupted her presentation a few times with short comments. In writing to Eunice Murray some days later, Chrystal Macmillan admitted that their silence had been somewhat unnerving:

> It was rather terrible their never interrupting. You know how much more animated I can be when I'm heckled or opposed. I daresay it was partly consideration, but it was what I most dreaded. The first day I spoke 50 minutes with no interruption and the second day, I think I must have had one spell of two hours without a remark. As far as I could judge they all listened to every word. They all kept taking notes at intervals up to the end and kept their messenger, who runs for reference books, going all the time.[45]

Her letters to friends acknowledge the support she received from suffragists and others, while also revealing the naïve pleasure she felt at being in the limelight:

> I don't know how I did so well. It is the special providence which looks after suffragists. If I had not gone to London when I did and stayed with Miss Hooper; and if she had not understudied the Lord Chancellor for several nights till I found the best way to arrange my notes; and if it had not happened that we brought up Mr Mair[46] to look up references and be at my elbow; and if it had not happened that I had only an hour to start off with and a day's interval between, the whole thing might have been a crisis.[47]

> It is wonderful to think it has all gone off so well and I've had no end of nice things said. The fact that the press agrees with these kind people makes it more probable that they really mean what they say. It is quite true about my voice being good. The first day especially I had never before felt it sound so well. It is a delightful room to speak in. I may never have another opportunity but one of my correspondents addresses me to the House of Lords to which he says I would be a valuable addition!![48]

She added, 'the Newspaper Reports are delightfully entertaining. I've ordered a good many copies of the best and more amusing and will send you a selection on Monday.'[49] Not all the press coverage was complimentary, however. *The Nottingham Evening Post* remarked that 'With the childlike petulance which is excused in a pretty woman Miss Chrystal Macmillan B.Sc. still insists that "person includes woman" but she must have been more logical in the examination room or she would not have earned her degree.'[50]

The Law Lords did not call upon counsel for the universities and the women's appeal was dismissed, as had been expected, but when delivering his Judgement on 10 December 1908, the Lord Chancellor complimented the appellants on their skill in presenting their argument: 'This appeal has been argued temperately, with evident knowledge that your lordships have to decide what the law is, and nothing beyond that simple question.' In setting out the reasons for dismissal, he admitted that two judges were reported as saying that women might vote at parliamentary elections, but he contended 'these are dicta derived from an ancient manuscript of no weight'. Noting that these issues had been fully discussed in *Chorlton* v. *Lings*, he said that if a legal disability was to be removed it must be done by Parliament.

In dismissing the argument, Lord Ashbourne argued from the point of custom that 'The Parliamentary Franchise has always been confined to men, and the word "person" cannot by any reasonable construction be held to be prophetically used to support an argument founded on a statute passed many years later.'[51] In this, he was supported by Lord Robertson who added that 'the question whether women should vote for members of Parliament is at least a grave and important question for Parliament to decide'.[52]

THE REACTION OF FELLOW SUFFRAGISTS

Although the women graduates lost their case, suffrage activists were delighted with the publicity that followed as it brought to wider attention the fact that in the eyes of the law women were not regarded as 'persons' and that, along with children and lunatics, they were subject to 'legal incapacity'.

Suffragists hoped that such a categorisation would raise awareness of the prejudice that existed against women, and that more people would come to accept that women should have the same voting rights as men. In her report to the IWSA Congress in London in 1909, Millicent Fawcett announced that 'The decision was not unexpected, but it was felt that the action of the Scottish graduates had been able and dignified and that it had been effective propaganda.'[53]

At this time, Chrystal Macmillan and Frances Simson became heroines, enjoying the prestige and honour following their appearance at the House of Lords. Chrystal Macmillan was already known as a speaker and campaigner in the suffrage movement but now she became an inspirational figure among the network of women who had supported the graduates' action. She received a standing ovation when she attended a rally for industrial and professional women at the Queen's Hall in London a few days after the hearing:

> It is inspiring to hear thousands of people cheer and wave for two or three minutes before they let me begin to speak as they did. It made me realise how avidly the case is known. The chairman did not announce my name clearly so I suppose the audience must have recognised my hat![54]

However, as she confessed to her friend Sylvia Murray, 'I felt rather solitary because I had not a single friend in the hall. Tickets were not to be had and even my hostess had such a cold that she could not come out.'

Later in November, both she and Frances Simson were given an accolade by Sarah Siddons Mair, President of the Edinburgh National Society for Women's Suffrage (ENSWS), who hosted an event held in their home city by the United Suffragists of Edinburgh. Guests at the meeting included representatives of the Women's Freedom League (WFL) and the Women's Social and Political Union (WSPU):

> Miss Mair said it was a very brave act these ladies performed when they went up to London to plead that case in person . . . It was a great contribution to the cause that these Scottish graduates had been able to render. They were waiting to hear the result of the case, but whatever happened they would always be grateful for that great contribution made to their armoury of argument. They had brought very prominently before the public the extraordinary judgment that some people had of brains – those people who judged them, not by the quantity or quality, but by the sex of their possessors.[55]

It was perhaps surprising that Chrystal Macmillan opened her speech with a reference to rumours that the 'Mrs Grundy[56] of Edinburgh' disapproved of the women graduates taking the case further than the Court of Session in Edinburgh, highlighting the fact that some Scottish people believed that there should be no appeal made higher than to the Scottish court.

In her response to the enthusiastic reception she received from the audience in Edinburgh, Chrystal Macmillan paid tribute to the many woman suffrage supporters who had made possible their actions, including the other appellants in the case, namely Margaret Nairn, Elsie Inglis and Frances Melville, and all the Scottish women graduates who had cooperated through the Graduates Committee. She also noted the 'generous grant' from the Edinburgh Suffrage Society[57] and a subscription from Priscilla Bright McLaren.[58] In an article about her speech, the *Edinburgh Evening News* related the way in which she had engaged and entertained her audience:

> There was one little secret she would like to tell that meeting. As she came to the middle of one of her sentences in the course of her speech in the House of Lords, she felt that the sentence was going to finish with the words, 'Votes for Women'. (Laughter) She determined that she should say that little bit of the sentence very clearly and distinctly and she said it with a great deal of expression. But nobody noticed it, not even the appellants in the pew. It was of interest, however, to know that these terrible words had been said aloud by a woman in the House of Lords. (Laughter and applause)[59]

CONCLUSION

The Scottish Women Graduates' Case represented yet another stage in the suffrage mission to educate the public about women's claim for equal treatment with men regarding voting rights in Parliamentary elections. The novelty of two women taking a legal appeal to the House of Lords caught the imagination of the press, which gave the case considerable coverage, both in the quality newspapers and in those with popular appeal. The reports expressed surprise at the capability of a young woman – Chrystal Macmillan – to argue a legal case so competently, while also giving notice that women graduates wanted their fair share in public life and were not going to remain silent.

The suffrage movement took pride in the women's skilled presentation of the case, particularly that of Chrystal Macmillan, and sent messages of support as well as contributions to the women's legal costs. Many women were shocked by the ruling that they could be considered 'not to be persons' under the voting laws and this phrase was included in their propaganda to put more pressure of the government to grant women the vote.

Through this sequence of landmark court appearances, first in the Court of Session in Edinburgh, then in the House of Lords in London, Chrystal Macmillan became a well-known figure, not only in Scotland but throughout Britain. She was to build on this reputation and use it to help sustain the suffrage cause until, in 1928, women over the age of 21 were given electoral equality with men.

Notes

1. Sheila Hamilton, 'The First Generations of University Women 1869–1930', in Gordon Donaldson (ed.), *Four Centuries: Edinburgh University Life 1583–1983* (Edinburgh: Edinburgh University Press, 1983), p. 103.
2. For fuller discussion, see Lindy Moore, *Bajellas and Semilinas: Aberdeen University and the Education of Women 1860–1920* (Aberdeen: Aberdeen University Press, 1991), pp. 20–36.
3. For further information on Elsie Inglis, see Ewan et al., *The New Biographical Dictionary*, p. 210.
4. Ibid., p. 314.
5. One of eight women who were first to graduate from Edinburgh University in 1893.
6. One of eight women who were first to graduate from Edinburgh University in 1893, and first Warden of Masson Hall, a women's hall of residence, Edinburgh University; a post she retained for forty years. See Hamilton, 'The First Generations'.

7. Representation of the People (Scotland) Act 1868 c.48 Part III Elections in Universities Section 33.
8. First Graduation of Female Students, 1893 – Our History, https://ourhistory.is.ed.ac.uk/index.php?title=First_Graduation_of_Female_Students,_1893.
9. *The Student* VIII, Feb. 1894, p. 244.
10. Letter Helen Waddel, *The Scotsman*, 20 Dec. 1905.
11. *Dundee Evening Telegraph*, 29 Jan. 1906.
12. *The Scotsman*, 1 Feb. 1906.
13. Edinburgh University Court Minute, 12 Feb. 1906.
14. Letter Chrystal Macmillan to Millicent Fawcett, 14 Feb. 1906 (Manchester Archives. Local Studies M50/3/1/38).
15. Letter E. Wolstenholme Elmy, 16 Feb. 1906, fol. 211. Elmy refers to the case of *Chorlton* v. *Lings* 1868 where the Appeal Court in England decided that a woman was ineligible to vote: the judges argued that Common Law placed women 'under legal incapacity' to vote.
16. Ladies' Column, *Midlothian Journal*, 2 Mar. 1906.
17. *The Dundee Courier*, 19 Mar. 1906.
18. Letter Chrystal Macmillan to Helen McIlquham, 9 Mar. 1906: Elizabeth Wolstenholme Elmy Papers. London: British Library.
19. *Aberdeen Press & Journal*, 28 June 1906.
20. The Lord Ordinary's Opinion in *Nairn* v. *University Courts of St Andrews and Edinburgh* 1908 S.C 113, pp. 115–18, quoted in Leah Leneman, 'When Women Were Not "Persons": The Scottish Women Graduates' Case, 1906–8', *Juridical Review*, Pt 1 (April 1991), pp. 109–18.
21. 1868 SLR 6-100.
22. 1868 L. R. 4 C., p. 374.
23. *Nairn and Others* v. *the University Courts of St Andrews and Edinburgh and Others*. Court of Session 45 SLR 122.
24. *Women's Suffrage Record*, 1 July 1906, p. 9, quoted in Leneman, 'When Women Were Not "Persons"'.
25. 'Women Graduates' Appeal in Edinburgh', *Women's Franchise*, 7 Nov. 1907.
26. *Aberdeen Press & Journal*, 23 Oct. 1907.
27. *Northern Whig*, 18 Nov. 1907.
28. *Nairn* v. *University Courts of St Andrews and Edinburgh*, 1908. S.C. 113.
29. *Votes for Women*, 6 Dec. 1907.
30. *Dundee Evening Telegraph*, 9 Dec. 2007.
31. *Aberdeen Press & Journal*, 17 Mar. 1908.
32. Edith Hooper had a flat in Chenies Street Chambers, Ladies' Residential Dwellings set up for professional women in Bloomsbury in the 1880s. Founders of the scheme included Agnes Garrett and her sister Dr Elizabeth Garrett Anderson – see Elizabeth Crawford, *Enterprising Women: The Garretts and their Circle* (London: Francis Boutle, 2002).
33. Letter Chrystal Macmillan to Eunice Murray, 19 Nov. 1908 (London: Women's Library, LSE).

34. *Daily Chronicle*, 4 Nov. 1908.
35. 'Preface' to *Report of the Scottish Women Graduates' Appeal in the House of Lords November 10th and December 11th, 1908*. London: Woman Citizen Publishing Society. Leneman, 'When Women Were Not "Persons"', notes that the full text of proceedings was also reproduced in *Women's Franchise*.
36. School boards were the earliest form of public office for which women in Scotland could vote and stand: these women were also concerned with women's suffrage – see Esther Breitenbach, 'Edinburgh Suffragists: Exercising the Franchise at Local Level', *Book of the Old Edinburgh Club New Series* 15 (2019), pp. 63–80.
37. *Report of the Scottish Women Graduates*, p. 12.
38. Ibid., p. 45.
39. Ibid., p. 24.
40. Ibid., p. 36.
41. Ibid., p. 47.
42. Ibid., p. 49.
43. Ibid., p. 51.
44. Letter Chrystal Macmillan to Eunice Murray, 9 Nov. 1908. Microfiche TWL6.1 (London: Women's Library, LSE).
45. Ibid.
46. John Mair, junior advocate who 'devilled' for Lord Alness in Edinburgh – see obituary for Chrystal Macmillan by Lord Alness, *The Scotsman*, 24 Sept. 1937.
47. Letter Chrystal Macmillan to Sylvia Murray, 18 Nov. 1908, Microfiche TWL 6.1 (London: Women's Library, LSE).
48. Ibid., 19 Nov. 1908. Microfiche TWL 6.1 (London: Women's Library, LSE).
49. Cuttings can be seen in Eunice Murray's scrapbook in the Women's Library, LSE, London.
50. *Nottingham Evening Post*, 11 Dec. 1908.
51. *Report of the Scottish Women Graduates' Appeal in the House of Lords*, 1908, p. 55.
52. Ibid., p. 57.
53. IWSA Report of Fifth Congress, London 26 April–1 May 1909, p. 103.
54. Letter Chrystal Macmillan to Sylvia Murray, 18 Nov. 1908.
55. *Edinburgh Evening News*, 23 Nov. 1908.
56. 'Who is Mrs Grundy?', *Linlithgowshire Gazette*, Oct. 1896.
57. *The Scotsman*, 23 Nov. 1908.
58. Priscilla Bright McLaren, first president of the Edinburgh Women's Suffrage Society. See entry on her in Ewan et al., *The New Biographical Dictionary*, s.v.
59. *Edinburgh Evening News*, 23 Nov. 1908.

3

Women, Suffrage and Parliament

CHRYSTAL MACMILLAN'S CAMPAIGN FOR WOMEN'S SUFFRAGE IN SCOTLAND

The women's suffrage movement in Scotland had started to take shape during the 1860s. Many middle-class women who had experience of campaigning for other issues, and particularly for temperance or the abolition of slavery, turned their attention to the women's suffrage campaign. In November 1867, the ENSWS was established, with Priscilla Bright McLaren as its first president:[1] this society held meetings and sent speakers around Scotland from 1870 to 1890. Local branches were formed in many parts of Scotland, and members regularly raised petitions for presentation to MPs and to Parliament,[2] where women's suffrage was debated eleven times between 1870 and 1884.[3] There followed a lull in Parliamentary activity until 1906, when the suffrage movement in Scotland was revitalised and active campaigning began again.[4]

The ENSWS was affiliated to the National Union of Women Suffrage Societies (NUWSS), led by Millicent Fawcett, with headquarters in London. Chrystal Macmillan was a member, and her campaigning took her all over Scotland, to Greenock, Campbeltown and Glasgow in the west; Aberdeen, Dundee, Edinburgh and Fife on the east coast; and into the Highlands and Northern islands of Orkney and Shetland. Sometimes she represented ENSWS, at other times the Edinburgh University Women's Suffrage Society (EUWSS): later, after 1909, she acted on behalf of the Scottish Federation of Women Suffrage Societies (SFWSS), sometimes known as the Scottish Union of Women's Suffrage Societies, which was also affiliated to the British organisation, NUWSS.

NUWSS, formed in 1897, was the oldest of the three main women's suffrage organisations campaigning in Britain: its membership increased from 8,000 in 1908 to 54,592 by 1914.[5] Members of the organisation, including Chrystal Macmillan, believed in campaigning by 'constitutional' non-violent methods, such as holding public meetings, presenting petitions to Parliament, holding processions, lobbying MPs and leading deputations to Ministers: they came to be known as 'suffragists'.

There were two other main suffrage organisations campaigning in Scotland, the WSPU, established in 1903 by Emmeline and Christabel Pankhurst, and the WFL, formed in 1907 by a group of women who split from the WSPU in protest at the authoritarian regime imposed by the Pankhurst leadership. The members of these two militant organisations came to be known as 'suffragettes'.

Prior to 1909, all the suffrage organisations cooperated with one another in their campaigns. NUWSS regularly reported on WSPU activities in their journal *The Common Cause* and members of non-militant organisations had articles published in *Votes for Women*, the WSPU journal. For example, Chrystal Macmillan wrote an article on the 'Scottish Graduates' Case' for *Votes for Women*.[6]

Following her success in arguing the case for Scottish women graduates (see Chapter 2), Chrystal Macmillan was invited to give a lecture in London on the day of the opening of Parliament, 16 February 1909. The text of this speech was published by the WSPU in a pamphlet entitled 'The Struggle for Political Liberty', and in it, Chrystal Macmillan condemned the fact that the King's Speech contained no reference to women's demands for the franchise, and presented an analysis of their political struggle:

> When the history of the twentieth century comes to be written, it will be told how its first years witnessed a great revival of interest in and enthusiasm for the fundamental principles of liberty, and freedom and justice, an awakening to the fact that, if in theory men hold these things good for all, in practice they are a monopoly of certain privileged classes . . . [T]hose born to the ruling class unwillingly yield to the pressure of the people. They resist always in the belief that they are acting only for the good of the people, and as anxious to save them from responsibility . . . The governing class bases its hereditary claim on the natural or divine order of things and shuts its eyes to the fact that what it takes to be the natural order is merely a passing political custom.[7]

This might seem an unusual statement from a middle-class woman with a private income, but she herself may have felt uncomfortable working with the aristocratic women in the suffrage movement who could exercise influence through their husbands or other family members, whereas her family wealth was derived from 'trade'. She may have been directing her criticism at the rule of men at that time when women played no public part in political life.

In her speech, she reviewed the history of men's struggle to widen the franchise, from the Divine Right of Kings to the limitation of the franchise to landowners, but strongly condemned those men of her time who were unwilling to share with women the responsibility of electing MPs, thereby refusing to share the responsibility of governing the country. She observed that women in many countries had started

> . . . to ask for the franchise on the same terms as it is now, or may be, exercised by men, leaving any required extension to be decided by the men and women together. Be the franchise wide or be it limited, it must not exclude women on the ground of sex. In other words, women demand that they should be recognised as 'the people'.

The wide-ranging speech, published in full by WSPU, concluded with a demand for a Women's Charter to give women the same privileges as men, including the right to vote in Parliamentary elections. She continued to voice her vision of a Women's Charter throughout her career including a response to the League of Nations (see later in this chapter).

At this time, members of these different suffrage organisations shared platforms and took part in each other's processions. In 1907, the Edinburgh suffrage procession and demonstration was organised by ENSWS and had speakers from NUWSS, WSPU and WFL: women travelled from Glasgow and Dundee to march wearing the NUWSS colours of red and white.[8] This cooperation between the suffrage organisations continued until 1909.

Chrystal Macmillan, a member of EUWSS, and her friend Eunice Murray, a member of WFL, often campaigned together in 1908, and Eunice Murray described the experience in her diary:

> She and I have been having an outdoor campaign on the Clyde. We have visited Rothesay, Dunoon, Gourock, Greenock and Campbeltown. She so tall and stately, and me so willing to do my best.
> The first day she vanished into a shop and came out and handed me a piece of chalk or pipe clay. 'What's that?' said I. 'For you to chalk the pavement', said she. 'I'll do one side and you can do the other'. I had no idea what she meant but soon found my fate was to stoop down and write 'Votes for women meeting on esplanade 3.30'. As soon as I got one written someone came along and rubbed it out, or a crowd gathered round and jeered. Beastly job!
> Chris didn't seem to mind. I looked over and there she was, her scarf floating gracefully behind her, not choking her as mine did, but most

marvellous of all she was quite indifferent to the attentions of the crowd that surrounded her, so I remembered the hymn and took fresh courage and finished my part.[9]

In Campbeltown it was noted in the press that the two women arrived by the turbine steamer, the *Queen Alexandra*, and spoke from a waggonette to a sympathetic audience, mainly of fishermen.[10] It was recorded as the first time a suffrage meeting had been held in the town. In Greenock they spoke to a small audience at the outset but gradually the numbers increased, along with some heckling. By the time the women were joined by Elsie Inglis to speak in Dumfries in March 1909, they were well able to handle the heckling, and the local newspapers reported the speeches in full, noting that Chrystal Macmillan had a pleasant voice, and answered all the questions. By now a competent speaker in public, she confidently confronted her audiences with a robust challenge, declaring on one occasion that

> All the different societies in the movement are working for the same object and that is the granting to women of votes on the same terms as it is granted at present to men. (booing) . . . Men who have the necessary qualifications are debarred at present only if they are paupers, criminals or lunatics . . . Men have made a more comfortable world for boys and men than for girls and women, and the women now want the power to make the world more comfortable for the girls and women, without doing any harm to the boys and men (laughter and cheers).[11]

That year, 1909, Chrystal Macmillan extended her speaking tours throughout Scotland and, occasionally, into England. During September she became the main speaker for the suffragist campaign in the north of Scotland and the Northern Isles. As she reported back to her colleagues:

> Mrs Wilson M.A. (Aberdeen) and I held an outdoor meeting in Dingwall and at Ullapool – a town 30 miles from a railway [where] we had a crowded meeting in the Drill Hall . . . At Lybster and Halkirk in spite of short notice our halls were well filled. At Wick the Drill Hall was packed – it seats 800 – and all the available standing room was full. This was the first indoor Suffrage meeting that had been held here and everyone prophesied a rowdy meeting. It was almost too quiet. The audience seemed so anxious to hear everything. Provost Ross very kindly presided as did Provost Durran at Thurso the following evening. Here too, the largest hall in the town was packed to overflowing.[12]

These reports remind us that there was great public interest in the woman suffrage campaign, and the only way for the public to learn more was to attend a public meeting. But speakers had to be ready to face noisy opposition and able to handle the hecklers.

When Chrystal Macmillan spoke in Orkney and Shetland, the audiences were not always as attentive. In Kirkwall it was reported that

> Miss Macmillan had a very poor hearing on account of an uproar caused by some boys who obtained admission to the gallery . . . Sir Victor Horsley expressed regret that the meeting had not given Miss Macmillan a better hearing for the question, he assured them, was a national one of supreme importance.[13]

Moreover, her travel arrangements did not always go to plan. She described the difficulties faced by campaigning suffragists:

> I have had a busy week, as distances are great, and the steamers by no means regular. This not only affects one's ability to go from place to place, but means that posts are more uncertain, and halls have generally to be taken by wire . . . On Tuesday, I had planned to go to Stronsay, but the wind and sea were so high that a six hours' journey in a small steamer seemed out of the question.[14]

Despite the difficulties of travelling to remote areas, the efforts made by the women were often rewarded by the formation of local suffrage societies in the places where they had spoken. For example, after several successful meetings in Orkney, and encouraged by Chrystal Macmillan's visit, twelve local women came together to form the Orcadian Women's Suffrage Association.

Her meetings in Shetland drew very different responses from the two local newspapers, *Shetland News* and the *Shetland Times*.[15] The former reported that the hall was so full at a meeting in Lerwick that some people had to be turned away. The paper also included a full account of her speech in which she emphasised her status as a graduate member of the Scottish University Women's Suffrage Union (SUWSU). Her speech also exemplified the fact that early women graduates felt that they owed it to the next generation to continue to improve the situation for women:

> Women who had benefitted by the opening of the universities felt they should do something that would benefit future generations of women . . . So far, their intellects had been allowed to develop, but at present they were not allowed to develop their sense of responsibility towards the State . . . Men could not be expected to see things from a woman's point of view, and they could not have a just government until they had both men and women's views represented, and the only means of making that possible was to give women the vote.[16]

In this speech Chrystal Macmillan voiced her view that women cannot expect men to understand the female perspective and therefore cannot represent women's point of view in government, and that government will be improved once women play their part, working alongside men in the governance of the country.

In contrast to the *Shetland News* report, the *Shetland Times* published a reader's letter excoriating the women's movement, while a columnist dismissed the suffragist campaign without even attending the meeting, basing his article on a chance meeting in the street:

> I felt that it would have been pleasant to be scolded by so charming a young girl. There was nothing of the 'blue stocking' about Miss Macmillan. She looked just 'a bright sonsy wise-like Scotch lassie'. The picture of health, she set one's mind a-thinking of lowing cattle, of teeming fields, of cackling hens and all the one hundred and one sounds and sights of the farmyard; and the very last thing one would have associated her with was Women's Suffrage ... And I could not but help imagining that it would be all the better for the race, for the country and for the Empire, if such big, healthy, strong lasses had all their attention glued to the nursery, rather than gadding about the country following a kind of will-o'-the-wisp, and procuring a sort of cheap notoriety as 'pioneers' and 'martyrs' in the 'cause'.[17]

This press report takes the anti-suffrage perspective, outlining a more appropriate role for women as wives and mothers, and linking this perspective to the then current ideals on the promotion of the British race and their role in the ruling and sustaining of the British Empire – certainly not a view of Empire that Chrystal Macmillan shared.

From the Northern Isles, Chrystal Macmillan travelled to the Scottish mainland and rushed back to Edinburgh to take part in the WSPU Suffrage procession on 9 October 1909.[18] The newspapers reported that a considerable number of women graduates participated and that the Edinburgh University Women's Suffrage Union had participated in the organisation of the procession. However, Chrystal Macmillan participated as an individual, as ENSWS cooperation had been withdrawn on account of the first acts of violence committed by WSPU members.[19] (A re-enactment of the 1909 procession was held in Edinburgh in 2009 to commemorate the event and encourage women's current political participation.[20])

After participating in the Edinburgh procession, and before returning to the campaigning, Chrystal Macmillan took part in a deputation of women to Edinburgh Town Council to object to Prime Minister Asquith being given the Freedom of the City, on the grounds that they found his implacable anti-suffrage views unacceptable. The Council allowed the women to speak, as 'rate payers', but dismissed their objection.

Chrystal Macmillan then returned to the north of Scotland to continue the suffrage campaign, speaking to crowded meetings in Helmsdale, Brora, Golspie, Dornoch, Cromarty and Alness.[21] By January 1910, prior to the general election, she was the principal worker in the Fife suffrage campaign against Herbert Asquith, leader of the Liberal Party, 'not because he is a Liberal, but because he is unfavourable to women's suffrage'.[22] Throughout the spring of that year, she addressed meetings in Dundee, St Andrews, Cupar, Falkirk and Galashiels. July was the month of two mass meetings, a joint NUWSS, WSPU, WFL and SUWSU demonstration on Calton Hill in Edinburgh[23] and an NUWSS demonstration in Trafalgar Square in London:[24] she was a main speaker at both events. Referring to MPs and the passage of the Conciliation Bill in her Trafalgar Square speech, she said:

> Time was when a man, when he said he approved of Women's Suffrage and did nothing, was considered a supporter. That time is past. Unless he uses all his strength and all his power to put that measure on the Statute Book, he is no supporter of ours.[25]

This speech intimates the change in attitude of the suffrage movement toward Liberal and Conservative politicians who said they supported women's suffrage but then, when the parliamentary party demanded that MPs support the government policy of not granting the parliamentary vote to women, these MPs would support the party line and vote against bills designed to widen the franchise to include women. This change in attitude later led to the development of the NUWSS policy of supporting Labour candidates.

HARMONY AND DISCORD WITHIN THE SUFFRAGE MOVEMENT

Speaking in Shetland in 1909, Chrystal Macmillan spoke of the cooperation between the suffrage organisations: 'There are seven of eight different societies in the country working for Women's Suffrage and although they all work on different lines, it is a remarkable thing that they [are] all agreed in what they are asking for.'[26] However, the cooperation of the suffrage organisations was not to last: in the later months of 1909, members of the non-militant organisations began to question the violent activities of the WSPU, and the press fanned the flames by trying to set the two sides against one another.[27] For example, the *Aberdeen Press &*

Figure 3.1 Frances Simson, unknown, Chrystal Macmillan, NUWSS march, London, 1909 (Christina Broom photo © London Museum)

Journal published an article unfavourably comparing the women graduates with their militant sisters:

> The difference between Miss Chrystal Macmillan and Miss Frances Simson, the leaders of the little band of ladies from St Andrews, and the Drummond-Pankhurst combination, is as wide as it possibly could be. Miss Macmillan, the lady who conducted the hearing before the Lord Chancellor and his colleagues, is of quiet and refined manner, not at all like the representatives of the 'Shrieking sisterhood' who have caused so much trouble recently; and the appearance and the behaviour of herself and her companions showed that the claim to a right, real or supposed, need not be accompanied by a species of female hooliganism.[28]

An un-named writer for *The Common Cause* challenged the press claim that, by their actions, the militants were preventing the voice of more moderate women from being heard:

> To be a woman, who wants the vote, is to be classed at once as disorderly, and to ask a perfectly orderly question in a perfectly orderly way is (if the question relates to women) to be thrown out of a meeting with every accompaniment of brutality, even if you are a man . . . [The newspapers] fill their

pages with record and comment on the militants and leave unrecorded our reasonable propaganda and demonstration.[29]

When challenged to say whether she supported 'the tactics of the ladies who smashed the windows of Mr Asquith's house', Chrystal Macmillan answered that she had only seen press reports and reports were not always correct. But she also expressed sympathy for the militant suffragettes as they were unable to get the vote by constitutional means. Moreover, violence had been shown against the women and they were now just 'turning the violence in another direction'.[30]

The issue of violence by and against members of the WSPU was discussed at the NUWSS Quarterly Council Meeting in Cardiff when a resolution 'condemning the use of violence in political propaganda' was passed.[31] The report of the meeting noted that the discussion was long and without rancour. It acknowledged that the actions of the militants had brought much more public awareness to the women's cause, and they refused to condemn the women, though they did condemn the violence: 'It was felt that they are "good women" and you do not condemn the good . . . The militants do what they think right, and what they do is very hard and very terrible in its results for them, and we cannot condemn them.'[32]

Addressing the Aberdeen University Women's Suffrage Association, Chrystal Macmillan expressed her sympathy for the WSPU women who had been 'arrested and thrown into a cell with stone floors without being convicted', and commended the actions of the local MP for Aberdeenshire who had helped the women. However, she also emphasised that she believed that it was better to 'have faith in the power of persuasion' than in violence.[33]

MAKING POLITICAL PROGRESS?

By 1911, despite the vigorous and arduous campaigning by women since the 1860s, there was still no sign of the government changing its position on granting women the franchise, and women's frustration was mounting. Writing to *The Common Cause* in 1911, Chrystal Macmillan entreated suffragists to continue to educate the electorate but also to seek out other methods of campaigning – and 'put Suffrage before Party'. This sounded like a reasonable campaign slogan but one that Chrystal Macmillan was going to find difficult to accept when, the following year, NUWSS decided to support the only political party which included women's suffrage in its manifesto, namely the Labour Party.

From 1910 through to 1912, three 'Conciliation Bills' were introduced to Parliament, based on the work of the Conciliation Committee, a committee of MPs representing all shades of opinion on suffrage within the House of Commons.[34] At an NUWSS-led deputation of Scottish women to the Lord Advocate at Parliament House, Edinburgh, Chrystal Macmillan pressed him to support the second reading of a Conciliation Bill:

> Introducing the group, the local organiser, Miss Lisa Gordon, said that they were members of the constitutional society which had 30,000 members. Chrystal Macmillan who was, by this time, an experienced speaker and lobbyist, spoke on behalf of the group: the principal object of the deputation was to ask the Lord Advocate if he would give his vote for the second reading of the Conciliation Bill, the voting on 22nd March being of the utmost importance as it was the first expression of opinion on the question in 1912. The Lord Advocate stated that he had been a believer in Women's Suffrage all his life and though he had not spoken for it, he had been a constant supporter. He understood that the NUWSS did not support the Conciliation Bill as an ideal but as a practical measure and he pledged himself to vote for its second reading.[35]

Chrystal Macmillan and members of NUWSS, alongside women of other suffrage organisations, threw their weight into campaigning for the Conciliation Bill: 'NUWSS had written letters, organised deputations, courted politicians, collaborated with political associations and devised countless other lobbying strategies.'[36]

When the Speaker of the House of Commons announced that a women's suffrage amendment to the Conciliation Bill would not be possible – which meant that a measure for women's suffrage within the foreseeable future was swept away – women's enthusiasm turned to anger. In Scotland, this failure had a devastating effect on the Scottish Women's Liberal Federation, which had conducted a robust campaign, working consistently to promote a women's suffrage clause, making contact with every Liberal constituency and directly with every Scottish Liberal MP, as well as Prime Minister Asquith.[37]

MEMBERSHIP OF THE NUWSS EXECUTIVE COMMITTEE

In 1912, Chrystal Macmillan was elected to the Executive Committee (EC) of NUWSS. She attended and spoke at the regular NUWSS weekly meetings in London even though she was still resident in Edinburgh and continuing to campaign in Scotland. She became chair of the NUWSS Organisation Committee dealing with national administration of the organisation, such as the appointment and training of paid organisers, as well as the administration of their salaries and grants to local sections for paid secretaries: it was no surprise when she was later appointed Assistant Treasurer.

She was also a member of the NUWSS Parliamentary Committee, so her voice carried some weight in committee and with members. Nevertheless, her concerns were not always shared by her colleagues, and she became embroiled in internal dissensions over several issues.

In June 1912, the NUWSS EC decided that they would no longer support Liberal candidates who, although expressing sympathy with the cause, then voted against measures in the House of Commons. The NUWSS Parliamentary Officer, Catherine Marshall, proposed that the National Union should change its non-party policy and work with Labour candidates in by-elections, as the Labour Party had become the only party to adopt a commitment to some measure of women's suffrage as party policy.

This caused much heart searching in constituencies where NUWSS members had been supporting and working with sympathetic Liberal MPs. Chrystal Macmillan felt that Catherine Marshall's proposal was a step too far and she initially abstained from supporting the policy.[38] Her concern was that if the NUWSS ceased to be a non-party organisation to one supporting a particular party, that is the Labour Party, this would drive away women sympathetic to the Liberal Party – and indeed Vice-President Lady Aberdeen later resigned from NUWSS because of the change in policy.[39]

However, the EC resolved that the NUWSS 'would support Labour candidates in all cases except where he is personally unsatisfactory in his views on Women's Suffrage', and it was agreed to set up an Electoral Fighting Fund (EFF) to support Labour Party candidates in by-elections, while the women worked out the policy in practice.

At the Midlothian by-election in September 1912, NUWSS implemented a campaign to support the Labour candidate, which resulted in the loss of the Liberal seat to the Conservative candidate.[40] After the election, Chrystal Macmillan took issue with the NUWSS's decision to support a Labour candidate, regardless of his attitude to the Reform Bill provisions: at the EC meeting in July she moved, seconded by Eleanor Rathbone,

> that the Committee considers that the Election policy of the Union was not correctly interpreted at Midlothian in view of the fact that the Labour candidate was supported by National Union when he had failed to pledge himself to vote against the third reading of the Reform Bill, should no women be included.

But she did not get the full support of the committee and the resolution was lost by seven votes to eleven.

The following year, when a by-election was held in Keighley, Chrystal Macmillan again raised concerns about the NUWSS policy of supporting the Labour candidate, noting that statements had been made by NUWSS workers that were positively party political, and that it had not confined its support to issues of women's suffrage; for example, the declaration that 'our business is to teach Suffrage and Labour'.[41] This was a clear departure from the original decision that NUWSS should be a non-party organisation, and so led to disharmony amongst members who held different political views.

The difficulty in implementing the EFF policy led to an even more serious disagreement when the Liverpool Suffrage Society questioned the decision to extend EFF policy to include general elections without having first held discussions or sought the approval of members at the National Council. When Eleanor Rathbone and three colleagues on the EC set up an informal committee to assess the feelings of members, they were accused of working against the NUWSS policy, and following an argument within the NUWSS EC, in 1914 the four women resigned. Although sympathetic to their unease about the implementation of the EFF policy generally,[42] Chrystal Macmillan did not join the informal committee led by Eleanor Rathbone, and she did not resign.

Arguments about general policy continued through the early months of 1914. When Margery Corbett Ashby suggested it was not good tactics to ask for women to be eligible to stand for Parliament, Chrystal Macmillan replied that it was undesirable for NUWSS to say it did *not* want women to be eligible for election.[43] She asked again for the phrase to be dropped from the resolution, but the committee overruled the objection and agreed the wording: 'It is not good tactics to include a demand for women to be eligible for Parliament', much to Chrystal Macmillan's disapproval.

When war was declared in August 1914, the NUWSS EC were committed to the organisation of relief work but unsure as to whether they should formulate a policy recommending that officers remain neutral in their publicly expressed views or one recommending that individuals could decide for themselves. Eventually Millicent Fawcett pointed out that according to the rules and constitution, the desire for enfranchisement of women was the only thing which united the members of the Union.[44]

From September 1914 through to 1915, the NUWSS EC continued to wrestle with the individual differences in members' attitudes towards the war. The NUWSS Annual Council met in London over three days in February 1915 when members of the EC hoped that the resolutions presented to the members of the Council would clarify the policy of the organisation and differences would be resolved. However, although the delegates voted for the resolutions supporting the view that war caused unnecessary suffering and was a poor way to resolve international disputes, they did not support any programme of work or give guidance on how the resolutions could be carried into action.

At the Executive meeting on 18 March 1915,[45] the women discussed the invitation to send delegates to the International Congress of Women (the lead up to the Congress and Chrystal Macmillan's role as one of the organisers is discussed in Chapter 4). Millicent Fawcett felt strongly that it was undesirable for the suffrage movement to be seen supporting a peace conference and that 'the time to be agitating for peace was so inopportune that to do so was almost treachery'. The EC meeting voted that delegates should not be sent to the Congress.

Millicent Fawcett and the right-leaning members of the EC raised the straw argument that the women who did not agree with them were proposing to 'work for peace now, including an immediate truce'. Catherine Marshall and Katherine Courtney had proposed that NUWSS should start a discussion on peace education, linked to the development of a policy that defined the kind of settlement that women would want to be introduced at the end of the war. Despite this proposal, Millicent Fawcett continued to present the discussion as an argument between those who wanted to focus on supporting the British war efforts and those who wanted 'peace at any price now'. Over the following four weeks, ten members of the EC decided to resign in protest, not only because the peace education proposal was excluded but also in protest against the undemocratic decision to exclude it from further discussion.[46]

Chrystal Macmillan, who was at this point helping to organise the International Women's Congress at The Hague, did not participate in the discussion about the Congress at the March EC meeting but she was present and proposed the motion that affiliated societies and federations were not at liberty to pass resolutions either in support of or against the war, nor were they free to express an opinion on the war when speaking on behalf of NUWSS: this motion was carried.

Although other members of the EC resigned, Chrystal Macmillan did not resign. Writing to Evelyn Atkinson, NUWSS Secretary, she gave her reasons:

> I hold strongly and have at many times fought for the opinion that a member of the Executive is responsible, not to the Executive as a whole, but to the

Council which elects her, and therefore, her voting in minority is one of the strongest reasons why she should not resign. She should remain on in order to fight for the point of view whenever possible. She is right to assume the Council put her there for the purpose.[47]

And so, despite their differences, Chrystal Macmillan and Millicent Fawcett continued to work together on the NUWSS EC and in the IWSA Headquarter Committee throughout the war.

POLITICS AND TENSIONS BETWEEN THE SCOTTISH FEDERATION AND NUWSS EXECUTIVE

Chrystal Macmillan continued to play an active role in the Scottish suffrage movement after becoming resident in London in 1913 and was expected to present 'the Scottish point of view' to the NUWSS EC – an impossible expectation, given that the Scottish societies that were affiliated to NUWSS did not all share the same views. For example, from the early 1900s, the Glasgow and West of Scotland Association for Women's Suffrage (GWSAWS) and the ENSWS differed in their interpretation of NUWSS campaign policy.

Tensions between staff at the London HQ and the GWSAWS arose when the Glasgow committee proposed setting up the Scottish Federation of Women's Suffrage Societies. Although the London-based committee initially disapproved, SFWSS was established, with an office in Edinburgh, in November 1909. Sarah Siddons Mair was elected president, Andrew Ballantyne of the Glasgow Society became the chair and Dr Elsie Inglis the secretary. The societies in Inverness and Nairn were initially unhappy about the new organisation and applied to NUWSS HQ to form a Northern Federation, though they did eventually join the Scottish Federation. The SFWSS attracted 30 to 40 delegates from branches all over Scotland to the monthly meetings and the organisation oversaw much of the campaigning for women's suffrage in Scotland.

In late November 1913, tensions eased when the Scottish Federation focused on developing a strategy for the inclusion of a women's suffrage clause in the Scottish Home Rule Bill: they asked MPs and all Scottish Parliamentary candidates to 'press for the inclusion of women as electors in the Scottish Home Rule Bill and oppose any such Bill where women are not so included'. During 1914 they lobbied MPs, both in the constituencies and the House of Commons, until the clause was inserted into the Bill. Not unexpectedly, the Bill failed to gain passage through Parliament, but the Scottish Federation's efforts were clearly appreciated

Figure 3.2 Scottish Federation of Women's Suffrage Societies, Glasgow, October 1913
Front row from left: Mrs Laurie, Millicent Fawcett, Miss Henderson, Miss S. E. S. Mair, Dr Elsie Inglis, Miss K. W. Lindsay, Miss Low, Miss Gordon; back row: Miss Chrystal Macmillan (centre), Mrs Hunter, Mr Ballantyne (courtesy Women's Library, LSE)

by Millicent Fawcett who recorded her 'very hearty congratulations upon the success scored about women in Scottish Home Rule Bill. It was more than I dared to expect, whatever I hoped. I know how splendidly the Scot Fed have worked for it.'[48]

The interpretation of EFF policy continued to be a source of tension between the Scottish suffragists and NUWSS HQ in London throughout 1913 and 1914.[49] The ENSWS, which was happy to work directly with NUWSS HQ in London, provoked further disharmony when, at a meeting of the Scottish Federation in November 1913, it gave notice of its proposed resolution: 'That the Edinburgh Society asks leave of Executive Committee of the Scottish Federation to have complete control of EFF work in its own area and to arrange all details regarding such work directly with EFF Committee in London.'[50] This did not meet with the approval of the Scottish Federation which, when the issue was debated two months later, voted by twenty votes to six that 'EFF work in Scotland should be carried on under the auspices of Scottish Federation'.

When Chrystal Macmillan was elected chair of the Scottish Federation in March 1914, she inevitably had to deal with this divisive issue, being in the unenviable position of both leader of the Scottish suffrage organisations and representing the Scottish Federation on the NUWSS Executive based in London. She did, however, continue to have the support of the Edinburgh society (ENSWS), as expressed in the minutes of their 1913 annual report:

> [She] is an invaluable member of the Central Committee of the N.U.W.S.S. She ably represents the Scottish point of view on that Committee and interviews the Scottish Members of Parliament when any crisis in the political situation occurs.[51]

In April 1914, the Scottish Federation decided to accept a proposal from the NUWSS EFF Committee to form special committees in by-election constituencies where campaign work was to be undertaken along EFF guidelines. These committees would consist of equal numbers of the local society (if it was willing to undertake the work) and of the Federation. It was agreed that a Central EFF Committee of the Scottish Federation must be formed to coordinate all EFF work in Scotland – this committee to be in close touch with the NUWSS EFF Committee and to carry out work approved and initiated by them.

The Scottish Federation passed a resolution claiming 'the right under National Union constitution to appoint its own committees and carry out election work in its own area and maintains that that right cannot be taken away without an alteration in NUWSS Constitution'. In the following July, a conference was called in London to consider the delegation of EFF work: the Scottish Federation, represented by Chrystal Macmillan, Elsie Inglis and Mary Henderson, continued to claim the right of the Scottish Federation to conduct all election work in its own area. No vote was taken on the issues, but Millicent Fawcett acknowledged the position of the Scottish Federation, proposing that that the discussion should continue – the issue of the point of difference between the EFF Committee and the Scottish Federation being left open.

The outbreak of war brought an end to the tensions between London HQ and the Scottish Federation: it fell to Chrystal Macmillan to explain to members of the Scottish Federation that the NUWSS Executive had decided to suspend all political work and to request that the societies focus their activities on relief work.

The formidable energy and organisational skills of the Scottish Federation soon focused on fundraising and various relief works: their secretary, Elsie Inglis, proposed the formation of a Hospital for Services abroad, but when Chrystal Macmillan, as chair of the Scottish Federation, initially raised the issue at the NUWSS Executive meeting on 6 August in London, the proposal was dismissed. It took several weeks to get members of the Executive to change their minds; what they wanted was to take over the hospital scheme and call it the National Union of Women's Suffrage Societies Scottish Federation Hospital. However, the Scottish Federation held firm and recommended that the name of the project should be the Scottish Women's Hospital for Foreign Service, and it was agreed that 'NUWSS' would be used in the headings of all papers, letters and appeals and that the project would be advertised nationally with a public appeal for funds. The first chair of the committee was Chrystal Macmillan.

The Hospital Committee of the Scottish Federation grew in stature, with the appointment of a new chair and a treasurer dedicated to fundraising and furthering the work of the hospitals, with the Scottish Federation staff being paid for three months to assist with administration. Elsie Inglis, who was the driving force behind the project, was anxious to retain the support of the whole NUWSS and arranged to speak for the Scottish Women's Hospital at a Kingsway Hall meeting in London, calling her talk 'How women can help in time of War'. She proposed that a committee be formed in London to facilitate hospital work, and the Scottish Federation agreed to ask the London Society to appoint one.

In September 1915, Chrystal Macmillan resigned as chair of the Scottish Federation: she was no longer able to travel to Scottish meetings due to pressure of work as the organiser of the International Women's Relief Committee based in London.

CONSULTATIVE COMMITTEE OF CONSTITUTIONAL WOMEN'S SUFFRAGE SOCIETIES

The Consultative Committee of Constitutional Women's Suffrage Societies, known as the Women's Consultative Committee (WCC), was formed in 1916 and worked throughout the First World War to improve the representation of women in public life. At its first meeting in May that year, the chair of the committee, Eleanor Rathbone, welcomed the representatives from twelve constitutional suffrage societies, and listed the WCC objectives: to maintain the links between societies; to monitor government proposals for any change in suffrage registration; to make plans for demonstrations after the war; and to promote the representation of women on government committees.

Chrystal Macmillan was an active member of the WCC. She attended most monthly meetings and was popular with the twenty-to-thirty regular attenders from sixteen suffrage organisations, contributing to many resolutions and frequently accepting amendments proposed by others. She was elected to the Joint Parliamentary Committee of MPs and women representatives to consider an Equal Franchise Bill.

The WCC was a hard-working committee, pressing for women's suffrage to be brought to public attention and constantly lobbying the government and individual MPs. As a member of WCC, and with their backing, Millicent Fawcett wrote to Prime Minister Asquith in May 1916, drawing his attention to the change in public attitudes to women's enfranchisement, and a 'marked change of tone in the press'. She reminded him of all the work being undertaken by women 'to sustain the vital energies of the nation', especially noting the work of the Scottish Women's Hospital Service, and advised him that the continued exclusion of women from representation would be impossible after the war.

Amidst rumours of the government's intention to change the electoral register to include soldiers and sailors, members of individual suffrage societies were encouraged to write to their MPs, and branches were urged to write to the Select Committee on Registration and Electoral Reform to remind them of women's claim for representation.

Under competing pressures to reform the electoral register, the government agreed in October 1916 to set up a Conference under the leadership of the House of Commons Speaker to review the issue of registration and franchise and make recommendations to Parliament.[52]

After twenty-six sittings, the Conference made many recommendations, including the extension of the franchise to women on the Local Government Register. In an effort to ensure a majority of male voters, the Conference recommended that only women over the age of thirty be considered eligible.

The WCC acknowledged that the proposed legislation did not achieve what the suffrage movement wanted but it was the best chance to get some measure of women's suffrage passed into law. A period of intense activity followed: WCC members met regularly, to endorse letters to MPs, elect members to meet with sympathetic MPs and review the compromises necessary to ensure the passage of the proposed legislation, the Representation of the People Bill. At a WCC meeting in April 1917, Chrystal Macmillan proposed:

> That we, the undersigned representatives of our respective Societies, welcome the fact that the Electoral Reform Bill is to contain a provision for Woman suffrage; . . . and urge that the Government shall make itself responsible for the retention of Woman Suffrage in the Bill.[53]

Chrystal Macmillan studied the Bill carefully and produced a leaflet in 1918 that gave detailed information about which women would be eligible to vote under the Representation of the People Act:[54] this was the first guide to be published for women voters.[55] She continued to monitor the situation and in 1922 wrote an article for *The Women's Leader* urging women to check whether they were eligible to vote and whether they were on the electoral register.[56]

WOMEN'S WORK FOR EQUAL FRANCHISE 1918–1928

With the passing of the Representation of the People Act in 1918, the women's suffrage movement saw some changes. The following year, Millicent Fawcett resigned as president of NUWSS and the organisation, now under the leadership of Eleanor Rathbone, changed its name to the National Union of Societies for Equal Citizenship (NUSEC). Chrystal Macmillan continued as a member of the EC.

As far as the members of NUSEC were concerned, the granting of the vote to some women in 1918 was only the start of what had long been their ambition for women to have the same voting rights as men. In her lively account of the Parliamentary path to Equal Franchise, Mari Takayangi notes that 'between 1919 and 1927 there was not one year when an Equal Franchise Bill did not come before Parliament and in some years, there were more than one'.[57]

The NUSEC committees had to continue their energetic campaigning for another ten years to obtain the extension of the vote to all women over the age of 21. In 1922 the NUSEC Equal Franchise Committee, with Chrystal Macmillan as chair, met nine times,[58] and by 1923 this Committee had not only considered their campaign strategy, but also the registration of voters, the candidature of women for Parliament and proportional representation. In 1924, NUSEC had to employ more staff to cope with the influx of 'press enquiries, demand for publications, and requests for information, speakers and local workers'.[59]

When the Equal Franchise Act was passed on 2 July 1928, giving women electoral equality with men, and giving the vote to all women over 21 years old, Chrystal Macmillan was there with her suffrage colleagues in the House of Lords to witness the moment: it must have given them all cause to celebrate!

CHRYSTAL MACMILLAN'S RELATIONSHIPS WITHIN THE SUFFRAGE MOVEMENT

As chair of the Organisation Committee that directed the work of the paid NUWSS workers, Chrystal Macmillan could sometimes be over-pedantic: she frequently asked questions that annoyed the NUWSS leaders, such as, were decisions in line with the constitution, or what exactly had been agreed at NUWSS Council? She could also be high-handed, not always considering whether or not her questions or proposals would receive the backing of her colleagues, and occasionally raising issues that were regarded by them as being 'outside the scope of the NUWSS'.

In a committee meeting in March 1912, her decision to question Catherine Marshall's right, as Assistant Parliamentary Secretary, to sit and vote on the NUWSS EC inevitably caused upset: it neither endeared her to Catherine Marshall nor to other committee members, who voted against her proposal to limit Catherine's right to participate. And she again met opposition when she criticised NUWSS officers' decision to send a letter to the government, copied to the press on the eve of the committee meeting, without waiting to consult the committee. This made her unpopular both with the NUWSS officers and the other members of the committee who unanimously endorsed the officers' action.

However, despite these shortcomings, Chrystal Macmillan's honesty and knowledge of constitutions and regulations were beyond doubt and never questioned: she was one of two committee members appointed to review necessary changes to the rules of the organisation, and took on the role of the awkward person of independent thought, claiming that minority views should always be considered. This was a view that, when put into practice, came to annoy Millicent Fawcett, president of the NUWSS, and Carrie Chapman Catt, president of the IWSA, though neither of them was quite so explicit in their criticism as Adela Coit, a member of the London Society for Women's Suffrage:

> I quite agree with your view of Chrystal Macmillan's character. She is absolutely honest, but so often absorbed in her own particular view of a case that nothing will make her see anything else and she will go on spinning her own thread quite unconscious and unimpressed by what another person says and thinks. She is most tenacious in her own schemes and often absolutely non-committal when the scheme originates in anothers [sic] brain: see her withholding her vote in C[ommi]ttee when it is not her proposal.[60]

Such misgivings did not prevent Chrystal Macmillan from being given crucial roles within the NUWSS, in which she was acknowledged as a capable and trusted organiser. In January 1913 she was entrusted with the establishment of an Information Bureau, setting up the constitution and hiring paid staff. Another major success included planning and organising the NUWSS 1913 summer schools, one in Oxford and the other in St Andrews, where she gave two lectures: 'Parliament & Parliamentary Procedure' and 'Women under the Law'.

Moreover, she provided an important link with other organisations. By 1911 she was the trusted proxy for Millicent Fawcett at the IWSA Congress in Stockholm and two years later she was one of twelve British delegates to the IWSA Congress in Budapest, where she was elected Second Recording Secretary (see Chapter 6). And as a member of the NUWW EC, she reported back regularly to the NUWSS on matters of common interest, and vice versa. For example, she ensured that support was gathered within NUWW for the resolution, passed by the NUWW National Council in 1913, confirming that 'without the firm foundation of the Parliamentary Franchise for women, there is no permanence for any advance gained by them'.

ASPIRATIONS TO ENTER PARLIAMENT

'Miss Chrystal Macmillan, B.Sc., M.A. has also ambitions towards the green benches of the House of Commons' – so the *Dundee Courier* asserted in December 1919. However, there is no evidence of her seeking nomination to Parliament till many years later, in 1935. By that time, she was very experienced with Parliamentary procedures, learning when best to lobby MPs, advising MPs and various committees on how to write the

Figure 3.3 NUWSS Scottish Summer School, St Andrews, 1913. Chrystal Macmillan holding Edinburgh Banner (courtesy Women's Library, LSE)

first draft of Bills to be presented to the House of Commons, and giving evidence to Select Committees.

In November 1935, the North Edinburgh Liberal Association adopted her unanimously as their candidate for the forthcoming Parliamentary elections. She, like her father, who was elected to the EC of the Midlothian Liberal Unionist Association in 1895,[61] had always inclined towards the Liberal Party, and for the 1935 election she stood as a Free Trade Liberal, in support of the Liberal leader Sir Herbert Samuel's policy. Her opponents were the Unionist, Alexander Erskine, and Gerald Crawford for the National Labour Party.[62]

Among the motives for choosing her as the candidate may have been the fact that of the 46,786 electors in the constituency, 26,009 were women, to whom a female candidate might be assumed to have special appeal. That may have been the reason why, in 1929, the Labour Party also chose a woman candidate, Eleanor Stewart, who was an active member of the STUC and founding member of its Women's Advisory Committee. However, in neither case was the woman elected.

In the absence of letters or other evidence, it is only possible to speculate why Chrystal Macmillan decided to stand for Parliament, though one of her obituarists probably came closest to the mark:

> Miss Macmillan demanded one law for men and women, and fought out-of-date legislation and proposals which from that point of view are reactionary. Indeed, it was partly because she desired fuller scope to fight in the House of Commons for the women's cause that she stood as Liberal candidate in North Edinburgh.[63]

While this may indeed have been her reason to stand for parliament, she may have been well aware that her chances of winning the North Edinburgh seat were very slight, given that it had long been solidly Conservative, and the Liberal Party's popularity was waning. As reported in *The Scotsman* at the time:

> Miss Chrystal Macmillan's belated entry into the contest will no doubt have some effect on the distribution of the votes but is not likely to alter the constituency's selection. She is all for the League and peace but on this point, there is no divergence with the National Government representative. Miss Macmillan also stands, as one would expect, for the same rights for women as for men throughout the political and social sphere.[64]

Judging from newspaper notices announcing the hustings to be held in her constituency, Chrystal Macmillan's appearances were few, but, as an anonymous 'women journalist' observed, 'being a barrister,

[Chrystal Macmillan] has, of course, the trained legal mind, and those who listen to her cannot but be impressed with her clear statement of a case, her reasoned approach to the matter under discussion'.[65] Interestingly, this was the first general election to be contested by the Scottish National Party (SNP), and in an election address given by Chrystal Macmillan on 12 November 1935, a comment she made appeared to suggest her sympathy for the SNP agenda: 'Home Rule, delegating to a Scottish Parliament power to manage purely Scottish affairs, would hasten the solution of many of the problems particularly affecting Scotland.'[66]

In her election address, in Leith Walk School, Chrystal Macmillan began with reference to a matter close to her heart, that of disarmament. She was highly critical of the current National Government for its stance on disarmament, arguing that by failing to give a lead at the Disarmament Conference they 'had not only failed to bring disarmament nearer, but had done much to bring about the present rearmament of Germany and to make general disarmament more difficult'. She pointed out that the government had opposed proposals by France, supported by Sweden, Japan and Denmark, for stopping the private manufacture of arms and the putting of state manufacture under international inspection, and that in May 1933 they had refused Germany's offer to destroy all its armaments if others did likewise.

She also attacked the government in relation to its position on barriers to international trade, arguing that the world would not only gain in prosperity, but one of the causes of war would be removed, by getting rid of such barriers. In her view, free trade would do more than any other policy to improve people's general welfare, and to 'foster good relations with other countries on which that welfare so greatly depends'.

The other issue addressed in her speech was, inevitably, that of gender equality: 'The granting of the same rights to women as to men throughout the whole political and social system would enable women more fully to develop their personality and make a greater contribution to the life of the community.'[67] She went on to cite examples of inequality arising from decisions taken by the government, and pointed out that under its regulations, 275,000 married women had been denied their unemployment benefits, towards which they had contributed. Furthermore, the unemployment assistance scheme proposed by the government, but not yet adopted, would mean that women would receive one or two shillings less than men per week.

In a rousing finale, she passionately denounced

> The growing and dangerous practice of conferring arbitrary powers on a Minister to deal by regulations with matters in which our rights ought to be clearly defined by law, [which] is encroaching on our civil liberties. No discretionary power should be conferred which could be used to discriminate between man and woman.[68]

Impressive as she would undoubtedly have been as an MP, it is unlikely that she could have won as a Liberal candidate in 1935.[69] Given past results, it would have been unlikely for anyone other than the National Conservative Party candidate to win in Edinburgh North: in the event, Erskine achieved a huge majority, with 20,776 votes. Crawford came second with 8,654 votes and Chrystal Macmillan third with only 1,798 votes, which meant she lost her deposit.

CONCLUSION

Chrystal Macmillan's skilled presentation of the Scottish women graduates' case in the House of Lords in 1908 both raised her public profile and gained her popularity as a speaker for the women's constitutional suffrage campaign throughout Scotland, from 1909 until 1913. She campaigned alongside members of the militant organisations but, after the end of 1909, when the more militant WSPU members began to undertake violent actions, Chrystal Macmillan and her colleagues no longer cooperated with WSPU, even although they expressed sympathy for individual WSPU activists.

Chrystal Macmillan moved to London in 1913 to continue her work on suffrage issues, collaborating closely with Millicent Fawcett in the work of NUWSS and IWSA. Although she felt more comfortable working with the internationalist perspective of the IWSA, she was often expected to present the Scottish view on suffrage matters to the NUWSS EC, especially in the early months of 1914 when she took on the role of chairing the SFWSS.

At the start of the First World War, when NUWSS stopped political activity, Chrystal Macmillan became an active member of the WCC, an organisation representing several women's organisations, including NUWSS. This organisation continued to lobby the British Government to extend the parliamentary franchise to women, working successfully with the House of Commons Speaker's Conference to achieve parliamentary votes for some women over the age of 30, in 1918.

It took another ten years and a long campaign by NUSEC for women's equal treatment in the political sphere to eventually achieve success with the passing of The Representation of the People (Equal Franchise) Act 1928, which gave women in Britain the same voting rights as men. For Chrystal Macmillan, who had played such a major part in the campaign of the constitutional suffragists, both in her native Scotland and in the wider context of British politics, this was an achievement to celebrate, and she and her suffrage colleagues took much pleasure in the occasion by attending the House of Lords to witness the moment when the Act was passed.

Notes

1. Leneman, *A Guid Cause*, p. 12
2. Elizabeth Crawford, 'Scotland', in *The Women's Suffrage Movement in Britain and Ireland: A Regional Survey* (Abingdon: Routledge, 2006), pp. 225–34.
3. Millicent Fawcett, 'England: The Women's Suffrage Movement' (1883), in Theodore Stanton (ed.), *The Woman Question in Europe: A Series of Original Essays* (London: Sampson Low, Marston Searle & Rivington, 2015), pp. 1–29; Martin Pugh, *The March of the Women: A Revisionist Analysis of the Campaign for Women's Suffrage 1866–1914* (Oxford: Oxford University Press, 2002).
4. Leneman, *A Guid Cause*, p. 40.
5. Martin Pugh, *Votes for Women in Britain 1867–1928* (London: Historical Association, 1994), p. 254.
6. *Votes for Women*, 17 Dec. 1908, p. 190.
7. Macmillan, *The Struggle for Political Liberty*, p. 1.
8. *Dundee Courier*, 7 Oct. 1907, p. 5: later NUWSS colours were red, white and green.
9. Eunice Murray, Aug. 1908, *Diary (1895–1918)*.
10. *Greenock Telegraph and Clyde Shipping Gazette*, 11 Aug. 1908.
11. *Dumfries & Galloway Standard*, 27 Mar. 1909.
12. *The Common Cause*, 23 Sept. 1909.
13. *The Orcadian*, 25 Sept. 1909.
14. *The Common Cause*, 30 Sept. 1909.
15. Marsali Taylor, *Women's Suffrage in Shetland* (self-published, 2010), https://www.lulu.com/shop/marsali-taylor/womens-suffrage-in-shetland/ebook/product-1j9g25mv.html?q=Marsali+Taylor&page=1&pageSize=4.
16. *Shetland News*, Sept. 1909.
17. *Shetland Times*, 10 Oct. 1909.
18. *Orkney Herald, and Weekly Advertiser and Gazette*, 20 Oct. 1909.
19. *The Scotsman*, 9 Oct. 1909.

20. Gude Cause Archive (Edinburgh: National Library of Scotland).
21. *The Common Cause*, 14 Oct. 1909.
22. *St. Andrews Citizen*, 1 Jan. 1910.
23. *Edinburgh Evening News*, 22 July 1910.
24. *The Vote*, 16 July 1910.
25. *Bath Chronicle and Weekly Gazette*, 14 July 1910.
26. *Shetland News*, 25 Sept. 1909.
27. Maria DiCenzo, 'Unity and Dissent: Official Organs of the Suffrage Campaign', in Maria DiCenzo, Lucy Delap and Leila Ryan (eds), *Feminist Media History: Suffrage, Periodicals and the Public Sphere* (London: Palgrave Macmillan, 2011), pp. 76–119.
28. *Aberdeen Press & Journal*, 11 Nov. 1908.
29. *The Common Cause*, 16 Sept. 1909.
30. *Shetland News*, 25 Sept. 1909.
31. Ibid., 14 Oct. 1909.
32. Ibid.
33. *Aberdeen Press and Journal*, 16 Oct. 1909.
34. Sandra Stanley Holton, *Feminism and Democracy: Women's Suffrage and Reform Politics in Britain 1900–1918* (Cambridge: Cambridge University Press, 2002), pp. 69–70.
35. *Linlithgowshire Gazette*, 22 Mar. 1912.
36. Leslie Parker Hume, *The National Union of Women's Suffrage Societies* (New York and London: Garland Publishing, 1982), p. 134.
37. Minutes Scottish Women's Liberal Federation (Edinburgh: National Library of Scotland).
38. NUWSS Executive Committee minutes, 20 June 1912 (London: Women's Library, LSE).
39. Ibid., 25 June 1914.
40. *London Evening Standard*, 13 Sept. 1912; *Western Times*, 13 Sept. 1912.
41. NUWSS Executive Committee Minutes, 6 Mar. 1913 (London: Women's Library, LSE).
42. Pedersen, *Eleanor Rathbone*, pp. 135, 409.
43. NUWSS Executive Committee Minutes, 19 Mar. 1914 (London: Women's Library, LSE).
44. NUWSS Minute 15 Oct. 1915 (London: Women's Library, LSE).
45. NUWSS Minute 18 Mar. 1915 (London: Women's Library, LSE).
46. The minutes of the EC debates leading up to the resignations are in the Katherine Marshall archive. Letters of resignation from the EC are in the NUWSS archive in the Women's Library, LSE. Issues are discussed fully in Jo Vellacott, *Pacifists, Patriots and the Vote: the Erosion of Democratic Suffragism in Britain during the First World War* (Basingstoke: Palgrave Macmillan, 2007).
47. Letter Chrystal Macmillan to Evelyn Atkinson, NUWSS Secretary, *The Common Cause* 7.324, 25 June 1915.

48. Quoted in SFWSS Minutes, 30 May 1914 (Glasgow: Mitchell Library).
49. Holton, *Feminism and Democracy*, p. 107.
50. SFWSS Minutes, 29 Nov. 1913 (Glasgow: Mitchell Library, TD1734/1/1/1).
51. ENSWS, 45th Annual Report, 1913, p. 14.
52. Parliamentary Archives, PHO/11/2/36/3.
53. Minutes Consultative Committee of Constitutional Women's Suffrage Societies, 18 April 1917 (London: Women's Library, LSE, 2/CSS).
54. Chrystal Macmillan, *And Shall I Have a Parliamentary Vote?* (London: NUWSS, 1918).
55. Véronique Molinari, 'Educating and Mobilizing the New Voter: Interwar Handbooks and Female Citizenship in Great Britain, 1918–1931', *Journal of International Women's Studies* 15.1 (2014), pp. 17–34. Available at: http://vc.bridgew.edu/jiws/vol15/iss1/2.
56. Chrystal Macmillan, 'The Registration of Parliamentary Voters', *The Woman's Leader* 14.1, 3 Feb. 1922, p. 3
57. Mari Takayangi, 'The Path to Equal Franchise: The Passage of the Equal Franchise Act 1928, and Earlier Attempts', in 'Parliament and Women, c.1900–1945' (PhD thesis, Kings College London, 2012), chapter 4, 2012_Takayanagi_Mari_1069335_ethesis.pdf (kcl.ac.uk).
58. NUSEC 1922 Annual Report, p. 13.
59. NUSEC 1924 Annual Report.
60. Letter Adela Coit to Millicent Fawcett, 3 Sept. 1915 (GB127.M50/2/22/44), Manchester Local Archives, quoted in Jo Vellacott, *From Liberal to Labour with Women's Suffrage: The Story of Catherine Marshall* (Montreal and Kingston: McGill–Queen's University Press, 1993), p. 213.
61. *Edinburgh Evening News*, 30 June 1899.
62. *The Scotsman*, 1 Nov. 1935.
63. *The Scotsman*, 24 Sept. 1937.
64. *The Scotsman*, 9 Nov. 1935.
65. Ibid., 13 Nov. 1935.
66. Ibid., 12 Nov. 1935.
67. Ibid., 13 Nov.
68. Ibid.
69. Catriona Burness, 'Count up to Twenty-one: Scottish Women in Formal Politics, 1918–1990', in Esther Breitenbach and Pat Thane (eds), *Women and Citizenship in Britain and Ireland in the Twentieth Century* (London: Continuum International Publishing Group, 2010), pp. 45–77.

4

Working for World Peace

Chrystal Macmillan was one of the organisers of the International Women's Congress which met at The Hague in 1915, during the First World War, and was attended by 1,200 women from twelve countries. And, as Secretary of the Congress, she guided the formation and establishment of the WILPF, the oldest women's peace organisation which continues to campaign today.

For Chrystal Macmillan, as for many of her colleagues, working for peace was a natural extension of her commitment to women's suffrage,[1] which she believed would lead to a fairer world. Firm in that belief, many women argued that if they were able to engage fully in political life and international negotiations, there would be an end to war.

Writing in September 1914, one month after the outbreak of the First World War, Millicent Fawcett expressed the view that,

> If the political citizenship of women in all the countries concerned had become an established fact long enough to secure its organisation into concrete political power, it is impossible to doubt that this power would have been used to ensure such a political reorganisation of Europe as would have rendered it certain that international disputes and grievances should be referred to law and reason, and not to the clumsy and blundering tribunal of brute force.[2]

Despite this insight, Millicent Fawcett felt it necessary to fully support the British government's decision to engage in the war till a military victory could be achieved. However, Chrystal Macmillan continued to advocate for mediation to resolve disputes between the warring nations and proposed that, in order to avoid future wars, further study and discussion on the causes of war were required.

Chrystal Macmillan's peace initiative was grounded in her experience of working in two international women's organisations, the ICW[3] and the IWSA,[4] both of which promoted international friendships and good working relationships between women of different nations: by 1914, both organisations had established vibrant international networks.

PEACE WORK WITH THE INTERNATIONAL COUNCIL OF WOMEN (ICW)

'Peace and Arbitration' was an item on the agenda of the ICW Conference in Rome in May 1914. The ICW president, Lady Aberdeen, reminded delegates that a resolution advocating International Arbitration was first passed unanimously at a public meeting of ICW Congress in London in 1899 and later affirmed at the ICW Congress in Toronto in 1909. The report of the ICW Peace and Arbitration Committee was presented in Rome in 1914 and the following resolution was passed at the end of the well-attended public meeting:

> The International Council of Women supports warmly the effective application of the resolutions passed at the Hague Conferences[5] for the peaceful settlement of international conflicts and declares its sympathetic desire for the conclusion of treaties through which the Governments pledge themselves in the case of disputes of every kind to enter into negotiations for mediation.[6]

The Hague Conferences of 1899 and 1907 had produced a series of international treaties and declarations, including the first formal statements of the laws of war and war crimes in the body of secular international law.[7] These conferences were organised by men and all the delegates were men: women were not admitted, so the ICW provided an international opportunity for women to voice their approval of the resolutions passed by the men.

The women attending the ICW Congress in Rome, who were aware of the gendered violence that accompanies conflict, decided that as the men had not considered that aspect of war at the Hague Conferences of 1899 and 1907, they would draw attention to it themselves:

> The International Council of Women protesting vehemently against the odious wrongs of which women are the victims in time of war, contrary to international law, desires to appeal to the next Hague Conference to consider how a more effective international protection of women may be secured which will prevent the continuance of the horrible violation of womanhood that attends all wars.[8]

Chrystal Macmillan was not a member of the Peace and Arbitration Committee, but she was an active member of the ICW EC, and a member of the Committee on Laws regarding the Legal Position of Women. She was a regular attender at ICW Congress and would have been aware of the debates that informed the resolutions on peace and mediation that were passed by the ICW Congress in 1904, 1909 and 1914.

PEACE WORK WITH THE INTERNATIONAL WOMAN SUFFRAGE ALLIANCE (IWSA)

When she became IWSA secretary, working at the head office in London, Chrystal Macmillan was at the very centre of the women's international suffrage network. In July 1914, the IWSA EC became alarmed at the impending crisis in diplomatic relations across Europe and decided to issue an International Manifesto of Women, which was signed by Millicent Fawcett, IWSA vice-president, and Chrystal Macmillan, IWSA secretary, and delivered by them to the Foreign Office and all the foreign embassies in London:

> We, the women of the world, view with apprehension and dismay the present situation in Europe, which threatens to involve one continent, if not the whole world, in the disasters and the horrors of war . . . We women of twenty-six countries, having banded ourselves together in the International Women's Suffrage Alliance with the object of obtaining political means of sharing with men the power which shapes the fate of nations, appeal to you to leave untried no method of conciliation or arbitration for arranging international differences which may help to avert deluging half the civilised world in blood.[9]

The Women's Manifesto was ignored by the political leaders, and by the time the text was published in *Jus Suffragii*, the war was underway.

On 4 August 1914, immediately after Britain declared war on Germany, the IWSA women attended a meeting which had been organised by the NUWSS at the Kingsway Hall in London, before the declaration of war: this became the occasion for women to voice their objection to war, and emotions were running high. Many British women's organisations were represented – the NUWW (later known as the National Council of Women – NCW), the National Federation of Women Workers, the Women's Cooperative Guild and the Women's Labour League. The speakers who came from France, Germany, Hungary, Finland and Switzerland as well as Great Britain voiced their opposition to war, calling for a negotiated settlement of the conflict and condemning the senseless war-driven destruction of 'women's treasures', not pieces of canvas, the icons of art, but each woman's family and native land.[10]

Appalled by the declaration of a war in Europe, women suffragists in the USA held a peace parade in New York at the end of August: no music was played apart from muffled drums, no banners were displayed, only white flags of peace, and marchers were asked to wear black, or white with black armbands.[11]

CANCELLATION OF IWSA CONGRESS TO BE HELD IN BERLIN IN 1915

But the women's calls for mediation, and for political leaders to make more of an effort to avoid war, went unheeded and the war activities increased on every side. By September 1914, the women of the German section of the IWSA felt they had no alternative but to cancel the International Congress meeting which had been due to take place in Berlin in June 1915.[12]

In response, on behalf of the Dutch national committee, Dr Aletta Jacobs wrote to *Jus Suffragii* in November 1914 to suggest that the Congress could be held in the Netherlands, which was a neutral country: 'In these dreadful times in which so much hate has been spread among different nations, the women have to show that we at least retain our solidarity and that we are able to maintain mutual friendship.'[13]

Responding to Dr Jacobs' suggestion, as IWSA secretary, Chrystal Macmillan put forward a proposal 'that NUWSS propose to Mrs Catt [IWSA president] that a business Congress be summoned for 1915'. This proposal was carried with only two dissentients, one of whom was Millicent Fawcett, who was strongly opposed, believing that 'it would hardly be possible to bring together the women of the belligerent countries without violent outbursts of anger and recriminations'.[14]

Next, Chrystal Macmillan wrote to each of the twenty-six suffrage societies in the IWSA urging them to agree to meet in the Netherlands to 'discuss the principles on which peace should be made and, if so, to act internationally'. She suggested that suitable subjects for discussion might be international arbitration, control of foreign policy, principles for transfer of territory, reduction of armaments, establishing an international federation, and international levies for restoration of devastated territories.

In a letter to Sylvia Pankhurst, she insisted that the meeting would be a 'Congress of Women' and not a 'Peace Congress'.[15] This idea was reinforced by Aletta Jacobs in her opening speech to the Congress: '[We] have never called it a *peace congress* but an international Congress of Women assembled to protest against war, and to discuss ways and means whereby war shall become an impossibility in future.'[16]

When the IWSA leaders appeared less than enthusiastic to Chrystal Macmillan's proposal, she provided three alternative plans for meeting:

- That the IWSA could have its regular convention with a business meeting afterwards: or
- That the IWSA could call a convention attended by different women's organisations: or
- That a conference could be summoned for individual women.

Members of the national committees responded in favour of these suggestions, but the leaders of the organisation were opposed to any meeting at that time. Millicent Fawcett became alarmed when she received a letter from the Government Minister Lord Robert Cecil, a supporter of women's suffrage, in which, referring to the IWSA meeting at Kingsway Hall, he threatened to withdraw his support if Millicent Fawcett continued to talk of peace.

> Permit me to express my great regret that you should have thought it right not only to take part in the 'peace' meeting last night but also to have allowed the organisation of the National Union to be used for its promotion. Action of that kind will undoubtedly make it very difficult for the friends of Women's Suffrage in both the Unionist and Ministerial parties. Even to me the action seems so unreasonable under the circumstances as to shake my belief in the fitness of women to deal with great Imperial questions and I can only console myself by the belief that in this matter the National Union do not represent the opinions of their fellow countrywomen.[17]

This letter had a crucial effect on Millicent Fawcett as it questioned not only women's capacity to use the vote wisely but also women's commitment to the Empire. Historians have argued that for many women and men in this era, 'conceptions of national identity were closely linked to Britain's status as an imperial power'.[18] From this point on, Millicent Fawcett avoided any statements that could be construed as undermining support for the war effort. In a letter to *Jus Suffragii*, she defended her decision not to support the proposed Congress:

> Each nation engaged in this war feels its very existence is at stake: each believes its cause to be the cause of justice and freedom: each has suffered and sacrificed much, and is prepared to suffer and sacrifice much more, because each feels, rightly or wrongly that it is fighting for its very life. This intense National feeling causes a diminution in the glow of Internationalism . . . We should run the risks of outbursts of uncontrollable Nationalism as opposed to Internationalism.[19]

The sentiment expressed in this statement by Millicent Fawcett was shared by the IWSA national leaders but not by the members of the executive committees.

PLANNING AN ALTERNATIVE CONGRESS

As the majority of IWSA committee members were not opposed to an international conference, Chrystal Macmillan and four other British women met with Belgian and German women alongside a Dutch committee led by Dr Jacobs in February 1915, to discuss the practicality of inviting individual women to an International Congress of Women and to draft possible resolutions. It fell to Chrystal Macmillan to help organise invitations to 'women of all nations', and despite postal disruptions caused by the war, they were sent out to organisations and to individual women. Travel and accommodation arrangements for the attendees were made, and the preliminary three-day programme for an International Women's Congress at The Hague, from 28 April, was finalised and published in *Jus Suffragii* on 1 March 1915.

Despite lack of support from the leaders of the suffrage movement and bitter criticism from the press, 180 British women applied for passports to travel to The Hague. They faced a dangerous crossing as the North Sea and the English Channel had been declared a war zone with the threat of submarine attacks on all shipping. Moreover, the women had great difficulty in obtaining passports from the British government; only after lobbying by Catherine Marshall did the Home Secretary, Reginald McKenna, grant twenty passports 'to the more sensible women'.[20]

The women set off to Tilbury to catch the ferry but the naval conflict between Britain and Germany escalated and it was announced that the North Sea and the Channel were closed to all shipping. Only three British women reached the Congress: Chrystal Macmillan and Kathleen Courtney, who had travelled to the Netherlands earlier to assist with the preparation of the Congress, and Emmeline Pethick-Lawrence, who travelled from the USA with the American contingent.[21]

The courage of these women in voicing dissent is remarkable, as the public atmosphere in the belligerent countries was demanding a show of patriotic commitment. In Britain, and throughout Europe, war fever was spreading 'like measles':[22]

> All London is placarded – the walls of buildings, billboards, even the base of Trafalgar monument. The windshield of every 'bus and taxicab carries its complement – narrow strips with endless variations of appeals to the

'young men of Britain' to enlist for 'King and country' . . . The poster campaign is supplemented by various appeals to the popular imagination – brass bands, companies of soldiers on parade, street corner speeches and mass meetings.[23]

Despite knowing the dangers, the delegation of forty-two American women set sail from New York on the *Noordam* on 13 April, spending their time on board discussing and amending the resolutions proposed for the Congress. When the ship reached the English Channel, it was stopped by British warships and held there for four days without explanation. It was finally released on 27 April, so that the women arrived only just in time to join the first evening of the Congress.

INTERNATIONAL WOMEN'S CONGRESS AT THE HAGUE, 1915

Approximately 1,200 women attended the Congress from twelve countries, both neutral and belligerent, and there were always women representatives of different countries on the top table. Those women who signed up to attend the Congress had to agree to two statements of principle:

- That international disputes should be settled by pacific means, and
- That the parliamentary franchise should be extended to women.[24]

The women worked through three days with a programme of debates and discussions, some lectures given in public, some debates conducted in committee. Speeches were generally short and inspirational, delivered in English, French and German, and meetings were competently chaired. Women from the twelve countries worked in groups, with someone acting as translator and interpreter, with the aim of reaching agreement on twenty resolutions. Mary Sheepshanks, editor of *Jus Suffragii*, described the behind-the-scene dynamics of the international meeting:

> The Resolutions Committee consisting of two representatives from each country with Miss Macmillan as convener met before, throughout and after the Congress, and considered amendments and new resolutions and drafted the programme and final arrangements of resolutions.[25]

The twenty resolutions were arrived at through discussion and have a vibrancy that continues to resonate today (see Appendix 2 for list of the resolutions). They were grouped under seven headings: Women and War, Action towards Peace, Principles of Permanent Peace, International Cooperation, The Education of Children, Women and the Peace Settlement Conference, and Action to Be Taken.

Figure 4.1 International Women's Congress, 1915, platform party
From left: Mme Thoumaian, Armenia; Leopoldina Kulka, Austria; Miss Hughes, Canada; Rosika Schwimmer, Hungary; Dr Anita Augspurg, Germany; Jane Addams, USA; Eugenie Hamer, Belgium; Dr Aletta Jacobs, Netherlands; Chrystal Macmillan, Great Britain; Rosa Genoni, Italy; Anna Kleman, Sweden; Thora Daugaard, Denmark; Louise Keilhau, Norway (courtesy Women's Library, LSE)

Chrystal Macmillan's Resolution Committee faced a particular challenge in framing a resolution on peace in such a way as to avoid any accusation that the women were seeking 'peace at any price':

> There was hardly a country which did not contribute something to the Peace Settlement Resolution which was moved as substitute for that entitled 'To call a truce'. The difficulties of members who did not wish to ask for peace if there were any doubt as to justice of that peace, and of those who felt that the whole Congress would be a failure if no demand was made to end the war, were met by putting into one resolution the demand for an end to bloodshed, for the beginning of peace negotiation and for the establishment of peace based on the principles of justice adopted by Congress.[26]

As well as chairing the Resolution Committee and participating in discussions, Chrystal Macmillan contributed to a debate in which she recommended the establishment of various means to improve international cooperation in future, including the establishment of International Courts and a League of Nations: 'We do not want a peace that is a negation of war, but a peace that is living and growing and active.'[27] She was also responsible for the onerous task of organising the resolutions into an understandable order, coordinating the work of the Congress, and writing the final report.

In the meantime, the press continued their attacks on the women meeting at The Hague:

> 'Blundering Englishwomen' (*Daily Graphic*)
> 'Folly in Petticoats' (*Sunday Pictorial*)
> 'This mischievous and futile committee' (*Globe*)
> 'The babblers from this country' (*Evening Standard*)
> 'This shipload of hysterical women' (*Globe*)
> 'Those feminine busybodies' (*The People*)
> 'Pro-Hun Peacettes in their sixth floor Eyrie' (*Daily Express*)[28]

Even the British Prime Minister Herbert Asquith spoke contemptuously of 'the futile pacifists whose whispers are like the twittering of sparrows while storms and tempests shake the world to its foundations'.[29]

These attacks affected the attitudes of the leaders of the suffrage organisations who feared a nationalistic backlash against women's suffrage. The chair of the ICW Peace and Arbitration Committee had changed her mind and decided not to accept the invitation to the Congress and the president of IWSA had voted against sending representatives of the organisation. When president Millicent Fawcett vetoed any NUWSS representation at the Congress, ten members of the EC voiced their concern, later resigning in protest against the undemocratic decision not to send representatives to the Congress nor undertake any peace education.[30] Surprisingly, Chrystal Macmillan, one of the main organisers of the Congress, did not resign, arguing that she considered voting in the minority was a strong reason not to resign. She remained on the NUWSS EC to fight for her point of view and continued to work with Millicent Fawcett throughout the war.[31]

ENVOYS FROM THE CONGRESS TO GOVERNMENTS

As the Congress neared its end, Rosika Schwimmer gave an impassioned speech urging the women to act to bring about the end of the fighting. Chrystal Macmillan and several colleagues expressed doubts about the practicality of Rosika Swimmer's proposal that a delegation of women should carry the message expressed in the twenty resolutions of the Congress to the rulers of the belligerent and neutral nations of Europe and the President of the USA. Schwimmer suggested that the elected delegates visit the political leaders in person to urge them to put an end to the bloodshed and begin peace negotiations; she so inspired the Congress that the women voted for this final resolution.

When the Congress ended on 1 May 1915, almost all the women returned home, leaving the five delegates, elected by Congress, to plan their travel across a war-torn Europe to meet with the heads of state of all the belligerent and neutral countries. The five women organised themselves into two groups: three from the warring countries were delegated to visit neutral countries while the two women from neutral countries set off to belligerent countries.

Chrystal Macmillan, Emily Balch, Rosika Schwimmer and two companions set off northwards to make contact with heads of state in the neutral and Scandinavian countries – Norway, Sweden, Denmark and Russia. One of the companions in the party was the Canadian Julia Grace Wales, who had proposed a method of negotiation, 'Continuous Mediation without Armistice',[32] and with this plan in mind the delegates advocated that a conference should be called by the neutral nations of Europe.

> This International Congress of Women resolves to ask neutral countries to take immediate steps to create a conference of neutral nations which shall without delay offer continuous mediation. The Conference shall invite suggestions for settlement from each of the belligerent nations and in any case shall submit to all of them simultaneously reasonable proposals as a basis of peace.[33]

The President of the Congress, Jane Addams, accompanied by Dr Aletta Jacobs and two companions, all being from neutral countries, set out to visit political leaders of the warring nations – Germany, Austria, Hungary, Italy, France and Great Britain. The two groups proposed to meet up later to exchange information from the various political leaders they would interview, and to plan how best to seek an interview with the US president.

The two groups of women travelled back and forth across Europe for two months, meeting face to face with all the heads of state, talking with some leaders more than once. In all, fourteen countries were visited and the women delegates were received by twenty-one ministers, two presidents, one king and the pope. They presented their proposals for summoning a neutral conference for continuous mediation to bring the war to an end and laid out the details of their proposals, inviting the statesmen to respond. The women took notes of the conversations, and checked their understandings with each other and with the interviewees to confirm or clarify meanings. They also asked the political leaders to sign a written statement outlining initiatives that would be acceptable to them and their governments. (See Appendix 3 for a list of their visits.)

The women worked with diplomats and civil servants to set up formal meetings with political leaders, and they also made contact with women's organisations. In Sweden, they addressed massive public meetings organised by women and men who wanted to encourage their government to initiate peace mediations. In Great Britain, they were welcomed by members of the Women's International League who were setting up a national organisation to promote the resolutions passed at the International Congress of Women at The Hague.

All the delegates made light of their travel difficulties, but it was a formidable experience, as Rosika Schwimmer described:[34]

> You have to go in and be searched. You have to undress. We women have to take down our hair and shake out to show there is nothing in it . . . my shoes were put down and I was asked what are these numbers . . . This powder paper here . . . in Europe one has to have paper to clean one's face, because one does not get towels or soap. This paper has passed the censor twice. It has been taken away from me because it had the maker's name on it, and I had to leave it at the station.[35]

As British citizens, Chrystal Macmillan and Julia Grace Wales could not travel to Scandinavia through Germany, they had to find a boat and a captain prepared to take them. When they found a fishing boat willing to do so, there was room for only one passenger at a time, so Julia Wales travelled first, and Chrystal Macmillan returned to The Hague for one week to complete work on the Congress Report, joining the group later.

In Norway, the driver hired to take them to an appointment with the king circled the palace twice as he did not believe that unaccompanied women would be allowed to speak to the monarch. But the king did speak with them for over an hour-and-three-quarters, and took particular interest in their mediation plan.

When they travelled to Russia, they had to undertake a three-day journey by train through the north of Sweden and Finland to Petrograd. While waiting three weeks for an appointment to see Sazonoff, the Minister of Foreign Affairs, they visited various places in Petrograd, including the nurse training school organised by the Russian League for Equal Rights of Women.

Initially, not one of the ministers in the neutral countries of Europe would agree to call a conference for fear that this would bring their neutrality into question. But the women persisted in their diplomatic work, travelling back and forth, encouraging ministers to consider issuing invitations, not from just one country but from a group of five neutrals,

Figure 4.2 IWC envoys waiting to meet King of Norway, 1915
From left: Emily Greene Balch, USA; Cor Ramondt-Hirschman, Netherlands; Rosika Schwimmer, Hungary; Chrystal Macmillan, Great Britain (courtesy Collection IAV-Atria, Institute on Gender Equality and Women's History, Amsterdam)

Figure 4.3 IWC delegates with graduating class, Nursing School, Petrograd, 1915 (courtesy Collection IAV-Atria, Institute on Gender Equality and Women's History, Amsterdam)

namely Denmark, the Netherlands, Norway, Sweden and Switzerland. At the meeting in Petrograd, Sazonoff, the Russian Foreign Minister, agreed to sign a statement written out by Chrystal Macmillan, to the effect 'that it would not be unacceptable to Russia if the neutral nations called a conference and made proposals of possible terms of peace and offered mediation to the belligerents'.[36]

This achievement by the envoys to the neutral counties was matched by that of their colleagues to belligerent countries who had procured agreement from leaders of those countries that they would not oppose the calling of such a conference, even though they could not call for such a meeting themselves. The envoys acknowledged that 'if the side in the strong position were to ask for peace, the weaker side would resent mediation because it would be thought that the stronger wanted to dictate terms; while, were the weaker side to ask for peace, it would be considered as a confession of defeat'.[37] In July 1915, Von Jagow of Germany supported this analysis, adding that 'at this moment neither side is strong enough to dictate terms and neither side is so weakened that it has to sue for peace'. He said that Germany would not oppose a conference organised by neutrals.[38]

On 14 July 1915, Chrystal Macmillan, accompanied by Emily Balch, met with Lord Crewe at the Foreign Office in London. In a letter to Chrystal Macmillan, written on behalf of Lord Crewe, Eric Drummond confirmed Lord Crewe's statement of the British position – that the British government would not place any obstacle in the way of the formation of a League of Neutrals or make any protest against its existence, should it come into being.[39] The envoys initially expected that US President Wilson would be the right person to act as mediator but they found that German leaders did not consider him to be neutral as US industrial corporations were supplying munitions to Britain. Moreover, several leaders in European countries did not consider President Wilson suitable as they believed he knew little of European political issues or European ways of working.

The women had agreed to meet in Amsterdam in August to review their progress but, without consulting her colleagues, Jane Addams sailed for America – a change of plan that disrupted the women's relationships. Dr Jacobs then set off to the US, suggesting that the other delegates remain in Europe. However, Chrystal Macmillan and Rosika Schwimmer soon followed, all hoping for an interview with President Wilson and his backing for a conference organised by the neutral nations. When Chrystal Macmillan and Rosika Schwimmer gave press interviews on landing in the USA, Dr Jacobs expressed her anger, accusing them of jeopardising the meeting with President Wilson. But they did meet with the president who, disappointingly, reserved his judgement on the proposal, privately informing his colleagues that he would only offer his support when mediation could be guaranteed success.

On October 15, 1915, the women envoys issued a manifesto to the press in America, giving a brief description of their findings, emphasising that they had heard 'much the same words in Downing Street as in Wilhelmstrasse, in Vienna as in Petrograd, in Budapest as in Le Havre'. They had shown that there was room for mediation if the political leaders willed it, and concluded with an appeal to all political leaders to work toward finding a way to stop the war.

> The excruciating burden of responsibility for the hopeless continuance of this war no longer rests on the wills of the belligerent nations alone. It rests also on the wills of those neutral governments and people who have been spared its shock but cannot, if they would, absolve themselves from their full share of responsibility for the continuance of war.[40]

The manifesto was welcomed by the press who acknowledged that the calling of a neutral conference for mediation had become a matter of serious discussion by government officials, the press and public in all the countries concerned. However, no action was taken by any head of state and the war continued unabated. All the women who had attended the Congress in The Hague earlier in the year were heavily criticised on their return to their own countries and several were temporarily imprisoned in Germany.

Undaunted, Chrystal Macmillan resumed the task of writing up the report of the Hague Congress, and formulated the twenty resolutions into an orderly sequence which shows some resemblance to President Wilson's later formulation of Fourteen Points. Although Jane Addams, the president of WILPF, was unsure how much they had influenced the president, she knew he had read them:

> I had the pleasure of presenting those Hague resolutions to President Wilson in 1915. He was very much interested in them, and when I saw him three months later, he drew out the papers I had given him, and they seemed to have been much handled and read, 'You see I have studied these resolutions', he said, 'I consider them by far the best formulation which up to the moment has been set out by any body.'[41]

Chrystal Macmillan was inspired by the formation of the new organisation, which she hoped would allow women to take a share of the responsibility for the future:

> Looking to the future the Congress founded an International Committee of Women for Permanent Peace [ICWPP] to organise international support for the Resolutions and to ensure that a Congress of Women be held at the same time and at the same place as the Conference of the powers which shall frame the peace-settlement after the war. Believing that women must take their full share of responsibility in all national and international questions it asks that in this Conference women shall be included and that the Conference shall pass a Resolution advocating the extension of the parliamentary vote to women in all countries . . . The Congress has made a beginning. Let us now each in our own country carry on this international work to ensure that a just and lasting peace shall soon be established.[42]

At the Hague Congress, Chrystal Macmillan had been elected secretary of the new organisation, and from 1915 to 1918 she made several unsuccessful attempts to organise an international meeting of members of the EC. In the meantime, Rosa Manus, based in the Amsterdam office, was able to collect sufficient information to publish a newssheet, *Internationaal*, throughout the war, although she complained that Chrystal Macmillan, as secretary, should have been in Amsterdam to help her.

Figure 4.4 Chrystal Macmillan and Jane Addams, WILPF Congress, Zurich, 1919 (courtesy Collection IAV-Atria, Institute on Gender Equality and Women's History, Amsterdam)

At the end of the war, in 1919, Chrystal Macmillan worked with colleagues to organise the ICWPP Congress in Zurich. As stated in a resolution of the 1915 Hague Congress, this 1919 Congress had been planned to take place side by side with the official Peace Conference at the end of the war. However, when the leaders of the Allied countries set the Peace Conference in Paris, the women refused to set theirs there as women delegates from the Central Powers (Germany, Austria, Hungary) would not be permitted to enter France. ICWPP refused to go along with this exclusionary tactic and organised their conference in Zurich, Switzerland, in a neutral country.

The Treaty of Versailles was published just as the women gathered: they were so appalled by the terms of the Treaty that they sat up all night discussing them, and the next morning sent off a telegram to members of the Peace Conference:

> This International Congress of Women expresses its deep regret that the terms of peace proposed at Versailles should so seriously violate the principles upon which alone a just and lasting peace can be secured, and which the democracies of the world had come to accept.
>
> By guaranteeing the fruits of the secret treaties to the conquerors, the terms of peace tacitly sanction secret diplomacy, deny the principles of self-determination, recognise the rights of the victors to spoils of war, and create all over Europe discords and animosities which can only lead to future wars.[43]

The women recognised that the terms of the Treaty were harsh and would lead to bitter feelings among the people of Germany, Austria and Hungary. Their telegram of warnings was ignored by the men working at Versailles on the details of the settlement.

The three main committees of the Zurich Congress – the Political, the Feminist and the Educational Ethical Committees – were then asked to consider practical proposals to put to the Peace Conference.[44] The Political Committee brought forward resolutions on a League of Nations which were debated: on the third day of the Congress, Chrystal Macmillan moved a resolution, introducing it as follows:

> This Congress of women holds that the peaceful progress of the world can only be ensured when the common interests of humanity are recognised in the establishment of a League of Nations for the promotion of international cooperation.[45]

The Congress agreed several resolutions: on 'Famine and the Blockade'; the 'Treaty of Peace'; 'League of Nations'; 'Women's Position in a League of Nations', including the need for a 'Women's Charter'; 'Military Action in Russia and Hungary'; and an 'Amnesty for War Prisoners'.

Chrystal Macmillan was one of four women elected by the Zurich Congress to take these messages in person to Versailles, where they presented copies of all the 1919 Zurich Congress resolutions. They also included their criticisms of the Peace Treaty, their comments on a League of Nations, and their proposals for a Women's Charter and women's employment. In her report of the deputation, Chrystal Macmillan noted that they had been received by several members of the Peace Conference, and that Lord Robert Cecil had stated very definitely that women would certainly be eligible for every position in the League of Nations.[46]

As the national sections of the ICWPP were showing such vitality, it was agreed that the formation of a permanent organisation was now necessary. The name was changed to the WILPF, and its aims were 'to organise support for the resolutions passed at the Women's International Congress at The Hague in 1915 and Zurich in 1919, and to support movements to further peace, internationalism and the freedom of women'.[47]

Three special committees were appointed at the Zurich Congress: one on finance, one on education, and one to deal with the nationality of married women, with Chrystal Macmillan as chair of the nationality committee. It was a role in which she continued for the rest of her life, later being elected chair of a joint committee of IWSA and the ICW on this issue. She felt strongly that a woman should not lose her nationality by marriage when a man in the same situation could not: it struck at the heart of her understanding of the rights of citizenship and she believed that this had to be remedied by reform of international law (see Chapter 8).

She resigned from the WILPF International Committee in 1920, but continued as a Council member of the British section, the Women's International League, from 1925 to 1927. This resignation gave her more time to undertake further work with the ICW and IWSA, including organising the IWSA Congress in Rome in 1923 and advising both these, and other organisations, on legislative matters. In 1924, after many years of campaigning for women's admission to the legal profession, she was called to the Bar in London: she was among the first group of women to qualify as a barrister in England (see Chapter 7).

CONCLUSION

For some women, there is a logical connection between feminism and pacifism, but many who consider themselves feminists do not accept this connection, nor do they consider peace to be an issue for discussion.[48]

However, many women, including Chrystal Macmillan, who might not call themselves 'pacifists', are committed to ideas of peace and oppose militaristic responses to international disputes.

In April 1915, 'for the first time in history, women of different nations met together at a time of war to express their opposition [to war] and consider ways of ending the conflict'.[49] Facing up to criticism not only from Government and family but also from the leaders of NUWSS and IWSA, Chrystal Macmillan showed considerable courage when she organised invitations to IWSA members to attend the International Women's Congress at The Hague. As Sandi Cooper wrote, 'What the congress in 1915 did was brave a torrent of hostility in order to meet – as well as brave some serious physical dangers.'[50]

At The Hague in 1915, Chrystal Macmillan helped to organise the agenda and chaired the committee that studied the various resolutions put forward, bringing them together in an acceptable form to present to Congress. After the Congress finished, she consolidated the twenty resolutions passed by the Congress and wrote the report in a structured style that was to be retained by WILPF for many years. She was also one of the envoys who travelled around northern Europe to persuade the political leaders of the neutral countries to set up negotiations for a mediated settlement of the war. Again, in 1919, she helped to organise the Women's Congress in Zurich, where she chaired the Resolutions Committee and took an active part in the debates. At the end of the Congress, she was one of the elected members of the delegation deputed to speak to the men meeting in Paris to devise the Peace Settlement to end the First World War.

Although she did not take part in any further WILPF Congresses, Chrystal Macmillan left an organisation that was well established with a working constitution; it has continued to this day as an active women's international peace organisation that has gained consultative status with the UN Economic and Social Council. WILPF members have continued to campaign resolutely for over 100 years, providing a gendered analysis of the causes of each war, a feminist perspective on how to resolve international disputes by peaceful means and a dialogue on how nations might prevent international conflict in the first place.

Notes

1. Ruth Roach Pierson (ed.), *Women and Peace: Theoretical, Historical and Practical Perspectives* (London: Croom Helm, 1987).
2. *Jus Suffragii* 8.13, 1 Sept. 1914, p. 159.

3. The ICW was established in 1888, had a well-organised structure of ten committees, one of which was 'Peace and Arbitration', and regularly passed resolutions on peace at ICW Quinquennial Congresses.
4. The IWSA was the organisation formed in 1904 to share campaigning strategies for women's suffrage. As the women worked together at the international level to exchange ideas and build campaigns for obtaining the franchise in their respective countries, they also discussed other issues of concern to women.
5. The Hague Conferences of 1899 and 1907 produced a series of international treaties and declarations including the first formal statements of the laws of war and war crimes in the body of secular international law.
6. *Report of ICW Congress*, 1914, p. 207.
7. For definition and discussion on the 'law of war', see https://en.wikipedia.org/wiki/Law_of_war.
8. *Report of ICW Congress*, 1914, p. 209.
9. *Jus Suffragii* 8.13, Sept. 1914, p. 159.
10. Ibid., p. 160, reprint from 'Protest against War', *Votes for Women* 7.335, 7 Aug. 1914, p. 680.
11. Anne Wiltsher, *Most Dangerous Women: Feminist Peace Campaigners of the Great War* (London: Pandora Press, 1985); David S. Patterson, *The Search for Negotiated Peace: Women's Activism and Citizen Diplomacy in World War One* (New York: Routledge, 2008).
12. *Jus Suffragii* 9.3, 1 Dec. 1914, p. 200.
13. Ibid.
14. Letter Millicent Fawcett to Carrie Chapman Catt, IWSA president, 15 Dec. 1914. Quoted in Sybil Oldfield, *Spinsters of this Parish* (London: Virago, 1984), p. 190.
15. Sylvia Pankhurst, *The Home Front* (London: Cresset Library, Century Hutchinson, 1987 (first pub. 1932)), p. 15.
16. *Report International Congress of Women The Hague, 28th April–1st May 1915* (Amsterdam: International Women's Committee of Permanent Peace), p. 7.
17. Letter Robert Cecil to Millicent Fawcett, 5 Aug. 1914 (London: Women's Library, LSE, 9/01/1091); quoted in Jo Vellacott, 'Feminist Consciousness and the First World War', in Pierson (ed.), *Women and Peace*, p. 122.
18. Heloise Brown, *The Truest Form of Patriotism: Pacifist Feminism in Britain, 1870–1902* (Manchester: Manchester University Press, 2003), p. 180.
19. *Jus Suffragii* 9.4, 1 Jan. 1915.
20. *Birmingham Daily Gazette*, 23 April 1915.
21. A centenary re-enactment of the women's efforts to reach The Hague has been made into a documentary, 'These Dangerous Women', and can be viewed at https://www.youtube.com/watch?v=0a2xYvXwGiw&feature=youtu.be.
22. Lucy Thoumaian speaking at Kingsway Hall, 4 Aug. 1914, reported in *Jus Suffragii* 8.13, Sept., p. 208.

23. Christina Merriman, 'British War Posters' *The Survey* 34.10, 5 June 1915, p. 223.
24. Helena Swanwick, 'Women's Congress at The Hague', *Jus Suffragii* 9.12, 1 Sept. 1915, p. 357.
25. Report on 'International Congress of Women', *Jus Suffragii* 9.9, 1 June 1915, pp. 301–4.
26. *Report of the International Congress of Women*, 1915, p. xlvi.
27. Ibid., p. 140.
28. Evelyn Sharp, 'The Congress and the Press', in *Toward Permanent Peace: A Record of the Women's International Congress* (London: British Committee of the Women's International Congress, 1915), pp. 20–1.
29. *Liverpool Echo*, 2 Mar. 1915.
30. NUWSS Minutes 1914–15, Katherine Marshall Papers (Carlisle: Cumbria Archive, DMAR/3/45–48).
31. Letter Chrystal Macmillan ('in train en route to Petrograd') to Atkinson, 7 June 1915. Quoted in Vellacott, *Pacifists, Patriots and the Vote*, p. 79.
32. Julia Grace Wales, 'Mediation without Armistice: The Wisconsin Plan' (Madison: Wisconsin Peace Society, 1915), quoted in full in Mary Jean Woodward Bean, *Julia Grace Wales: Canada's Hidden Heroine and the Quest for Peace, 1914–1918* (Nepean, ON: Borealis Press, 2005), appendix 1.
33. *Report of International Congress of Women 1915* (Amsterdam: International Women's Committee for Permanent Peace), p. 37.
34. A report of the journeys in Scandinavia and Russia, *The Survey*, 4 Sept. 1915.
35. Note by Rosika Schwimmer, 1915, quoted in Wiltsher, *Most Dangerous Women*, p. 106.
36. Memorandum by Rosika Schwimmer and Chrystal Macmillan, August 1915; handwritten notes by Emily Balch re interview with Sazonov in Petrograd, June 1915 (Boulder, Colorado: Archive, WILPF Series 1), Box B Folder 2.
37. Remark by one of the envoys, Rosika Schwimmer and Chrystal Macmillan, *Memorandum on Delegations to Governments* (Boulder, Colorado: Boulder Archive, WILPF Series II), Box 1, Folder 1, Addams 1915.
38. Von Jagow, quoted in Rosika Schwimmer and Chrystal Macmillan, ibid.
39. Letter Eric Drummond on behalf of Lord Crewe to Chrystal Macmillan, 22 July 1915, in Rosika Schwimmer and Chrystal Macmillan, ibid.
40. Jane Addams, Emily Balch and Alice Hamilton, 'Manifesto', in *Women at the Hague* (New York: Humanity Books, 2003 (first edition, 1915)), p. 134.
41. Jane Addams's speech to Congress, *Report of the International Congress of Women, Zurich* (Geneva: WILPF, 1919), p. 196.
42. Chrystal Macmillan, 'The History of the Congress' (1915), in *Report of the International Congress of Women 1915* (Amsterdam: IWCPP), pp. xlvii–xlviii.
43. Text of telegrams, quoted in Gertrude Bussey and Margaret Tims, *Women's International League for Peace and Freedom 1915–1965: A Record of Fifty Years' Work* (London: George Allen & Unwin, 1965), p. 31.

44. A centenary re-enactment of the 1919 Zurich Congress has been made into a documentary film 'The Return of the Dangerous Women', https://www.youtube.com/watch?v=Gavbkc2PdHI.
45. *Report of the International Congress of Women, Zurich* (Geneva: WILPF, 1919), p. 83.
46. Chrystal Macmillan, 'Deputation to the Peace Conference', *Towards Peace and Freedom*, Aug. 1919, p. 17 (*Towards Peace and Freedom* was a journal providing a record of the International Women's Congresses in 1915 and 1919).
47. Ibid.
48. These issues are examined from various perspectives in Pierson, *Women and Peace*.
49. Bussey and Tims, *Women's International League*, p. 17.
50. Sandi Cooper, 'Women's Participation in European Peace Movements: The Struggle to Prevent World War I', in Pierson, *Women and Peace*, p. 67.

5

Working with National Issues and British Organisations

All her adult life, Chrystal Macmillan was involved with movements seeking equality and human rights: she worked on two fronts, national and international, and through membership of several women's organisations. In this chapter, the focus is on her work on the executive committees of four British voluntary organisations – the NUSEC (formerly NUWSS), the NUWW, the AMSH and the National Council for the Unmarried Mother and her Child (NCUMC). Among the tasks she undertook on these committees, one was to advise and campaign on legal issues that particularly affected women. As a former colleague noted, 'She was always on the alert to "spot" clauses which were prejudicial to women, or which differentiated their treatment from that of men.'[1]

NATIONAL UNION OF SOCIETIES FOR EQUAL CITIZENSHIP (NUSEC, FORMERLY NUWSS)

After 1918, when some women over the age of 30 were granted the vote, suffragists continued to campaign for full and equal franchise. They also renewed their efforts to review legislation that affected women, working with sympathetic MPs to amend the many British laws that discriminated against women.

From 1919 through to 1926, Chrystal Macmillan regularly attended NUSEC EC meetings where she worked with Eleanor Rathbone on several of the subcommittees and regularly drafted preliminary Bills, based on the work of the committees, to illustrate to MPs what the women were proposing. The committees discussed issues where they felt new legislation was needed and reviewed proposed legislation: Widow's Pensions & Equal Guardianship; Equal Moral Standard; Status of Wives and Mothers; Economic Independence of Women; Married Women

(Parliamentary Bills); and Coverture Disabilities (Abolition) Bill. In 1920, Chrystal Macmillan and Edith Bethune-Baker, also a member of NUSEC EC, collected evidence and, on behalf of NUSEC, presented it to the Joint Committee on Criminal Law Amendments Bills. Two years later, Chrystal Macmillan was one of four NUSEC women on a deputation to the Home Secretary, the Minister of Health and other members of the Cabinet, on the Guardianship of Infants Bill. She also prepared a memorandum for MPs on 'Inequalities in Civil and Criminal Law between Men and Women'.

The year 1924 was increasingly busy for the NUSEC committees, with an additional Legislative Committee for Scotland being set up to monitor and deal with Scottish Bills. The Annual report for 1924/25 noted that 'additional staff had been engaged at headquarters, reinforced by more voluntary workers to cope with the influx of Press enquiries, demands for publications, and requests for information, speakers, and workers'.[2]

Despite being called to the Bar that year, Chrystal Macmillan found time to be actively involved in several NUSEC committees, each dealing with different pieces of legislation: the Status of the Married Woman Bill (Domiciles, Torts & Contracts); the Guardianship of Infants Bill; Separation and Maintenance Orders Bill; Married Women's Income. This work required a detailed knowledge of the law and legal terminology, so Chrystal Macmillan's legal training was a great asset to the committees. Six members of the NUSEC Married Women (Parliamentary) Bills Committee, of which Chrystal was chair, took it upon themselves to study the legal differences between men and women in Contract and Tort: Domicile. After some highly technical discussions the secretary resigned on the grounds that she could not 'hear sufficiently well to follow the business of the meeting'![3]

That year, 1924, a Joint Select Committee was appointed by Parliament to consider and report on the Guardianship of Infants Bill, which proposed to give mothers equal legal authority with fathers. When the Committee started to take evidence, Chrystal Macmillan and Eva Hubback, both representing NUSEC, gave evidence in favour of the Bill, meeting many of the points raised by previous witnesses.

The first witness, Sir Chartres Biron, Chief Magistrate of Bow Street, opposed the Bill as a 'revolutionary measure'. In her interventions, Chrystal Macmillan made it clear that NUSEC aimed to ensure that the law would treat women fairly and without a male bias:

> That is the point on which women's organisations and individual women who are not in women's organisations do feel strongly – the point that equality is

the necessary principle. The reason for putting in this phrase at the end, 'any rule of law or equity heretofore in force to the contrary notwithstanding', was because one has found by experience that when cases come before the Court, unless you not only state the thing positively where a woman is concerned, but also, as it were, rebut the common law, the decisions tend not to go in favour of the women ... [T]he Law Courts tend to interpret in another way and that is why that phrase was put in. I do not know if it is the sense in which all lawyers interpret it, but it is to make sure of the ground there. As far as I understood the Chief Magistrate this morning, he really objected to it on the ground that he objected to the alteration of the law. The object of it is to alter the law.[4]

Moreover, Chrystal Macmillan pointed out that the law should reflect the reality of mothers in the home with children:

> Sub-clause (d) introduces a new principle into the law. It has generally been assumed that the work of a woman in the home is not economic – that she is not a producer. This is to lay down the principle that the work that a woman does in the home with her children is of value ... We suggest that it is only reasonable that in estimating the contribution, the woman's work in the home should be considered as her contribution, and that it should not be considered that she is doing nothing for the children if she does not bring in money wages.[5]

The NUSEC Annual Report for 1925/26 noted that they had seen a 'real legislative harvest', seeing substantial improvements in the law on issues on which they had campaigned, such as pensions for widows and fatherless children, advances in the status of mothers regarding guardianship, custody and maintenance of her child, and separation and maintenance orders, all legislative changes which Chrystal Macmillan had worked to bring about.

> The fact that they fall short of the measures of perfection for which your Committee has been working for so many years, must not lead to an underestimate of their value ... Your Committee has to record a year of vigour and growth in the Union, and of a marked increase in the recognition accorded to its work in Parliament, in Government departments and in the Press.[6]

Despite these successes, by 1926 serious divisions over policy began to emerge between members of the NUSEC executive. The most divisive issue was whether NUSEC should support the introduction of protective legislation for the employment of women.[7] Chrystal Macmillan reacted critically to the proposed NUSEC programme for 1927. Although she had some sympathy for Eleanor Rathbone's proposed programme on birth control and family allowances, she felt strongly that these proposals were taking the Union away from their prime purpose:

> Equal Citizenship is Equal Suffrage, followed closely by our other demands for Equal Political Rights, namely membership of the House of Lords and Married Women's Nationality . . . The Union's special job is to build securely the foundations of the liberty and status of women.[8]

For her part, Eleanor Rathbone insisted that

> The task of NUSEC began but must not end with equality. The destruction of barriers must be followed by the reconstruction of conditions to fit the needs and aspirations of both sexes, instead of (as heretofore) one only. The question 'How to get for woman this thing that men have already?' though important, matters less than 'How to get for women this thing which is good in itself, whether men think so or not?' Bother men![9]

When Eleanor Rathbone won the support of membership for her proposed programme at the Annual Council meeting in 1928, Chrystal Macmillan and ten other women resigned from the NUSEC EC, several becoming founder members of the Open Door Council (ODC) that focused on the campaign for women's equality in employment.[10]

The NUSEC Annual Report of 1928 noted Chrystal Macmillan's resignation and paid tribute to her work for the organisation:

> The help given by Chrystal Macmillan, especially on legal matters on which her knowledge has always been freely placed at our disposal, calls for a special tribute. She has been identified with the Union for so many years that she has a place of her own in its affections, which no clash of opinions can alter.[11]

NATIONAL UNION OF WOMEN WORKERS (NUWW)

After graduating from the University of Edinburgh in 1900, Chrystal Macmillan spent a few months in Berlin but had to return to Edinburgh for her father's funeral in January 1901, and remained resident in Scotland until 1913. It was during this period in Edinburgh that she became a member of the NUWW, an affiliation that lasted for the rest of her life. The Union 'sought from the early 1890s onwards to create a supportive national network of individual women and affiliated associations committed to philanthropy, education and other forms of public service'.[12] Later known as the National Council of Women, it became what Julia Bush described as 'a broadly based body of mainly middle class, socially conservative reformers reunited around an agenda for advancing female citizenship'.[13]

By 1904 Chrystal Macmillan was honorary secretary of the Central District Union, which was part of the Scottish Branch of NUWW.[14] In 1908, in collaboration with the NUWW vice-president, Dr Maria Ogilvie Gordon, Chrystal Macmillan undertook a study of youth employment involving interviews with employers in Edinburgh and Leith.[15] However, by 1911 her attention became more directed towards London where she regularly attended the large monthly NUWW EC meetings, at which between forty and sixty representatives were often present. From her first attendance, representing the Scottish Standing Committee of NUWW, Chrystal Macmillan took an active part in discussions, regularly bringing forward resolutions.

NUWW and the National Insurance Bill

Due to her involvement in the Scottish women graduates' case (see Chapter 2), Chrystal Macmillan had become aware of the impact on women of the male interpretation of the law, and her awareness of implications in new and proposed legislation was increased and refined by her work as an elected member of the National EC (NEC) of NUWW.

An example of this was the work she did in relation to the National Insurance Bill. Initially, she spoke at a public meeting in Edinburgh, to raise awareness of the lack of provision for women under the proposed legislation.[16] Later that year, as a member of the NUWW subcommittee appointed to safeguard women's interests under the Bill, she successfully moved two resolutions at the NEC to protect women's rights under the terms of the Bill.[17]

Although she moved to London in 1913, she retained her interest in Scottish matters: when she attended the Scottish branch meeting in May that year, she suggested that, as amendments to the Insurance Act were shortly to be considered by Parliament, the secretary should write to members asking them to contact their local MPs, urging that 'one fourth of each insurance committee of representatives of insured persons should be women'.[18] Moreover, while visiting the Scottish branch she suggested that members be encouraged to lobby their local MPs to have at least one woman appointed as a salaried Commissioner to administer the Mental Deficiency Bill when it was enacted in Scotland.[19]

At the NEC meeting in London, she suggested that the NUWW might promote an amendment to the Home Rule Bill to extend the franchise to women in Scotland. She carefully framed her appeal to the somewhat conservatively minded NEC so that such an amendment might be supported by both suffragists and anti-suffragists, on the grounds that the proposed franchise would apply only to municipal and domestic elections and not to Parliamentary or imperial elections.

Learning about the law in the NUWW Legislation Committee

Given her interest and growing expertise in legislative matters, Chrystal Macmillan was an obvious candidate for membership of the NUWW UK Legislation Committee, to which she was duly elected in June 1912, and where she continued to learn how to use the law to advance women's rights. The committee monitored both draft legislation as it passed through Parliament, and government regulations, making representations to Parliament in cases where legal outcomes would disproportionately affect women.

In 1914, at the start of the First World War, Chrystal Macmillan brought to NEC attention the difficulties experienced by British-born women married to foreign men, difficulties brought about by the passing of the British Nationality and Status of Aliens Act 1914. She proposed two resolutions, both of which were passed: firstly, 'that the Executive Committee of NUWW urges the Government to instruct the local Distress Committees in making regulations to reduce unemployment and in administering relief, to treat British-born wives of aliens as British subjects', and secondly, 'that considering the many complicated questions arising out of the provision for alien men and women, both friends and enemies, the Executive Committee urges the Home Secretary to add women members to the Destitute Aliens Committee'.[20]

Later that year, she drew the committee's attention to a press report that five women had been court-martialled by the military authorities in Cardiff for contravention of an order prohibiting women from being out between 7 p.m. and 8 a.m. She asked members to move an emergency resolution protesting against this order, made under the war-time Defence of the Realm Act (DORA) regulations. The more conservatively minded members of the committee wanted more information before they would consider her resolution and she obliged them by telephoning the Town Clerk and local military officer in Cardiff. She then reported back to the committee, informing them 'that the order applied only to certain individual women of a certain class who had been often in prison'.[21] After further discussion, the committee voted to abstain from action, as military authorities were entitled to issue orders 'in fortified towns' under DORA. These orders were made to protect young soldiers newly recruited to military camp from being approached by prostitutes.

There was a general concern for public morality, as evidenced when the committee went on to discuss the need to discourage immorality in young women, voting by a large majority that

> ... the importance of establishing the principle that pensions should only be granted as of right to women who have been the lawful wives of deceased sailors or soldiers, and that in all cases of unmarried women claiming to have been dependent on sailors or soldiers, a pension or compassionate allowance should only be granted in special circumstances after full enquiry, and upon such conditions as may secure that the pension shall not be in effect an endowment of immorality and an encouragement to others to lead irregular or vicious lives.[22]

This resolution was proposed in opposition to a Local Government Board Circular recommending that 'no discrimination should be made between married and unmarried mothers'. Although this resolution penalising women and children in relationships where mothers were not legally married to military personnel was passed, it is unlikely to have been supported by Chrystal Macmillan, given her support for the NCUMC (see later in this chapter).

Following her involvement in the International Women's Congress at The Hague in 1915 (see Chapter 4), Chrystal Macmillan resigned from the NUWW NEC in April 1916 in protest at the decision by committee members to oppose sending NUWW delegates to the Congress. However, she later rejoined the committee and at a meeting on 18 January 1918 she was appointed to represent the NUWW Legislation Committee to advise in the drafting of a Bill arising from the Child Inquiry, organised by the Social Welfare Association. She was also asked to join a subcommittee considering whether closer cooperation was possible between the NUWW and the Joint Parliamentary Advisory Council.[23]

The work undertaken by Chrystal Macmillan and members of the NUWW Legislation Committee was supported by the reports of the Stansfeld Trust. This charitable organisation had been set up in 1896 to promote 'the equality of men and women before the law of the land', and employed Miss Chamney as Scrutineer.[24] Apart from monitoring Parliamentary activity, Miss Chamney's work involved publishing and distributing monthly reports on all Public and Private Parliamentary Bills wherein men and women were dealt with differently. The Scrutineer reports provided a solid basis for the NUWW and other women's organisations to organise interventions on all legislative matters negatively affecting women. This meant that whenever a question bearing on an issue of interest was likely to come up in Parliament, NUWW members, including Chrystal Macmillan, were well prepared to take action, to make representations to MPs and Ministers at Westminster, and inform and encourage NUWW members to lobby their local MP.

For example, when the Divorce Law Amendment Bill was being discussed in 1918, Chrystal Macmillan proposed that the NEC 'declare that any amendment of divorce laws shall provide that the same grounds of divorce shall be applicable to men and women; that the wife shall be adequately provided for; and that man and woman shall be treated equally as parents irrespective of the superior economic position of either'.[25] This resolution would be sent out to branches who could then decide whether to lobby their MP on the issue.

Throughout 1919 and the early 1920s, Chrystal Macmillan played a very active part on the NEC of the NUWW, proposing resolutions on the appointment of women as Justices of the Peace,[26] the separation of income tax between husband and wife,[27] and the registration of nurses;[28] and in 1921 she urged the government to extend the franchise to women under 30.[29] After July 1921, she no longer attended NEC meetings, but corresponded with them in her role as chair of the NUWW committee on the nationality of married women, becoming chair and coordinator of the Nationality of Married Women Pass the Bill Committee when it was formed in 1930 (see Chapter 8).

The NUWW regularly submitted petitions and memoranda to political leaders and sent deputations to Parliament. As an officer of the organisation, Chrystal Macmillan took an active part in monitoring the development and interpretation of proposed and existing legislation, and through such work she gained a greater understanding of the workings of the law, from the development of legislation to its implementation and administration.

It was due to her understanding of legal matters that, in 1915, the NUWW appointed her to the ICW International Standing Committee on the Legal Position of Women. Over succeeding years, her expertise was widely acknowledged when she contributed a chapter on 'The Present Position of Women Internationally' for the 1924 *Woman's Yearbook*[30] and, in 1929, when she wrote the section on 'The Legal Position of Women' for *Encyclopaedia Britannica*.[31]

THE ASSOCIATION FOR MORAL AND SOCIAL HYGIENE (AMSH)

Chrystal Macmillan became an active member of the AMSH EC in January 1917 where she formed a close working relationship with the secretary, Alison Neilans. The two women cooperated on several AMSH campaigns to reform the legislative provisions that affected women, including proposed amendments to DORA regulations and the Criminal Law Amendment Bill. Such campaigns for reforms were much needed as these laws were notorious for 'encapsulating many of the most fundamental social, legal and economic injustices that plagued women'.[32]

During the First World War there was a public panic about the spread of venereal disease, seen by military authorities as a threat to the efficiency of the troops.[33] Under Regulation 40D of DORA, it became a criminal offence for an infected woman to solicit or have sex with any member of His Majesty's Armed Services.[34] AMSH was concerned to expose the injustice of this regulation, which resulted in women and men being treated differently. Women could be subjected to medical examinations, and if found to be suffering from any venereal disease, could be imprisoned until cured. In contrast, men, including soldiers, were not subject to such legally authorised medical procedures. AMSH regarded this situation as discriminatory, and campaigned for the removal of this double standard of morality in order that the behaviour of men and women would in future be treated equally under the law.

In 1916, AMSH set up a subcommittee which organised a rota of members to observe court hearings involving women arrested for soliciting. This committee, chaired by Chrystal Macmillan, was known as the AMSH Police Court Rota Committee, and recruited and trained women volunteers to observe court proceedings and report back on the cases where women were convicted as 'common prostitutes' on the evidence given by a sole policeman. It was an important innovation at a time when courts were predominantly male environments; the judiciary, the lawyers and the jury were men, and frequently the magistrates and judges objected to a woman's presence in the court. Based on their experience of observing court procedures, members of the Police Court Rota Committee proposed 'that there should be for Police Courts a solicitor available without fee for the defence of any prisoner'.[35]

In 1919, AMSH issued a pamphlet, written by Chrystal Macmillan, urging opposition to the proposal to introduce Departmental Orders in place of government legislation for the compulsory notification of venereal disease. She noted that

> The custom of restricting the liberties of the subject by decree and not by Act of Parliament, may have been suffered in silence in war-time. Now that there is peace, such a method is inconsistent and intolerable in a democracy where the liberty of the subject is respected.[36]

She pointed out that the National Council for Combatting Venereal Diseases (NCCVD) had recommended that the provision of free and confidential treatment would produce better results in controlling the disease.

Chrystal Macmillan, supported by Helena Swanwick, was a prominent member of the AMSH Committee of Enquiry into Sexual Morality, which met from October 1918 to June 1920, dealing with questions around the prosecution of prostitutes.[37] The two women laid out the details of issues to be covered and those to be excluded, and the enquiry, chaired by Sir Charles Tarring, Chair of AMSH, heard evidence from various witnesses.

From one such witness, Mr Archibald Allen, a non-practising barrister, Chrystal Macmillan asked for an opinion on the court procedure whereby a woman could be convicted on the evidence of a policeman that she was a 'common prostitute'. She questioned whether it was unusual under British law for a 'serious charge which amounted to taking away the character of a woman, should be given in a police court without any real evidence'.

Archibald Allen replied that the evidence provided by the police that the woman was a common prostitute could be repudiated by the woman if she was able to produce evidence of her good character. His response was challenged by Chrystal Macmillan who asked him whether or not it was simply assumed that the accused woman was a common prostitute, and whether the evidence offered in court should be more robust and of a higher standard. In response, Mr Allen said that it was up to the police constable to give evidence that the accused was a prostitute, although in practice he believed that in 99 cases out of 100 the accused women did not deny the allegation.

Chrystal Macmillan then asked, 'When a case of stealing is proved, someone has to come and say plainly that the article belongs to them and so on but when a woman is proved to be a common prostitute no man is produced to say he has ever been with that woman. Is it really good evidence unless that is done?', to which Mr Allen replied that he thought it sufficient that the police witness swore that he had seen her going to a 'bad house'[38] (the use of this term refers not necessarily to a brothel but to a lodging house where poor women and women thought to be prostitutes might live).

When Sir Willoughby Dickinson MP was interviewed for the Enquiry, his response indicated the double moral standard of the age when he stated that

> If a girl over the age of consent and therefore not protected by it, solicited a man and she was thought to be a common prostitute, she becomes liable to the full penalties, but she is not protected after 16 either from being solicited

by a man or from being seduced. What is an offence in her, making her liable to three years imprisonment, is no offence in a man.[39]

Later in the Enquiry, Chrystal Macmillan asked a medical witness from the NCCVD whether there were any women on their EC, and when he admitted there were none, she suggested that they approach and recruit distinguished qualified women from the women's movement.

One of the questions posed by Chrystal Macmillan during the Enquiry resonates with the current change in attitude towards the prosecution of men who have sex with underage girls:

> I never quite understand how it is you can have girls declared prostitutes under the age of 16, the age of protection being 16. Do you know how it is there are never any prosecutions of the men who go with these girls who are under 16?[40]

The AMSH committee expressed concern when the volunteers of the Police Court Rota Committee reported back that not only were female volunteers being excluded but that all women were excluded from court hearings of child abuse cases. Female children were required to appear without any female support or legal representation in the totally male environment of the court. Moreover, the accepted defence put forward by several alleged male perpetrators was that they had been seduced by the child, who was of 'bad character and conduct', and that many courts and medical witnesses expressed doubts about the innocence of girls.[41] Evidence presented to the Enquiry became central to another AMSH campaign to strengthen the Children's Act to give children better legislative protection, and to have the age of consent raised.

During 1921, the AMSH Committee discussed issues arising from work undertaken by the League of Nations (see Chapter 6). Chrystal Macmillan moved a resolution that a letter be sent to Sir Eric Drummond, Secretary General of the League, asking that a woman be appointed to sit on the Mandates Commission.[42] Later in the year she reported on her informal meeting with Dame Rachel Crowdy, Head of the Social Questions and Opium Traffic Section of the League of Nations, who had been in London to attend the Traffic in Women Conference. As Rachel Crowdy had expressed a wish to have practical suggestions for the amendment of the White Slave Traffic Conventions, it was agreed that AMSH would immediately send a letter to Rachel Crowdy making certain suggestions.

Chrystal Macmillan resigned from the AMSH committees in April 1923 but continued to give advice in relation to its legal affairs. In an obituary for her, published in the AMSH journal, *The Shield*, special tribute was paid to her work for the organisation in relation to legal matters, to which she had brought considerable knowledge and skill:

> [She] took an active part in framing and promoting the Public Places (Order) Bill: a measure both to promote order and to rescue from injustice and bullying the woman of the streets. None who heard it will ever forget her evidence before the Street Offences Committee, in 1928, and her calm, relentless, ever recurring reminder to those who sought to rebut her plans for legal changes and substitute their own, that they could only do so if they were seeking to set up a 'Court of Morals': a course which the Committee had that very day explicitly rejected . . . She was actively interested in the Association . . . and gave legal knowledge and aid most generously whenever it was required . . . Many a Parliamentary Bill affecting women, or amendments to them, was drafted on her advice.[43]

NATIONAL COUNCIL FOR THE UNMARRIED MOTHER AND HER CHILD (NCUMC)

Chrystal Macmillan served on the Legal Subcommittee of the NCUMC from April 1918 until March 1920. The committee, under the chairmanship of Newton Crane, the barrister who later sponsored Chrystal Macmillan's application to be admitted to Middle Temple, worked to bring about changes in the law and administration to secure better provisions and overall protection for unmarried mothers and their children (and the widowed, or deserted mothers in need). Chrystal Macmillan, in cooperation with other members of the committee, worked with the magistrate and author Clarke Hall to introduce less punitive and more protective legislative provisions for children.[44]

CONCLUSION

Critics of Chrystal Macmillan have described her work for women's organisations in the 1920s and 1930s as that of a 'committee woman' rather than a 'campaigner for women's rights', but her activism must be set in the context of social changes of the early twentieth century. Writing in 1929, Vera Brittain described the gulf between pre-war and post-war feminism as follows:

> The young professional woman should realize that her own happy situation would never have come about if, for over half a century, women had not been prepared to spend, without remuneration, the greater part of their lives in committee rooms and on public platforms.[45]

During this period, women like Chrystal Macmillan were learning to understand the law and the implications of its interpretation and enforcement from a woman's perspective. Not only did they have to struggle against curtailment of their rights by long-standing custom and practice, they also had to work together to ensure that the opportunities offered under the Representation of the People Act (1918) and the Sex Disqualification (Removal) Act (1919) were used to secure women's progress to full citizenship rights. As Lady Rhondda argued, 'the women's movement was engaged in two battles, to achieve legislative progress for women and to change public opinion'.[46]

Notes

1. JS, *The Scotsman*, Sept. 24, 1937.
2. NUSEC Annual Report 1924/25, p. 5 (London: Women's Library, LSE), Annual Report of the National Union of Societies for Equal Citizenship 1924–5 (lse.ac.uk).
3. NUSEC Minutes, Married Women Drafting Committee, 18 June 1924 (London: Women's Library, LSE, NUSEC/A5/3(5)).
4. Minutes of Evidence to Joint Select Committee on Guardianship of Infants Bill, 1923, HMSO, para. 164.
5. Ibid., para. 171.
6. NUSEC Annual report 1925/1926, p. 3 (London: Women's Library, LSE), Annual Report of the National Union of Societies for Equal Citizenship 1925–6 (lse.ac.uk).
7. Cheryl Law, *Suffrage and Power: The Women's Movement, 1918–1928* (London: I.B. Tauris, 2000).
8. Statement of Views: NUSEC Annual Council Meeting 1927 (London: Women's Library, LSE, 2NSE/B/3/3).
9. Ibid.
10. *Yorkshire Post*, 7 Mar. 1927.
11. NUSEC Annual Report 1927/1928, p. 8 (London: Women's Library, LSE, Annual Report of the National Union of Societies for Equal Citizenship 1927–8 (lse.ac.uk).
12. Julia Bush, 'The National Union of Women Workers and Women's Suffrage', in M. Boussahba-Bravard (ed.), *Suffrage outside Suffragism: Women's Vote in Britain 1880–1914* (Basingstoke: Palgrave Macmillan, 2007), p. 105.
13. Ibid., p. 107.
14. NUWW Minutes St Andrews Branch, 1904. Special Collections, University of St Andrews GB227 msdep16.
15. Maria Ogilvie Gordon, *A Handbook of Employments Specially Prepared for the Use of Boys and Girls on Entering the Trades, Industries, and Professions* (Aberdeen: Rosemount Press, 1908).

16. *The Queen*, 1911; *Evening Telegraph & Post*, 10 July 1911, p. 5.
17. NUWW Minutes, 21 Nov. 1911. London Metropolitan Archive.
18. NUWW Minutes, 30 May 1913. City of Edinburgh Archive.
19. Ibid.
20. NUWW Minutes, 8 Sept. 1914. London Metropolitan Archives.
21. Ibid., 1 Dec. 1914.
22. Ibid.
23. NUWW Minutes, ibid., 18 Jan. 1918.
24. Stansfeld Trust, 1896 (London: Women's Library, LSE, 3JSM).
25. NUWW Minutes, 15 Feb. 1918.
26. Ibid., Feb. 1919.
27. Ibid., Mar. 1919.
28. Ibid., June 1919.
29. Ibid., Feb. 1921.
30. Chrystal Macmillan, 'The Present Position of Women Internationally' (1923), in Evelyn Gates (ed.), *The Woman's Yearbook 1923–1924* (London: Women Publishers, n.d.), p. 21.
31. Chrystal Macmillan, 'The Legal Position of Women', in *Encyclopaedia Britannica* (14th edn, 1929).
32. Julia Ann Laite, 'The Association for Moral and Social Hygiene: Abolitionism and Prostitution Law in Britain (1915–1959)', *Women's History Review* 17.2 (2008), pp. 207–23.
33. Letter to *The Spectator*, 25 Mar. 1916, p. 12.
34. Laura Lammasniemi, 'Regulation 40D: Punishing Promiscuity on the Home Front during the First World War', *Women's History Review* 26.4 (2017), pp. 584–96.
35. AMSH Minutes, 1917 (London: Women's Library, LSE, 3AMS/A/03/08).
36. Chrystal Macmillan, *A New Danger: Departmental Orders versus Legislation for Venereal Disease* (London: Association for Moral and Social Hygiene, 1919).
37. Laite, 'The Association for Moral and Social Hygiene', p. 217.
38. AMSH Minutes, June 1919.
39. AMSH Minutes, Nov. 1919.
40. Ibid.
41. Victoria Bates, *Sexual Forensics in Victorian and Edwardian England: Age, Crime and Consent in Courts* (London: Palgrave Macmillan, 2016).
42. AMSH Minutes, 18 Feb. 1921
43. Elizabeth Abbott, 'Obituary', *The Shield* 5.3 (Dec. 1937), pp. 134–5.
44. Minutes, Report of Legal Subcommittee of NCUMC, Dec. 1918 (London: Women's Library, LSE, 5OPF/02/12).
45. Brittain, 'Committees versus Professions', p. 105.
46. Viscountess M. H. T. Rhondda, quoted in Law, *Suffrage and Power*, p. 95.

6

Working with International Organisations

Chrystal Macmillan was a member of the ECs of the three most influential women's international organisations at the beginning of the twentieth century: the ICW, the IWSA and the WILPF.[1] She also undertook work with the International Federation of University Women (IFUW) and the Open Door International (ODI), which brought her into contact with the League of Nations, the organisation established in 1920 by the Versailles Peace Treaty which aimed to maintain world peace.

In her book charting the rise and development of the women's international organisations in the early years of the twentieth century, Leila Rupp argues that, although presenting as 'a federation of women of all races, nations, creeds and classes', ICW, IWSA and WILPF were strongly rooted in Europe and the USA.[2] However, in her work with these organisations, Chrystal Macmillan extended her reach to include women in Japan, India and Egypt.

As a woman of her time, she would undoubtedly be influenced by the ideology of the British Empire.[3] As Michelle Staff has noted, in her early days, Chrystal Macmillan saw Britain as the 'storm centre' of the enfranchisement movement.[4] However, she showed little prejudice, or belief in the superiority of the British culture, as was evidenced, for example, when her friend Eunice Murray expressed surprise in 1918 at Chrystal Macmillan's positive attitude towards the immediate self-determination for the people of India.[5] It was also evident in her long-term active engagement with various women's international organisations throughout the 1920s and 1930s that held 'a high degree of optimism and the belief that women could make a difference'.[6] And to this end Chrystal Macmillan travelled throughout Europe, Canada and America meeting with women through her work with the international women's organisations.

The growth in motor and railway transport at the start of the twentieth century made travel easier. European women, like Chrystal Macmillan, were able to travel to meet with other women, both within their own countries and more widely, across Europe and the Americas. As Charlotte Perkins Gilman observed, there was an awakening of cooperation between women: 'The most amazing thing in these great International Women's Congresses is the massing and moving of the hitherto isolated and stationary sex.'[7]

INTERNATIONAL COUNCIL OF WOMEN (ICW)

Chrystal Macmillan's introduction to work with international organisations started in 1904 with her appointment as honorary secretary of the Standing Committee of the Scottish District Unions of Women Workers, a branch of the NUWW which later became known as the NCW of Great Britain and Northern Ireland. The NCW was affiliated to the ICW, founded in 1888 in the USA with membership mainly in the USA and Europe, whose president and vice-president were for many years both Scottish women, Lady Aberdeen and Dr Maria Ogilvie Gordon, both of whom were well known to Chrystal Macmillan.

In June 1909, Chrystal Macmillan was chosen by her colleagues to be one of the British delegates to the ICW Quinquennial Congress in Toronto where she met delegates and heard reports of work undertaken in countries in Europe and the Americas, and in Australia – 18 countries in all. Five years later, in May 1914, she was again a delegate to the ICW International Quinquennial Congress when it met in Rome. This time she intervened in a debate, asking for a clause advocating the inclusion of women to be added to the resolution recommending that an intergovernmental meeting of immigration officials be called. The reply noted that, as there were no women officials in the immigration departments, there was no point in such an addition to the resolution.

Chrystal Macmillan's attempts to undertake international work under the auspices of ICW were sometimes limited by lack of support from the rather conservatively minded British committee. She had not yet learned the skills of two-level negotiation, between her British colleagues and international colleagues.[8] During the First World War, she frequently advocated a more international outlook on relationships with other ICW women members in foreign countries, especially in Germany, without getting any backing from her more nationalistically minded colleagues.

When she became one of the main organisers of the 1915 International Congress of Women at The Hague (see Chapter 4), she sent an invitation to the NUWW EC to appoint a delegate to the conference. In response to the invitation, a letter was sent to the EC from the ICW president, Lady Aberdeen, advising them that she would not recommend sending delegates to the Congress 'as she felt the moment was not opportune'. Elizabeth Cadbury, chair of the NUWW Peace and Arbitration Committee, stated that she, along with 150 others, had been supportive of the proposed conference, but that she had taken no part in the arrangements, and having reviewed the Agenda for the Congress had changed her mind: she would not be attending the Congress in The Hague. The president's letter and Elizabeth Cadbury's statement influenced the deliberations of the EC who passed a formal resolution that they would not appoint delegates, 'and further wish it to be understood that the Congress has no official connection with the International Council of Women'.

After an absence from meetings in 1915, Chrystal Macmillan resigned from the EC in April 1916. However, she was back and active on it again in October 1917, particularly focusing on issues concerning nationality and the illegitimacy of children. In November 1918, the NUWW international subcommittee considered a letter from her regarding an appeal for food for women and children, from the NCW in Germany: this was at a time when many German and Austrian children were suffering from severe malnutrition.[9] After a short discussion, members of the committee expressed the unanimous opinion, with one dissentient, that to take action in this matter 'would show a great want of faith in our Government': they were mindful that it was the British government policy of enforcing a naval blockade of Germany that led to the severe food shortages.

Although her legal expertise was appreciated, Chrystal Macmillan's international perspective on many issues was not shared by other members of the ICW national executive. While she continued to work with the British committee on national and international legislation issues, she did not progress to become an office-bearer in this international organisation.

INTERNATIONAL WOMAN SUFFRAGE ALLIANCE (IWSA)

Of all the organisations to which she belonged, it was to the IWSA that Chrystal Macmillan remained committed for more years than to any other organisation, from 1908 until her death in 1937. It was a remarkable commitment, perhaps sustained by the wide-ranging agenda of the organisation, as well as its international reach, which had always held a particular appeal for her. That range and reach is well illustrated by the following quote from Winifred Harper Cooley, an American delegate to the IWSA Congress in Budapest:

> It was not merely a dry discussion of ways and means to get the vote, but comprehensive studies of social and moral conditions, and of how women could better them. At almost every session one learned of the White Slave Traffic; of ways to protect young girls; of efforts of women legislators to raise the age of consent; of State insurance for mothers; of solutions of the problem of the illegitimate child; of better laws for working women; of the abolition of sweat shops and child labour.[10]

In 1908, as one of six delegates from the Edinburgh National Suffrage Society to the IWSA Congress in Amsterdam, Chrystal Macmillan spoke in the public debate which addressed the question, 'Why should representative governments enfranchise women?' She also participated in the general meeting, representing the ICW as a 'fraternal delegate'.[11]

The following year, at the IWSA Congress in London, and again acting as the fraternal ICW delegate, she caused a stir by challenging a resolution presented by the British NUWSS delegation. This resolution appeared to claim credit for all the progress on suffrage issues without giving any acknowledgment to the work undertaken by other suffrage organisations, such as the WFL or the WSPU. Chrystal Macmillan's challenge led to much debate, resulting in the passing of a more neutral resolution which was accepted by the NUWSS delegates.[12]

Clearly, her challenge to the NUWSS resolution did not shake their faith in her as, two years later, she was asked to act as proxy for Millicent Fawcett who was unable to attend the 1911 IWSA Congress in Stockholm. This was a busy and demanding occasion for her: she was appointed assistant secretary to the Congress, and took part in the public debate on municipal suffrage. Along with Marie Stritt and Maria Verone, she was appointed to compile a book of information on the different franchises already exercised by women around the world. Frau Stritt was responsible for the review of German and Scandinavian countries, Mme Verone for French-speaking, and Chrystal Macmillan for English-speaking countries. The resulting book, entitled *Woman Suffrage in Practice*,[13] was published in English, French and German in time for the 1913 IWSA Congress, and was later followed by a companion publication, *Facts versus Fancies on Woman Suffrage*, with Chrystal Macmillan as sole author.[14]

In 1913, when Chrystal Macmillan moved to London after she and her brothers had sold the family home in Edinburgh, she began working closely with Millicent Fawcett on NUWSS business and in the headquarters of the IWSA. She acted as both NUWSS and ICW fraternal delegate to the 1913 IWSA Congress in Budapest, where she was elected first recording secretary, and a member of the team to manage the IWSA journal *Jus Suffragii* based in London, alongside Adela Stanton Coit, Carrie Chapman Catt and Millicent Fawcett.

An issue frequently raised by Chrystal Macmillan was the need for women's organisations to establish good links with the press. At a meeting of the IWSA EC in July 1914, she put forward the following motion, which was approved: 'that the systematic collection of current news should be undertaken by the IWSA office to facilitate rapid communication on Woman Suffrage and the Women's Movement to national sections and for these sections to promote the publication of such news in their local press'.[15]

Figure 6.1 IWSA Board, Budapest, 1913
Standing from left: Katherine Dexter McCormick, USA; Adela Stanton Coit, GB; Anna Lindemann, Germany; Annie Furuhjelm, Finland; Signe Bergmann, Sweden; Chrystal Macmillan, GB; Rosika Schwimmer, Hungary; seated: Millicent Garrett Fawcett, GB; Carrie Chapman Catt, USA; Marguerite de Witt Schlumberger, France (courtesy Women's Library, LSE)

By the summer of 1914, women in the international organisations were becoming concerned that international relations between political leaders were deteriorating. As discussed in Chapter 4 on Peace, the two IWSA office-bearers, Chrystal Macmillan and Millicent Fawcett, jointly signed the International Manifesto of Women,[16] an IWSA plea to political leaders, made in July 1914, to make every effort to avoid war. The plea fell on deaf ears: war was declared by Britain one month later, on 4 August 1914.

Immediately war was declared, international suffrage work was suspended and the IWSA deployed their personnel and used their resources for relief work. For Chrystal Macmillan, this involved a huge commitment of time and effort, as recorded by Millicent Fawcett:

> Headquarters Committee have undertaken to extend help of various kinds to the large numbers of foreign women left stranded, and in some cases, penniless and friendless in London in the consequences of war. Our treasurer Mrs Coit and our recording secretary Miss Macmillan have been indefatigable in carrying out this work; they have been at the office every day and all day working ever since the war began.[17]

These efforts were formalised with the setting up of an IWSA International Women's Relief Committee, coordinated by Chrystal Macmillan.[18] This committee organised the repatriation of German women and children resident in England, and British women and children resident in Germany, escorting them across the Channel to their homes. The women were often foreign workers, the children often on school exchange, all of whom were stranded by the sudden outbreak of war.

After the fall of Antwerp in October 1914, there was an influx of 80,000 Belgian refugees to the small village of Flushing in Holland, and the IWSA committee responded to an appeal for food which 'reached the office by midday on 13 October':

> That very evening four great railway trucks of food were shipped to Flushing, including 20,000lbs of bread and large quantities of chocolate, condensed milk and biscuits. The direction of operations was taken by Chrystal Macmillan to whom the success of the whole transaction was due.[19]

> From the Belgian ambassador she obtained a guarantee of £200 with which to buy food. She and I went to Lyon's headquarters and then and there bought £200 worth of provisions. We saw the cases loaded onto lorries and sent off to the ship on which we were to take them to Flushing . . . We collected the

things necessary for a couple of nights and joined the ship. We were the only passengers, and the North Sea was empty of shipping as our boat was of people. We had one qualm when we saw a periscope, but it turned out to be a British submarine.

Flushing was a tragic sight, swarming with refugees. The walls were covered with notices of missing persons, and hundreds of families were sheltering in huge railway sheds, with the arc lights full on and Dutch soldiers keeping guard. The weather was damp and bitterly cold, and in the big square, tarpaulins were set up to give some shelter. We had difficulty finding beds for ourselves for the night, but finally the chef at one hotel let us have his private lodgings.[20]

This large consignment of relief for Belgian refugees, organised by Chrystal Macmillan under the auspices of IWSA International Relief Committee, was continued till the end of the year but by December, Mary Sheepshanks, editor of *Jus Suffragii*, was reporting that the situation in the Netherlands was changing. Again, Chrystal Macmillan was fully involved, and travelled widely to assist the relief effort:

Dutch arrangements for feeding these multitudes are fully organised, as they can now purchase foodstuffs it is more useful to send them money rather than food . . . Chrystal Macmillan visited Rotterdam, Amsterdam, Breda, Flushing and outlying towns and villages, and consulted the relief committees as to present conditions.[21]

By the end of 1915, when the government relief schemes were fully operational, the work of the International Women's Relief Committee came to an end, and Chrystal Macmillan resumed work on the establishment of the International Inquiry Bureau, cataloguing suffrage material and IWSA papers, building up a library and archive. By 1917, her attention turned to undertaking an international survey of laws on the Nationality of Married Women (see Chapter 8).

Throughout the First World War, the practical work of IWSA was undertaken from the London HQ office jointly by Chrystal Macmillan and Mary Sheepshanks, both of whom were committed to maintaining an international perspective. They corresponded with each other frequently and often collaborated to redraft documents and letters, as in 1919, when Chrystal Macmillan suggested rewording a document written by Millicent Fawcett, before it was issued: 'While agreeing to the idea here set forth, I think it has hardly been sufficiently transformed from the British to the international point of view.'[22]

The close working relationship between the two women is evident in Mary Sheepshanks' plea to Chrystal Macmillan to continue her work for IWSA in the aftermath of the First World War:

> I am truly thankful that you are not going to Holland. I really feel the IWSA work is now so critical that its existence depends on just the right thing being done now. Last week Mrs Fawcett and Mrs Coit both spoke of resigning at once! And whether they do or not, the whole question of a congress is imminent, and all depends on what action this committee recommends, then if there is a congress, there will be an agenda and all the proceedings at which you are supremely good and which I feel quite incompetent to handle singlehanded. I really felt quite consternated until I got your card this morning. It seems to me from experience of WIL and IWSA that you are very much more needed by the IWSA than by the WIL. They have several people available who could, if necessary, go to The Hague or Amsterdam but there is no possible person to take your place for IWSA.[23]

Both women were committed to the establishment of the League of Nations. Like many of her colleagues, Chrystal Macmillan was anxious that the League should promote an equal status for women and men. To the Conference on Women's Representation in the League of Nations, held in the Caxton Hall, London, on 4 and 5 September 1919,[24] she submitted the Draft of a 'Convention' or 'Agreement' between Nations for the Establishment of an International Women's Conference, holding annual meetings, and of an International Women's Office.

> The High Contracting Parties recognise that the status of women, social, political and economic is of supreme international importance. They hold that the natural relation between men and women is that of interdependence and cooperation and that it is injurious to the community to restrict women to a position of dependence, to discourage their education or development or to limit their opportunities.
>
> They recognise that difference in social development and tradition make strict uniformity with respect to the status of women difficult of immediate attainment. But holding as they do that social progress is dependent upon the status of women in the community, they think that there are certain principles which all communities should endeavour to apply. Among these principles the following seem to the High Contracting Parties to be of special and urgent importance:
> (1) That a woman should not be bought or sold but should have equally with men the protection of laws against slavery;
> (2) That on marriage a woman should not be under the tutelage of her husband but should have full personal and civil rights including the right to the use and disposal of her own earnings and property;

(3) That a mother should have the same rights of guardianship in her children as the father;
(4) That a married woman should have the same right to retain or change her nationality as a married man;
(5) That a woman should have the same right to education and opportunity for training for industries or professions as men;
(6) That women should have equal pay for equal work with men;
(7) That the equal moral standard should be recognised; the regulation of vice abolished; and the traffic in women suppressed;
(8) That the responsibility not only of the mother but of the father of a child born out of wedlock should be recognised;
(9) That the suffrage should be granted to women and their equal status with men upon legislative and administrative bodies recognised.[25]

This list of principles reflects Chrystal Macmillan's long-held view that there was a need for a 'Women's Charter' of legal rights.

A discussion then took place on the international representation of women. The meeting was unanimous in thinking that women should be represented everywhere, and on all bodies in connection with the League, but some difference of opinion arose as to whether a special machinery for representing women's views was required in addition. Some suggested that if women were to set up special machinery, they would appear to be claiming a special privilege and would weaken their claim to be included equally with the men. Others argued that women were so weak politically, as compared with men, that their representation would be inadequate to allow the few women in different departments of the League to have their views given sufficient weight. It was decided to refer the issue for further discussion at the newly formed Council for the Representation of Women at the League of Nations.[26]

Chrystal Macmillan then met informally with Sir Eric Drummond, Secretary General of the League of Nations, in January 1920 to discuss her plan to establish an International Women's Conference and an International Women's Office. She suggested to him that

> Just as the Labour Office in connection with the League of Nations was felt necessary in order to help improve the status of the worker so it seems that similar special machinery is necessary to help improve the status of women, which in all countries is low relatively to that of men.[27]

Drummond did not consider her draft plan to be feasible, saying that there was a 'great divergence of opinion among organised women as to the desirability or otherwise of the establishment of an organisation such as you suggest'. But the draft was used as a basis for discussion at the

IWSA Congress in 1920 which subsequently adopted it as a 'Programme of Women's Rights', defining 'reforms necessary for the establishment of real equality between men and women, under the heading of Political, Personal, Nationality, Domestic, Educational, Economic and Moral Rights'.

There was much discussion about the suitability of holding an IWSA Congress immediately after the war, both in relation to the financial burden on women to travel internationally and the suitability of meeting when so many women still suffered from war deprivations. Chrystal Macmillan travelled to Spain to discuss arrangements to hold the Congress in Madrid, but these were cancelled when permission to use the Opera House was denied owing to rumours that IWSA was an anti-Catholic organisation. Rapid rearrangement was needed, and with her usual competence, Chrystal Macmillan hurriedly took all the necessary steps to transfer the Congress to Geneva, to be held in June 1920.

Figure 6.2 Meeting of the International Committee at the IWSA Congress, 1920 Seated second from left, Aletta Jacobs; third from left, Eleanor Rathbone; fourth from left, Adela Stanton Coit. Seated first from right, Anna Lindemann; second from right, Carrie Chapman Catt; third from right, Chrystal Macmillan. Standing third from the right, Marguérite de Witt-Schlumberger; first from right, Marie Stritt (courtesy Collection IAV-Atria, Institute on Gender Equality and Women's History, Amsterdam)

In March 1920, Chrystal Macmillan wrote to Sir Eric Drummond, inviting an official representative of the League to attend the Geneva Congress. Miss Florence Wilson, the League's librarian, was appointed and wrote a full and positive report of the Congress.[28] Several governments appointed official delegates to the Congress and the IWSA was pleased to welcome the women 'from the East', and in particular from India, who were attending the Congress for the first time.

> It is a well-known fact that the women of India in days gone by possessed direct influence on public life; the state of subjection from which they are only now recovering was brought about by the constant internal wars and invasions of India.[29]

Chrystal Macmillan was unable to undertake her work as recording secretary for the Geneva Congress due to an eye infection, so asked the young Margery Corbett Ashby (who was to become president in 1926) to take her place. Chrystal Macmillan herself was elected second vice-president, replacing Millicent Fawcett who was retiring. It is evident from the large number of votes she received that Chrystal Macmillan was held in high regard across the organisation: of the twenty-nine nominations for ten office bearers, she received the second highest number of votes after Mme de Witt Schlumberger (France).

As vice-president, Chrystal Macmillan wrote to Sir Eric Drummond in April 1921 to express the IWSA's appreciation of the fact that the Constitution of the League of Nations included the statement that 'all positions under or in connection with the League, including the Secretariat, should be open equally to men and women'. She added that the IWSA appreciated that staffing at the League would give women equal pay with men, set the same examination tests for admission for women and men, and would not discriminate against married women. She wrote that she hoped that other public bodies would follow the same standards and urged the League to provide opportunities for women to gain promotion to senior posts.

At the following Congress, held in Rome in 1923, Chrystal Macmillan gave reports on the two IWSA committees which she chaired – the Committee on the Nationality of Married Women (discussed in Chapter 8), and the British Overseas Committee, which was set up to further the objectives of the IWSA in British Dominions and Dependencies. The British Overseas Committee not only reported on the establishment of new branches, but also noted successful lobbying of governments on women's suffrage, the abolition of child slavery in Hong Kong, and the protection of young girls in Jamaica. They were also successful in ensuring

Figure 6.3 Chrystal Macmillan speaking, IWSA Congress, Rome, 1923 (courtesy Collection IAV-Atria, Institute on Gender Equality and Women's History, Amsterdam)

that international law on trafficking of women and children was applied in British Mandates, and brought up issues relating to the regulation of prostitution in Palestine and Australia.

For reasons that are not recorded, Chrystal Macmillan resigned her role as vice-president in 1923 and did not stand again for election to the IWSA board. One reason for her resignation may have been her increased workload due to sitting the law examinations she needed for admission to the Bar, which she achieved early in 1924. Despite this extra demand on her time and energy, she nevertheless retained her role as chair of the IWSA Committee on the Nationality of Married Women, remaining in the role until her death in 1937, and giving full reports to Congress in 1926, 1929 and 1935.

Prior to the Istanbul Congress in 1935, it was agreed to change the name of the organisation to the International Alliance of Women for Suffrage and Equal Citizenship (IAWSEC) and to restructure the IWSA international committees: a new committee was formed – the International Standing Committee on the Civil Status of Women. When she provided a full report of the work of the Nationality Committee from June 1929 to January 1934, Chrystal Macmillan noted that the committee had been 'abolished in June 1930 and its members made members on this subject of the Committee on the Civil Status of Women with its chairman as Rapporteur'.[30]

This change in the IWSA committee structure reflected the changing ideas at the League, and the power struggles in the 'Joint Standing Committee of Women's International Organisations for securing the appointment of Women to the International and Expert Committees of the League of Nations', an organisation which, in 1936, amalgamated with the 'Liaison Committee of Women's International Organisations' to represent several international women's organisations: ICW, IAWSEC, WILPF, IFUW, Equal Rights International (ERI), Young Women's Christian Association (YWCA), World Union of Women for International Concord (WUWIC), World Women's Christian Temperance Union and La Fédération Internationale des femmes Magistrats et Avocats. As is discussed in Chapter 8, the focus of the women's international organisations at the League in 1936 was turning towards efforts to improve the status of women. By that time, at the age of 64, Chrystal Macmillan was less able to participate in international work as she was becoming unwell.

INTERNATIONAL FEDERATION OF UNIVERSITY WOMEN (IFUW)

The IFUW was founded in 1919 to promote understanding and friendship between university women of different nationalities. As a graduate of the University of Edinburgh, Chrystal Macmillan joined the organisation and, although not on the EC, was certainly known to its members.

In 1928, the Council of IFUW resolved to appoint a small committee of women jurists to collect information concerning the law governing the nationality of married women, with a view to making a presentation to the First Codification Conference of the League of Nations. The committee membership comprised Chrystal Macmillan, Mme Schreiber-Favre and Miss Ingeborg Hansen, with Chrystal Macmillan as its chair. The report she prepared for IFUW gave a brief outline of the history and practice of national and international law on women's nationality.[31] When the report was presented to the IFUW Conference in August 1929, several women lawyers present felt that they needed more time to study the issues, but the main principle of women's independent right to nationality was approved and the resolution carried by a large majority: 'That this Conference of International Federation of University Women declares that a woman, whether married or unmarried, should have the same right as a man to retain or change her nationality.'[32] When the Secretary General of the League asked various women's international organisations to each appoint two representatives to the League of Nations Consultative Committee on Women's Nationality in 1930, the

IFUW conducted a ballot, resulting in fourteen nominations: Chrystal Macmillan was one of the two to be elected and served on the League of Nations Consultative Committee for three years. (For more details, see Chapter 8.)

OPEN DOOR INTERNATIONAL (ODI)

The Open Door International for the Economic Emancipation of the Woman Worker (ODI) was established at a conference of women in Berlin in June 1929 when a manifesto and a Woman Workers' Charter were issued and several resolutions on women's working conditions were passed unanimously. Chrystal Macmillan, who had been a member of the Board of the British organisation the ODC, was elected president of the new international organisation.

The work of ODI was based on the belief that a woman had the same right as a man to be free to work as she chose, and that legal protection for the worker should be based on the nature of the work and not on the sex of the worker. This brought the organisation into conflict with the International Labour Organisation (ILO) and trade unions who were promoting legislation for the protection of the woman worker.[33]

Throughout the 1930s, but particularly in the latter years of the decade, the relationship between ILO protectionist policies on women's employment, and the feminist influence at the League to promote equality of rights between women and men, was complex. As Susan Zimmerman observed:

> The idea of an overarching international treaty or convention on women's status to be devised and adopted by the League of Nations . . . prescribing strict legal equality between women and men . . . [was intended to] delegitimize and reverse the international gender politics of the ILO.[34]

In their 1930 report, the ILO criticised the ODI for proposing 'to organise resistance to the special protection of working women'. In response to the criticism, the ODI sent a letter to the ILO Secretary General, signed by Chrystal Macmillan as ODI president and all nine members of the ODI International Board, refuting the detailed criticisms and stating that

> The tone of condescension to women which runs through this part of the report is hardly what would have been expected from the ILO, a new organisation with new tasks and new duties, founded at a time when great political and social reforms were being introduced in many countries. It is inconceivable that the Report would have referred in such terms to men's organisations

and it is equally unsuitable to adopt such a tone to women . . . [The ODI] does regret this general tone of patronage.³⁵

The ODI attracted the support of women from Europe and the USA. In January 1931, Chrystal Macmillan led an international delegation to the ILO to protest against the Night Work Convention, in so far as it discriminated against women.³⁶ The international nature of the organisation was further displayed when the second ODI Congress took place in Stockholm in August 1931. There were 200 people present at the opening session, including 116 members from ten different countries – women doctors, women industrial workers, a factory inspector and one well-known trade unionist.³⁷

Chrystal Macmillan gave the presidential address, in which she referred to the ODI's achievements in influencing proposed ILO legislation. For instance, the ILO proposal to ban women from working in bars in ports had been changed to a regulation to ban young people from working in such places. She also noted that the ODI had advised the ILO on a better method for governments to collect statistics on the textile industry: the statistics would no longer be collected in the two

Figure 6.4 Chrystal Macmillan, President ODI leads delegation, ILO, 1931
From left: Eugenie Meller, Hungary; Elizabeth Abbott, GB; Miss Beezen-Ostman, Finland; Chrystal Macmillan, GB; Anna Westergaard, Denmark; Alice Paul, USA; Dr Rosa Welt Straus, Palestine; Edith Rodgers, GB (photo: Wassermann, M., Geneva. Courtesy Schlesinger Library, Harvard Radcliffe Institute)

categories of 'men' and 'women and young persons' but would 'distinguish between the work of adults and persons of different ages, differentiating between men and women under each age group'. (As such, this was an early example of the promotion of gendered statistics, which were still uncommon up to the 1980s in the UK: in Scotland, the women's organisation Engender noted the gaps in gendered statistics in 1993 in their publication *The Gender Audit*.)

Chrystal Macmillan went on to warn of the attack on women's right to paid employment: 'In every country the cry is "Throw the women overboard." There are not enough jobs to go round, so women, especially married women, must give up their paid work. On all sides restrictions on women are proposed.'[38] She argued for rights in paid employment, not only for professional women such as teachers and civil servants, but also for poorly paid women employed as porters, miners, and textile and agricultural workers. She protested that pregnant women and mothers of very young children should not be banned from taking paid employment when, without it, they would suffer hunger and destitution.

When Chrystal Macmillan summarised the attacks on ODI policies as ill-informed, she based her argument on her personal experience as a suffragist:

> Our policy is condemned because it is new. But a new idea opposed to traditional policy has always been criticised, ridiculed and condemned. Twenty-five years ago, it was so with the new idea that women should have the political vote, which today is accepted as a commonplace.[39]

She concluded that the criticism that ODI did not represent working women and therefore that its policies had no merit, was in effect an attack not on the policies themselves but on the advocates of the policies which was 'a well-known ruse of the lawyer for distracting attention from the weakness of his case'. Later, she criticised *Women's Work*, the report published by the ILO, which suggested that women should not be employed in industry because of the 'injurious effects of labour on the female organism', and in response to the statement that 'the rhythm of machinery is not adapted to the female organism', she commented, 'I hope all housewives will at once dispose of their sewing machines and vacuum cleaners and never again enter a train or a motor bus or an aeroplane.' But she concluded that as the statistics quoted in the article are so 'obsolete and misleading' it brings the reliability of the whole report into question.[40]

However, the ODI came under attack for 'opposing legislation for the protection of women during pregnancy and childbirth'[41] and the organisation had to issue a statement that they welcomed the payment of a maternity grant and had 'no objection to grants being conditional on the woman herself deciding to give up her paid work but it is opposed to those clauses which make abstention compulsory'.[42]

When the ILO contacted Chrystal Macmillan in May 1932 to invite her to become a member of an ILO Committee of Experts on Women's Work to provide advice to the organisation, she gave a speedy response, questioning 'its scope and powers and the powers and responsibilities of individual members'. She was not impressed when further details emerged that the committee, to be formed of 100 members from different countries, would be 'purely advisory' and have no executive function.[43]

In July 1933, when the ODI met in conference at Prague, forty-eight delegates from ten countries and eight Government-appointed observers attended alongside 110 members (most member attendees were Czechoslovakian). In her Opening Address as ODI president, Chrystal Macmillan noted that with the growing economic depression, the attacks on women's right to work had increased and women were losing their jobs. Besides the ILO Conventions on Childbirth, Night Work and lead paint which imposed restrictions on the woman worker, there were more attacks on married women's rights and indirect attacks on the status of the woman worker through discriminatory national and international insurance schemes which treated the woman worker differently from the male worker. She noted that

> The conditions, status and pay of the woman worker everywhere are much worse than those of the man. We seek to improve these conditions and to increase that pay by raising the status of the woman as worker. We ask for equality of treatment for men and women in that field. We point out, too, that the present need for economic reconstruction should not be used as an excuse for postponing the raising of the status of the woman worker, but rather taken as an opportunity to build up a new system on a sound foundation of equality and justice.[44]

She expressed her concern that not only were married women being dismissed from their workplace, but there were also suggestions that some work was unsuitable for single women:

> The International Confederation of Christian Trade Unions . . . suggested the progressive elimination of women from all professions not specially suited for her, beginning with those which are morally dangerous. This Christian body has forgotten that the greatest of all dangers to morality . . . is poverty.[45]

Having noted the decision of the Permanent Court of International Justice confirming that the Convention on Night Work applied to all women, including those in manual posts and those in management, she raised the question as to whether this applied to nurses, doctors, journalists and engineers. The Conference passed two resolutions, one urging the ILO to 'adopt only such revised Night Work Convention . . . as provides that any prohibition or regulation of hours of work or of night work shall apply equally to men and women', and the other urging governments to opt out of the Convention until a new or revised Draft Convention removed the special prohibition of night work from women.

Talking of new insurance schemes, she noted that the ODI had been successful in its demand that the Old Age Conventions should not propose the payment of pensions at a lower age for women but regretted that legislation under the Conventions had not made it essential for governments to provide equality of treatment for men and women. She argued that this was disappointing as the ILO was supposedly committed to the improvement of the working conditions of both men and women based on its own equal-pay principle.

However, she welcomed the fact that the ILO were taking women's interests more seriously by appointing a Committee of Experts on Women's Work, although she warned that the ILO might view this panel of experts as individuals whom they could consult one-by-one to obtain views which supported the ILO policies. In contrast, she welcomed the ILO publication 'Women's Work and Labour Laws: A Survey of Protective Legislation', which indicated that serious consideration was at last being given to the work of women. Eventually, after consultation with the ODI Board, she accepted membership of the ILO panel.[46]

She went on to criticise the ILO for its 'overcrowded agendas which make for inadequate discussion' and which made a fetish of increasing the number of Conventions without ensuring that the new regulations would make the equal treatment of women essential. Giving an example of a less well-thought-through policy, she pointed out that in tropical countries, night work was less exhausting than work by day and therefore the imposition of the night work convention would be harmful to the woman worker.

Addressing the ODI conference in Copenhagen in 1935, she welcomed the support of the organised Trade Union women in Denmark who opposed the special regulation on the work of women under the guise of 'protection'. She expressed her dismay at the spread of regulations to promote the employment of men by excluding women from the workforce, and at the introduction of regulations and ministerial powers to 'protect' women by prohibiting their employment, whether married or unmarried, in work defined as heavy or dangerous to a woman's health or morals. She gave instances of governments such as those in Germany, Italy and Belgium which had introduced regulations to exclude women from work in the interests of fuller employment for men.

Providing a wide-ranging review of changes in international agreements affecting women workers, she deplored the extension of wage systems that fixed lower rates of pay and lower benefits paid to women workers compared with male workers. She reserved her strongest criticisms for the ILO's lack of clarity in its publications, for not providing full information on the effects of new regulations, nor naming those on whose advice they had based their decisions.

Looking to the future, she warned of new attacks on the woman worker and recommitted to the ODI policy:

> To continue our struggle to secure everywhere for a woman, irrespective of marriage, pregnancy or childbirth that laws and regulations affecting her work shall be based on the nature of the work and not upon sex so that she shall be free to work and [be] protected as a worker on the same terms as a man.[47]

From 1929 to 1936, as ODI president, Chrystal Macmillan worked closely with Winifred Le Sueur,[48] the secretary of the organisation. On learning of Chrystal Macmillan's serious illness in May 1937, Winifred Le Sueur was so distressed that she wrote to the ODI Board to say that she intended to resign and that the Fifth ODI Conference planned for July in Salzburg should be cancelled. After Chrystal Macmillan's death some months later, she was reconciled to the idea of continuing the work of ODI and helped to organise the postponed conference in Cambridge in 1938.

WOMEN AND WOMEN'S ORGANISATIONS AT THE LEAGUE OF NATIONS

British women were anxious to play their part in the establishment and development of the League.[49] Women from ninety-five women's organisations met at a conference at the Caxton Hall in London in September 1919 to discuss how they could be involved with the League. Five months later, in February 1920, the women met again with Dr Maria Ogilvie Gordon as chair when it was decided to form 'The Council for the Representation of Women in the League of Nations'. Dr Ogilvie Gordon was president from 1920 for over a decade, with Chrystal Macmillan as one of the vice-presidents from 1920 to 1923. This British women's organisation had considerable correspondence with the League and the British government: it was critical of the latter's failure to appoint women delegates and the lack of progress in the appointment of women to the higher levels of the Secretariat of the League.

But there were tensions and disagreements between the women's organisations as they vied for influence at the League, which had very few women officers and even fewer women acting as government representatives. Dr Ogilvie Gordon worked closely with the ICW president, Lady Aberdeen, who was keen that ICW should be acknowledged as the best organisation to represent women's views to the League: she wrote to the Secretary General in June 1919 suggesting that there was no need to set up a new organisation to represent women's views: a plan that was strongly opposed by Margery Corbett Ashby of IWSA.

The rivalry between women's organisations eased eventually and nine of them joined together to form a 'Joint Standing Committee of Women's International Organisations for Securing the Appointment of Women to the International and Expert Committees of the League of Nations'. In 1931, as the League continued to sideline the women's concerns, ten organisations formed a 'Liaison Committee of Women's International Organisations' to secure intercommunication between the member organisations and make a concerted effort to influence international policies being proposed by the League. Members of the Liaison Committee became involved in the crisis when Chrystal Macmillan and Margery Corbett Ashby resigned from the League's Consultative Committee on the Nationality of Women (see Chapter 8).

Although she was never a government delegate, Chrystal Macmillan made several contacts with the League of Nations from 1919 to the 1930s. Like most women, she was an 'outsider', using her position as a representative of the Women's International Organisations (IWSA, IFUW and ODI) to influence the League's international policy. It was her firm belief that women needed to be in positions to make and implement policies on an equal footing with men, and it was this that motivated her to make the following response to a request from the Secretary General in November 1931 for views on how the League might increase the collaboration of women in its work:

> Full and equal cooperation means a great deal more than being asked to supply information, or the mere doing of propaganda and educational work on a policy framed by bodies in which women are not included, or where they are in a very small minority, or inadequately represented. Full and equal

cooperation involves the power of directing effective criticism to policies in course of formation, with an effective voice in determining what these policies shall be. It also involves adequate representation among those who administer these policies.[50]

The memorandum concluded with recommendations on how the League of Nations could encourage women's cooperation directly by including more women on its committees, and by ensuring that women were included in the highest-grade appointments at the League. Recommendations were also offered on how women's cooperation could be gained indirectly by the League encouraging States Members to raise the status of women, giving them full civil, economic and political rights.

In 1935, representing ODI, Chrystal Macmillan participated in a deputation of international women organised by the Liaison Committee of International Women's Organisations to meet with M. Eduard Benes, president of the 16th Assembly of the League. In a prior statement, the ODI set out its arguments on the rights of women workers:

> . . . an international convention purporting to give equal status and equal rights as between men and women, such convention shall be so worded as to make it clear: (a) That the equal status and equal rights proposed include for a woman, irrespective of marriage or childbirth, equal status and equality of rights with a man in her capacity as a worker for pay, so that a woman shall be free to work and protected as a worker on the same terms as a man, under legislation and regulations dealing with conditions and hours, entry, training and payment (including minimum wages and insurance), which are based on the nature of the work and not upon the sex of the worker.[51]

CONCLUSION

As an activist in several women's international organisations, Chrystal Macmillan was a very busy woman. She was initiated into international work through the ICW, attending their 1909 Congresses in Toronto as a Scottish delegate. However, she became more involved with the international work undertaken by IWSA, promoting woman suffrage in all countries but also tackling issues where women's interests were ignored and needed to be considered. She was elected to, and sat on the IWSA Board from 1913 to 1920 and was vice-president from 1921 to 1925: she was also the organiser of their international Congresses in the early 1920s. From 1914 to 1919, she was one of the main organisers of the two International Women's Congresses which advocated mediation under the Wisconsin Peace Plan to bring a negotiated end to the First World War.

Chrystal Macmillan was at the forefront of women's international work as the League and the ILO developed their international standing, when women needed to make their voice heard and their perspectives considered by the new international organisation that was established and run by men. As a member of the IFUW, she was elected in 1930 to represent that organisation on the Women's Consultative Committee on Nationality (WCCN) at the League. All her international working experience proved useful when she became president of the ODI for the Economic Emancipation of the Woman Worker in 1929, guiding the organisation till her death in 1937.

What this chapter vividly demonstrates is that Chrystal Macmillan's commitment to the goals of equality, social justice, peace and women's rights persisted from her time as an Edinburgh undergraduate to her enthusiastic commitment to working with women's international organisations in her mature years, work which extended well beyond the bounds of her own country. She was above all a committed internationalist, engaging with women from countries around the world in their mutual determination to achieve these four goals.

Notes

1. For discussion about Chrystal Macmillan's work with the WILPF, see Chapter 4.
2. Leila Rupp, *Worlds of Women: The Making of an International Women's Movement* (Princeton: Princeton University Press, 1997).
3. Antoinette Burton, *Burdens of History: British Feminists, Indian Women & Imperial Culture 1865–1915* (Chapel Hill and London: University of North Carolina Press, 1994); Sharon Crozier-De Rosa, 'Emotions and Empire in Suffrage and Anti-Suffrage Politics: Britain, Ireland and Australia in the Early Twentieth Century', in Alexandra Hughes-Johnson and Lyndsey Jenkins (eds), *The Politics of Women's Suffrage: Local, National and International Dimensions* (London: University of London Press, 2021), pp. 309–30.
4. Michelle Staff, 'Women's Rights on the World Stage: Feminism and Internationalism in the Life of Chrystal Macmillan', *Journal of Women's History* 32,3 (Fall 2020), p. 44.
5. Murray, *Diary (1895–1918)*.
6. Marie Sandell, '"A Real Meeting of the Women of the East and the West": Women and Internationalism in the Interwar Period', in Daniel Laqua (ed.), *Internationalism Reconfigured: Transnational Ideas and Movements between the World Wars* (London: I.B. Tauris, 2011), pp. 161–85.

7. Charlotte Perkins Gilman, 'The Wonders of an International Congress of Women', *Jus Suffragii*, 15 July 1913, p. 6.
8. Robert Putnam, 'Diplomacy and Domestic Politics: The Logic of Two-Level Games', *International Organization* 42.3 (Summer 1988), pp. 427–60.
9. Francesca Wilson, *In the Margins of Chaos* (New York: Macmillan, 1945), pp. 114–20.
10. Winifred Harper Cooley, 'The Internationalism of the International', *Jus Suffragii*, 15 July 1913, p. 6.
11. *Women's Franchise*, 11 June 1908.
12. *Report of Fifth Congress, London, 26–30 April*, 1 May 1909.
13. Chrystal Macmillan, Marie Stritt and Maria Verone, *Woman Suffrage in Practice* (London and New York: National Union of Women's Suffrage Societies & National American Women's Suffrage Association, 1913).
14. Chrystal Macmillan, *Facts versus Fancies on Woman Suffrage* (London: NUWSS & P.S. King, 1914).
15. IWSA Minutes, 9 July 1914.
16. 'International Manifesto of Women', *Jus Suffragii* 8.13, 1 Sept. 1914, p. 159.
17. Ibid., p. 159.
18. Mary Sheepshanks, 'The International Women's Relief Committee', in ibid., p. 162.
19. Mary Sheepshanks, 'Belgian Refugees in Holland', *Jus Suffragii* 9.2, 1 Nov. 1914, pp. 194–5.
20. Unpublished Biography of Mary Sheepshanks, Women's Library, LSE, quoted in Joyce Marlow (ed.), *Virago Book of Women and the Great War* (London: Virago, 1999), pp. 59–60.
21. Mary Sheepshanks, 'International Women's Relief Committee', *Jus Suffragii* 9.3, 1 Dec. 1914, p. 212.
22. Letter Chrystal Macmillan to Mary Sheepshanks, 30 April 1919, IWSA/2/20 (Manchester: Rylands Library).
23. Ibid., 4 Mar. 1919.
24. Letter Chrystal Macmillan to Millicent Fawcett 7MGF/A/1/205. Papers of Association for Moral and Social Hygiene (London: Women's Library, LSE).
25. 'Draft of Women's Convention for Incorporation in the Treaty of Peace', first sent in a letter from Chrystal Macmillan to Mary Sheepshanks, 30 April 1919. IWSA/2/20 (Rylands Library, Manchester). Chrystal Macmillan introduced a similar Convention on a Women's Charter to WILPF Congress in May 1919 which was included in the Resolutions passed, *Report of International Congress of Women Zurich May 1919*, pp. 246–8.
26. 'Organised Women and the League of Nations', *Common Cause*, 12 Sept. 1919, p. 268.
27. League of Nations Archive R1356-23-1042-2668 (Geneva).
28. League of Nations Archive R1356-23-3554-5359.

29. IWSA Press Notice, League of Nations Archive R1356-23-3554-4377.
30. Report of Twelfth IWSA Congress, Istanbul 18–24 April 1935.
31. Chrystal Macmillan, 'The Nationality of Married Women', paper presented at 5th Conference of the IFUW, Geneva 13 August 1929.
32. IFUW Report of Fifth Conference, Geneva, Aug. 1929.
33. Draft Memorandum, 'Open Door Movement and the Protection of Women Workers', presented to Women's Advisory Committee of the Labour and Socialist International, Nov. 1929 (London: TUC Library Archives).
34. Susan Zimmerman, 'Equality of Women's Economic Status? A Major Bone of Contention in the International Gender Politics Emerging during the Interwar Period', *International History Review* (2017), http://dx.doi.org/10.1080/07075332.2017.1395761.
35. Letter ODI Board to ILO, 1 Nov. 1930.
36. ODI Deputation to ILO 30 Jan. 1931. Report in *The Open Door* 2.3, June 1931, p. 15.
37. Report of Proceedings ODI Second Conference, Stockholm, Aug. 1931, p. 12.
38. ODI Report, 1931, p. 10.
39. ODI Report, 1931, p. 7.
40. Chrystal Macmillan, 'Worse than Reactionary', *International Women's News*, Oct. 1931, p. 199.
41. *International Labour Review*, Sept. 1929, p. 389.
42. Open Door pamphlet, 'Maternity and Childbirth', 1929.
43. *The Open Door*, Aug. 1932, p. 26.
44. 'President's Address'. Report of Conference Open Door International, Prague, July 1933, p. 8.
45. Ibid., p. 8.
46. Chrystal Macmillan letter to H. B. Butler, ILO, Aug. 1932, published in *The Open Door* 10, Feb. 1933, p. 2.
47. Chrystal Macmillan, 'Presidential Address'. Report ODI Fourth Conference, Copenhagen, Aug. 1935, p. 13.
48. Little is known about the personal life of Winifred Le Sueur who was secretary of ODI from its formation in June 1929. She continued as secretary after the death of Chrystal Macmillan in 1937.
49. *The Common Cause*, 12 Sept. 1919, p. 268.
50. Full response in *The Open Door*, Aug. 1932, p. 30.
51. Statement Presented by the ODI for the Economic Emancipation of the Woman Worker, A.19.1935.V. League of Nations Archive R3756/3A/19841/13900.

7

Entering the Legal Profession and Life at the Bar

THE ROAD TO 1919

On the evening of 10 March 1913, Chrystal Macmillan presided at a dinner held at the Lyceum Club in London – what *The Manchester Courier* described as 'the well-known social resort of ladies'. The dinner was to honour what the same paper referred to as 'budding Portias who are desirous of entering the legal profession', under the headline 'Women as "Men of the Law"'.[1] Exactly seven years later, on 8 March 1920, she again attended a dinner, this time to celebrate the passing of the Sex Disqualification (Removal) Act 1919,[2] which enabled all 'budding Portias' at last to realise their ambitions. On this occasion, Chrystal Macmillan was invited to speak in place of the Lord Advocate for Scotland, who was unable to attend (see page 131).[3]

For Chrystal Macmillan, the 'road to 1919' had begun many years before, while she was living in Edinburgh. During that time, she joined the Scottish Federation of Women's Suffrage Societies (SFWSS) and the NUWW. She was elected honorary secretary of the NUWW Scottish Central Branch, and then secretary of the Scottish branch of the UK organisation in 1904. As noted in earlier chapters, her work for these organisations involved campaigning and public speaking all over Scotland, but the pivotal moment in her career was undoubtedly in 1908 when she spoke before the House of Lords as the appellant in the Scottish women graduates' case (see Chapter 2).

From then onwards, she was regularly referred to in the press as the 'Scottish Portia' – an apt sobriquet for someone who, like Shakespeare's Portia, had no formal legal training, was striking in appearance, highly intelligent, wealthy, and in her pleading before the Lords used the language of the law in her defence, rather than simply setting out the merits of her case. As argued by Laura Noakes, the House of Lords case was

> ... a culmination of Chrystal Macmillan's progressive outlook on life, which began in her childhood and developed throughout her feminist education. The feminist organisations in which she was involved provided her with professional mechanisms for advancing her activism. The arguments made in this case could only have been made by such a woman: one who knew the value of education, was determined to use the law to effect change, and held deeply ingrained suffragist beliefs.[4]

The background research required for the House of Lords case had introduced Chrystal Macmillan to the procedures and language of the law, and the realisation that legal argument and legislation were the most effective means of achieving the goals of social justice and equality for which she was to continue to campaign for the rest of her life.

In the absence of any written evidence, it can only be supposed that the experience she acquired through the Scottish women graduates' case was what prompted her to consider a legal career, which at that time was only open to men. She would also have been aware of women's early efforts to gain entry to the legal profession, both in Scotland and elsewhere. In Scotland, the most celebrated case was that of Margaret Hall[5] who, after leaving school, was employed in a solicitor's office and in 1900 petitioned the Court of Session in Edinburgh to be allowed to sit the first examination of the Incorporated Society of Law Agents. Her petition was refused on similar grounds to those cited by the Court of Session in the Scottish women graduates' case (see Chapter 2), namely that, according to 'inveterate usage', the term 'persons' referred only to male persons. The Court concluded that only 'if authorised by the Legislature' could women be admitted as law agents.

Chrystal Macmillan's involvement in the cause for women to be allowed to enter the legal profession began in earnest after her arrival in London in 1913. It was there that she came into close contact with women, including law graduates, who had for some years been pressing for women's entry to the profession, either as solicitors or barristers. Many of these women were present at the Lyceum Club dinner in 1913, including Gwynedd Bebb, Lucy Nettlefold and Karin Costello, who, together with Maud Crofts, were to challenge the Law Society in the High Court just three months later to demand a woman's right to be admitted to the preliminary examination of the Society. Known as *Bebb v. the Law Society*,[6] the case was dismissed on similar grounds to those cited by the Law Lords in the Scottish women graduates' case, namely that no precedent existed, therefore only a change in the law could alter the status quo. As Maud Ingram put it at the Club dinner, members of the legal profession, and specifically of the Bar, were 'entrenched behind the impregnable defence of immemorial custom'.[7]

This 'impregnable defence' had long been a barrier to women's entry to the Inns of Court. For example, in 1873, a group of women had petitioned unsuccessfully for admission to Lincoln's Inn, and in 1903 Bertha Cave[8] was refused entry as a pupil at Gray's Inn on the grounds of lack of precedent. The same fate was met by the suffragette and law graduate, Christabel Pankhurst, when she applied for admission to Lincoln's Inn in 1904. In her case, she was told that as women were not allowed to practise at the Bar, there was no point in her becoming a pupil.[9] The response was the same, regardless of whether or not the female applicant had a law degree, which a number of them did by this time. For example, in Scotland, two women – Eveline MacLaren and Josephine Gordon Stuart – had graduated as Bachelors of Law from Edinburgh University in 1909,[10] and would undoubtedly have been known to Chrystal Macmillan. Law graduates from universities elsewhere included Eliza Orme from the University of London (1888), Letitia Walkington and Frances Gray from Trinity College, Dublin (1889 and 1890), and Cornelia Sorabji from Oxford University (1892).[11]

To overcome these barriers, the support of sympathetic men in influential positions was crucial since they had the power to bring about change, both in the attitude of benchers in the Inns, and among Members of Parliament. Those men who did lend their support were not always successful, however. Notable among them was the barrister Holford Knight,[12] who in 1913 became chairman of a committee of barristers, including Lord Robert Cecil, its president, 'for the purpose of assisting the movement for opening the legal profession to women'. In the absence of records of the committee's endeavours, we can't know how they framed their arguments, but whatever they were, they failed to convince their fellow barristers. It was an up-hill struggle, given the reluctance of male members of the profession to 'share their power, privileges and professional space with women'.[13]

In Parliament, another champion of the women's cause was the MP Lord Wolmer, who, supported by parliamentary colleagues including Major John Hills and Lord Robert Cecil, failed to gain support for his Legal Profession (Admission of Women) Bill in 1913. An amended bill, which referred only to women becoming solicitors, not barristers, was later rejected at the Court of Appeal, but met with a favourable response from both Prime Minster Herbert Asquith and law officers of the Crown.

However, its further progress was made impossible at the time due to the outbreak of war.

Ironically, it was the war that provided a significant boost for the cause to admit women to the legal profession. At his speech to the Bar Council on 18 January 1917,[14] Holford Knight referred to 'the extraordinary capacity which had been shown by women' during the war, and the need to 'mobilise all the intelligence and capacity' available to 'carry on the country's work' after the war ended. However, even this pragmatic argument failed to find full support: of the 330 members present, only 21 voted in favour of Knight's resolution 'That the General Council of the Bar do consider and report upon the desirability of making provision for the admission of duly qualified women to the Profession.'

At the invitation of the Church League for Women's Suffrage, Holford Knight adopted an optimistic tone in an article he wrote for them on women and the legal profession. He opened with the comment that 'The renewed attempt to open the legal profession to women has failed, but the prospects of ultimate success were never brighter.' He went on to say:

> The declarations of popular gratitude to women for their great war services must lead to action. And that action must be prompt. Women must not be jobbed off (if that expression is permissible) by promises to carry out friendly intentions after the war. When matters are dealt with affecting men and women in the same way, such as the franchise, the sex discrimination of old must be abandoned in the spirit of the affirmations which the war service of women has evoked. It is idle to praise the civic and national work of women as showing their fitness to take a more active share in the control of the nation's life, while refusing to give effect to such admirable sentiments when the opportunity arises.[15]

While the support and actions by male politicians and others such as Holford Knight were critical in bringing about equality legislation after the war, it was women, acting both individually and collectively, whose relentless campaigning had provided the necessary impetus for change. As Rosemary Auchmuty observed, there was 'an interconnectedness and mutual support among feminist groups and campaigns at the time and the overarching feminist politics that located women's efforts to enter the legal profession within a wider struggle against male domination of public life'.[16]

Chrystal Macmillan's own campaigning activities had begun well before the war, when as a committee member of organisations such as the NUWW she was able to address and promote the cause for women's entry to the legal profession through articles and pamphlets and from lecture-hall podiums and conference platforms. For example, at the 1913 annual conference of the NUWW in Hull, she moved that 'the National Council urges Parliament to pass a measure to open the legal professions to women'. She went on to describe how some attempts made by women to enter that profession had been rebuffed, and concluded by saying that:

> There was no reason why women should not be lawyers. It was an honest employment (laughter) and if women were able to qualify themselves for it there was no reason why they should be shut out. (Applause) The admission of women would bring about reforms in much the same way the admission of women to the medical profession had done.[17]

Then in April 1914 she gave a lecture on 'Women and the Legal Profession' at the Women's Kingdom Exhibition in Olympia, London, in which she reviewed the attempts made in Great Britain to open the profession to women. She later became a founding member of the most focused of all the campaign groups, namely the COLPW. The committee was chaired by Major John Hills MP, and Ray Strachey, a prominent suffragist and elder sister of Karin Costello (see above), was its secretary. In 1917 the committee organised a petition, signed by 106 prominent women,[18] urging the government to give time to Lord Buckmaster's 'Solicitors (Qualification of Women) Bill' to allow women to become solicitors.[19] It was this Bill that was later augmented to include barristers (see below).

During the war, the arguments for women's suffrage and for their admission to the Inns had grown in intensity, and with the passing of the Representation of the People Act in February 1918,[20] which gave the franchise to women (with certain qualifications), aspiring women barristers approached the Inns with the high expectation of at last being admitted. But the Bar Council remained adamantly against it. When Helena Normanton applied to Middle Temple immediately after the new Act came into force, she was refused by the benchers, with no reasons given.[21] The minutes of the Middle Temple parliament record that the benchers yet again fell back on precedent in their defence, citing the Bebb judgement, even though that case related to solicitors, not barristers, and thus may not have been legally correct. The benchers of Lincoln's Inn were similarly disposed. According to Lord Buckmaster, speaking in a debate in House of Lords in March 1919,

> [Lincoln's Inn] said that the admission of women to be barristers was part of a wider national question, and that they did not think it was right for the Inns to act in a matter of that kind without receiving direction from Parliament ... It did not involve any acceptance of the view that they had not the power, if they wished to exercise it, but that they thought they ought not to exercise

such a power until Parliament had given them some indication that Parliament regarded it as in the national interest that women should be admitted.[22]

Helena Normanton was not easily put down: she appealed against the judgement of the Middle Temple benchers, and was widely backed in her efforts both by women's organisations such as the Women's Freedom League (WFL) and NUWW, and a few male members of the legal profession, including Holford Knight. Her appeal was not heard until a year after she had made her application to join the Inn, one possible reason for the delay being that a Bill had been introduced by Lord Buckmaster, namely 'The Barristers and Solicitors (Qualification of Women) Bill', which would have removed any barriers to women's entry to the legal profession. Buckmaster argued in the House of Lords that 'nobody thinks that the passage of this Bill is going to flood the legal profession with women. It will enable a few women, who are peculiarly qualified, to earn an honourable living.'[23] In April 1919, the Law Society met to consider the bill, and voted in favour of it by fifty votes to thirty-three, having concluded that it was very likely to be passed into law by the end of the year, as indeed it was.

Needless to say, many women's organisations did all they could to secure the passing of the bill. In January 1919, Ray Strachey, as secretary of COLPW, wrote to Bonar Law, Lord Chancellor and Leader of the House of Commons, urging the government to pass legislation to remove the legal disabilities of women.[24] Four months later, at a meeting in Central Hall, which Chrystal Macmillan was unable to attend and sent apologies, the following resolution was passed:

> This meeting calls upon the Government to give facilities for the passage through the House of Commons of the Barristers and Solicitors (Qualification of Women) Bill, which has already successfully passed through the House of Lords, so that it may become law at the earliest possible date. This meeting further asks that the Prime Minister, or Leader of the House of Commons, receive a deputation of women on this subject.[25]

Speaking in support of the resolution, Holford Knight noted that the Lord Chancellor, who had previously been strongly opposed to women's entry to the legal profession, had since changed his views, so he was optimistic for its success in the House of Commons. Chairing the meeting, Councillor Edith How-Martin expressed her hope that

> . . . if [the legal profession was] opened to women it was quite certain to lead to women sitting on the magisterial bench, to women becoming judges, and to women sitting on juries. Women were out to secure full equality of

opportunities and awards with men; it was essential that they should get inside the machinery of administration in this country, and the opening of the legal profession to women was one of the straightest paths to their goal.[26]

Another bill, the Justices of the Peace (Qualification of Women) Bill, which would have extended women's role in the legal world, was also passed by the House of Lords, but both it and Buckmaster's Bill were rendered obsolete by the passing of the Sex Disqualification (Removal) Act 1919, which finally removed any impediments to women entering the professions.[27] It was a moment of triumph for all those who had worked so hard for so long to secure women's entry to the legal profession, and it was fitting that it should be marked by a celebratory dinner at which so many of its champions, both women and some men, were present.

The dinner was a grand occasion, held in the House of Commons, and chaired by the Lord Chancellor, Lord Birkenhead, who was present as a guest of COLPW. The event was reported in *The Women's Leader* as follows:

> This dinner was the occasion for the heads of the great legal profession to welcome their new female disciples, and the warmth of their welcome added greatly to an already happy occasion. The Attorney General responded on behalf of the English Bar, and Miss Macmillan answered for Scotland. The Lord Advocate, who was unable to be present, may perhaps be alarmed at this proceeding but Major Hills, in asking her, said he was asking the future to reply for the present, and all who remember Miss Macmillan's famous pleading before the House of Lords will agree that some high place in the Scottish Bar would become her.[28]

It was a much-deserved tribute to Chrystal Macmillan, whose part in the remorseless campaigning had helped bring about this moment. As it was, Major Hills's presumption that her future lay with the Scottish Bar proved to be incorrect. Less than a year after the 1919 Act was given Royal Assent, she joined thirty-two other women as a pupil at Middle Temple. Five years later, in September 1924, she was called to the English Bar, just one year after Margaret Kidd, also a Scot, became the first woman to be called to the Bar in Scotland.[29]

WORKING WITHIN THE LEGAL PROFESSION

As suggested earlier in this chapter, it seems likely that it was her experience as the main appellant in the Scottish women graduates' case that prompted Chrystal Macmillan to consider a legal career as a barrister.[30]

Figure 7.1 Chrystal Macmillan, barrister, 1924 (courtesy John Herdman)

Another motivation was her belief that 'the existence and advancement of women lawyers will assist women in other walks of life'.[31]

She would also have been aware that women who became barristers would gain significant advantage when seeking advancement in a variety of fields that would otherwise be either closed to them or difficult to enter, including as Members of Parliament – an ambition held by Chrystal Macmillan (see Chapter 3):

> It is extremely likely that women, who intend to seek election to Parliament, will realise the benefit of an intimate knowledge of the Law. The Training will help them very materially in the task of influencing legislation and particularly legislation which specially concerns women. Furthermore, a great number of official positions are reserved to Barristers . . . Women barristers will . . . have open to them in future all the positions which are the special perquisites of barristers-at-law.[32]

Unlike some of the early women pupils in the Inns, Chrystal Macmillan had no law degree, and no close relations at the Bar. However, what she did have was a clear understanding of the advantages that a legal training could bring to her work for women's equality. As she put it in an article which she wrote for *The New Statesman* in 1917:

> Women will never learn just how the law affects them, or exactly how it works out in practice, and how new laws are likely to be interpreted, until women have been taking part in the practical work of interpreting the law and its administration . . . Many of the present abuses and inequalities in the administration of our courts cannot be remedied until women have a practical knowledge of the machinery of the law.[33]

It was a belief she put into practice, using her knowledge of the law not only as an advocate for justice in the courts, but for women in all spheres of life – prostitutes, factory workers, married women – indeed any women in need of legal advice.

By the time she applied to become a pupil at the Bar in Middle Temple, in 1919, Chrystal Macmillan was 48, single, had a private income – thanks to her inheritance from her father[34] – and was well acquainted with the business of lobbying parliament and with drafting and scrutinising proposed legislation on behalf of various women's organisations. For example, she was appointed to the UK Legislation Committee of the NUWW whose function was to monitor draft legislation and government regulations in cases where legal outcomes might adversely affect women. In 1915, her role within the NUWW was further extended when she was appointed to the International Standing Committee on the Legal Position of Women – a clear acknowledgement of her expertise in legal matters.

She also served on the Legal Subcommittee of the National Council for the Unmarried Mother and Her Child from April 1918 till March 1920, under the chairmanship Newton Crane, who later sponsored her application for admission to Middle Temple (see Chapter 5). She continued with this work during her time as a student at Middle Temple, often travelling abroad. For example, she was at that time heavily involved with the AMSH (see Chapter 5), being appointed in 1921 to its subcommittee for foreign affairs. That same year she drafted a 'British Nationality, Married Women' Bill for the Nationality of Married Women Committee, to which she devoted much of her time thereafter (see Chapter 8).

It was a heavy programme, one which could not easily have been undertaken without paid help to manage her household. At her residence at 71 Harcourt Terrace, Kensington, she had a housekeeper, Mrs Eliza Gibbons, and at 4 Pump Court, Temple, where she lived from 1929, her housekeeper was Mrs Edith Jones.

Not all women law students would have had the financial advantages that Chrystal Macmillan enjoyed (see Chapter 1), and for those who had neither a working husband nor a private income, a paid occupation was a necessity in order to pay for the not inconsiderable fees required for a Bar training. The Call fee in 1919 was £90, and at that time it was customary for students to read in the chambers of a barrister for about twelve months, the fee for which was usually £100.[35]

As Patrick Polden notes, 'Girls from humble backgrounds were a rarity at the bar and even those from modest ones were none too common.'[36] Polden also found that the number of women from Scotland who applied for admission to one of the Inns of Court was fifteen between 1919 and 1939.

> [They included] a very high proportion of mature women already enjoying a career; among the twelve whose ages are known, nine were over 30 . . . Already well known in the law was Chrystal Macmillan (MT 1920, aged 48) who had pleaded as a layman before the House of Lords in support of Scottish women's suffrage in 1908 and had as one of her ambitions to promote the access of women to the legal profession . . . Women admitted as bar students between the wars were mostly university educated. In the period 1919–1939, of Scottish graduates, seven were from Edinburgh, two from Glasgow and two from Aberdeen.[37]

Before being called to the Bar, students had first to pass examinations in various aspects of the law and to attend a fixed number of dinners at their Inn:

> The general rule is that every student before being called to the Bar must have kept twelve terms, which in effect means that he must have been a member of his Inn for three years before he can become a Barrister-at-Law. Terms are kept by eating dinners in the dining-hall. A student, who is also a member of a university has to eat three, and all other students six dinners each term.
>
> The system possesses the advantages of fostering the traditions of the Inns and of the Bar, of maintaining an *esprit de corps*, and of providing means for the members, who come not only from all parts of England but also from almost every section of the British Empire, of forming friendships which may last for life ... In fact an Inn of Court, as well as being an institution of learning, serves the purposes of a club.[38]

The arrival of women at the Inns clearly presented a challenge to the old-established and entrenched protocols, leading to various new rules to ensure that their presence would not be too disturbing. For example, at Middle Temple,

> On 16 January 1920, the benchers ruled that women members should lunch and dine at separate tables, doubtless feeling that was kinder to them than forcing them to mix with the men, some of whom were likely to be less than welcoming. On the next day the *Daily News* asked: 'Are the Benchers of the Middle Temple, after all, a little frightened of the women law students they have admitted? It seems rather like it. Five ladies had sat with men friends ten days ago.'[39]

The rules and regulations of the Inns were such that even women law students 'who held explicitly feminist commitments' could do little to bring about change: As a group

> ... they overwhelmingly accepted the dictates of the Inns and tried to accord with the societies' masculine culture. This compliance did not, however, undermine the goals of suffragists like Normanton or her colleague Chrystal Macmillan, who saw women barristers as uniquely poised to push forward women's rights in other areas.[40]

As a graduate, though not in Law, Chrystal Macmillan was well able to cope with the work involved in studying for the Bar exams. She gained a second class in Roman Law and Criminal Law and Procedure (Michaelmas Term 1921), first class in Constitutional Law and Legal History (Hilary

Term 1922), but only third class in Real Property and Conveyancing (Easter Term 1922).[41] For the final exam, taken in the Hilary Term 1924, she was awarded second class, which though not a brilliant result was still better than some achieved, including Helena Normanton, who only gained a third class in her finals. However, whereas Helena had taken only two years to complete the course, Chrystal took four, the difference most probably being due to her heavy work commitments with women's organisations.

It was customary for final Bar exam results to be published in some newspapers, including *The Common Cause*, which offered its congratulations to Chrystal Macmillan on passing her finals, adding the comment that her 'legal knowledge has long been regarded with awe by members – which awe will now be redoubled by its having received the seal of examination'.[42]

Her application for Call to the Bar was made on 15 January 1924, sponsored by Robert Newton Crane, a bencher at Middle Temple, and she was accepted thirteen days later. Records of what followed are sparse. The Law List names 5 Paper Buildings as her chambers in 1926, and 1 Crown Office Row from 1927 to 1929. Her residence until 1927 was 71 Harcourt Terrace, Kensington, where she had lived from 1919, and from 1929 she lived in a flat at 4 Pump Court, which remained her address until her death in 1937. Whether she was attached to a set of chambers between call and 1926, when she was elected a member of the Western Circuit, is not known. As Patrick Polden discovered,

> Information on women in chambers after call is also hard to come by, for the *Law List* did not show it in this form until 1966 . . . Before that date it gave only individuals' addresses and these are not a reliable guide since there were still some residences in the inns; Crystal McMillan [sic], for example, lived in the Temple without being in active practice.[43]

What is certainly true is that 4 Pump Court served both as Chrystal Macmillan's chambers and her residence; in fact, the electoral roll shows that she and her housekeeper Mrs Edith Jones were the only residents there, all the other people listed having residences elsewhere. However, contrary to Polden's assumption, court records attest that she was, from 1926 until 1935, most definitely in 'active practice'.

Her practice appears to have begun in 1926, after she was elected as a member of the Western Circuit Bar Mess (an association of barristers) on the occasion of its Grand Night, held in Winchester on 22 February.

She was asked to make a speech to the gathered company of the Mess,[44] presumably without notice, given this record in the Bar Mess minutes:

> Miss Macmillan denied that the young should be seen and not heard, but wished on the whole, that it was the rule here tonight. It would enable the younger members to learn from the older ones how to speak in any company in any subject at no notice.[45]

Had Chrystal Macmillan sought election to the Mess three years before, she might have met with opposition, for at a Grand Night meeting on 13 February 1923, the admission of women to the Circuit was still being considered. Both Helena Normanton and Beatrice Honour Davy were proposed and seconded for election that night, but the Mess members were unable to agree on whether or not to admit them. Some, such as E. B. Charles, KC, spoke in favour, as did Mr Emanuel, KC, who felt that women now at the Bar should have the same privileges as the men. However, Mr Hawke, KC, was less convinced, saying that he 'did not like the presence of young women in Mess dining with young men and hoped a scheme could be devised to distinguish between Circuit and Mess'. In the end, it was agreed to address the matter again at a meeting in London, where it was taken up a month later.[46]

The quibbling continued, with Mr Gregory, KC, pointing out that dinner was an essential custom of the Mess and if women were not admitted they couldn't be excluded from the public rooms, and if women were entitled to use public rooms, then the men could not be kept out. In the end, it was agreed to admit women to the Mess, and Beatrice Honour Davy was duly elected. Helena Normanton, however, was not. The grounds for this decision are not spelt out in the minutes, but when extracts from newspapers were read out to the Circuit members, their content convinced the majority present that her application should be refused.[47] Clearly, by the time Chrystal Macmillan was attending courts on the Western Circuit, the whole issue of women joining men in the dining room at Mess dinners must have been resolved, for she is recorded as having 'made a point of retiring from the mess when the port came round'.[48]

As well as becoming a member of the Western Circuit Bar Mess, Chrystal Macmillan also became a member of the Messes for the London Sessions and the Central Criminal Court and made frequent journeys between London and the South-West, turning up for Grand Night Circuit Mess events in both Winchester and Exeter between 1926 and 1929. She also attended Mess meetings for the Central Criminal Court, the records for which provide an interesting glimpse into the camaraderie that must have existed between the relatively few women who attended them. For example, at a quarterly meeting in March 1933, out of sixty-nine attendees, seven were women, and judging from the proximity of their signatures on the register, it would seem that they arrived together – Chrystal Macmillan with Miss H. Greenfield and Constance Colwill; Enid Rosser with Olive Crutchley; and Rita Reuben with Josémèé Greenwood.[49]

Camaraderie was not always evident among women barristers, however. It was a competitive world, and the question of seniority mattered – at least to some. For example, in June 1933 Chrystal Macmillan wrote to Helena Normanton to tell her that the Justices were to provide women barristers at the London Sessions with a special room, and that she had been given sets of keys for six lockers to be provided there. She proposed that the keys be given to women in the order in which they had joined one or other of the Sessions. What this meant was that Helena Normanton and four more women would be without lockers, though as she pointed out, it looked as if more lockers would be provided if requested. The letter met with a crisp response from Helen Normanton:

> I was not present at the discussion you had, and I think it is unfortunate to attempt to decide matters in the absence of any members of the Mess who might be affected thereby. In fact, it should be obvious that a matter cannot be validly decided in the absence of any person with a right to be heard, so that I regret to say that I consider this to be very undemocratic.[50]

Helena Normanton's reply went on to say that her own position was special in that she had been the first to apply to join the Sessions, but was rejected by the North London Sessions, and that this meant her second, successful application, came after those of the six women identified by Chrystal Macmillan. On top of that, she (Helena) had an injured ankle, which made carrying robes around very arduous.

There are no more letters relating to this incident, but the above exchange is sufficient to illustrate the tensions that could result from matters relating to committee procedures, and as a result of inadequate facilities. An inadequate supply of lockers was one thing, but lack of lavatories was even worse:

> No chambers could be obliged to take in a woman . . . there is little doubt that women often experienced difficulty at both stages . . . [Hannah Cross] applied to five or six sets for pupillage and was usually welcomed by the

head of chambers but found, once he had spoken to the clerk, that it was impossible because of the apparently insuperable problem of lavatory facilities. Eventually she found a sympathetic advocate in a KC who had had to make his own way in life and who got her a place at 1 New Square on her undertaking to use the public lavatories in Lincoln's Inn Fields.[51]

Venetia Stephenson used to advise always using the railway station lavatory upon arrival in a town in view of the likely want of such facilities in the court building.[52]

Court appearances

It was on the Western Circuit, at the Bodmin Assizes in Cornwall in June 1926, that Chrystal Macmillan made her first court appearance, as counsel for defence, where she succeeded in gaining a verdict of not guilty for Stanley Cole, accused of abducting a girl under 18 years old. She went on to act as counsel for defence in six more cases on the Circuit, in which the accused was found guilty in four cases, and not guilty in two. The first of the latter, taken at Bodmin Assizes in October 1929, was a case involving one Ruby Williams, accused of concealing the birth of her daughter by 'a secret disposition of its dead body'. In the second case, Edward Barnicoat was accused on two counts, one for the rape of Phillis Hooker, for which he was found not guilty, and the other for 'casual knowledge of her, she being above 13 and under 16 years', for which he was found guilty and committed to nine months' hard labour.[53]

It was almost certainly the Edward Barnicoat rape case that was recalled in an anecdote recorded (below) in *Circuit Ghosts*, as the court record shows that it was the only Poor Prisoner's Defence case (PPD) taken by Chrystal Macmillan in which the accused was male, and was found not guilty. Without any details of the case, it will never be known on what grounds Chrystal Macmillan was able to argue in Barnicoat's favour, but she must have presented a convincing enough case to persuade the jury to acquit him on the first charge.

> She [Chrystal Macmillan] was a lady of mature years with greying hair cut short in what used to be called an 'Eton crop'. On one occasion a prisoner wished to give a dock brief and was informed in the usual way that if he had the sum of £1.3s.6d. he could choose any counsel in court. His view of them was limited and he had not taken the prudent precaution, which the more experienced malefactors sometimes adopted, of consulting one of the warders (as they were then called) about which counsel he should choose. Scanning the row of heads, he announced after some hesitation, 'I'll have the nearest gentleman'. Chrystal Macmillan, who was the nearest, rose from

her seat. Out of a sense of fun, Ewen Montagu, who was sitting next to her, did too. 'Ho! Ho! Ho!' said Ernie Charles [the judge, the Hon Sir Ernest B. Charles] from the bench, 'The nearest gentleman is a lady. Now what are you going to do?' The prisoner gallantly said that he would stick to his choice of the nearest. So, she defended him, and she got him off![54]

What this quote tells us is that Chrystal Macmillan was chosen by the prisoner who wished to give a dock brief – that is, a brief from a prisoner who, unable to provide his or her own counsel, selected a barrister from among those present. For all newly qualified barristers, the value of dock brief and PPD cases could be measured only in terms of the experience they afforded, since the income they produced was very modest indeed. For Chrystal Macmillan, unlike many of her compatriots at the Bar, her private income released her from the necessity of waiting to be provided with briefs that would ensure a reasonable income from legal fees. For women barristers especially, briefs were hard to come by, especially ones that would bring some prominence, and thus the chance of advancement.

> The Chancery bar, with its preponderance of chambers work and a more conversational court style, seemed to some more suitable for women than the rough and tumble of the common law side. However, since it lacked any equivalent to the poor persons' procedure and dock brief, it was also harder to make a start and in fact very few women seem to have established themselves.[55]

> For those striving to start a career, there were two gatekeepers whose role was critical. One was the chambers clerk, who was sometimes a formidable obstruction. Even where they were not simply prejudiced, clerks were apt to regard women as a bad investment, whose probable lack of success would impact directly upon their own earnings.
> The other gatekeepers were the instructing solicitors. Only at the poorest end, where the Poor Persons' Procedure and the dock brief brought barrister and client into direct relationship, could the solicitor be bypassed.[56]

Of the forty-five cases in which Chrystal Macmillan appeared at the First Court of the London Sessions between 1927 and 1936, she acted as counsel for prosecution in thirty-four cases and for defence in eleven, ten of which were dock briefs, and the majority of those were for cases of larceny. In the Second Court of the London Sessions, she was counsel for prosecution in ten cases, and for the defence in ten, all of which were dock briefs. For the Central Criminal Court, she appeared as counsel for the prosecution in all but one case when, in June 1929, she defended a prisoner accused of GBH for whom, according to the record, 'legal aid under the Poor Prisoners' Defence Act 1903 is granted'.[57]

Records of any civil cases in which she took part are non-existent, so it is not known how many, or of what kind, she was involved with. However, in his obituary for her, her one-time head of chambers, Marshall Freeman, refers to the Poor Persons' Department, implying that she did more 'legal aid' work than the available court records reveal:

> She was an indefatigable worker, an ever-helpful colleague in chambers, never happier than when handling a case for the Poor Persons' Department, and untiring in her determination to secure justice if the opposite seemed to threaten. I have known her to spend days of research over such a case in the hope of finding adequate authority to support what she felt to be a just cause.[58]

Chrystal Macmillan's career as a barrister, while more active than some accounts have suggested, was not highly distinguished in that she took no celebrated cases of the kind that might have led to her advancement. However, as Polden found,

> ... the hard fact is that of something approaching 300 women who were called [between the wars] barely a score achieved what might be judged even modest success. It is true indeed that the making into KCs of Heilbron and Normanton in 1949 and the later promotion to the bench of Lane and Heilbron showed that women could reach the highest levels and encouraged the next generation, but they were isolated cases and studies in 1957 and in the early 1970s emphasised their rarity.[59]

Although not 'famous' in terms of celebrated cases, Chrystal Macmillan's performance in court was clearly admired by her colleagues:

> At the Old Bailey last Friday, the Recorder (Sir Ernest Wild) complimented Miss Chrystal Macmillan upon her speech in defence of a prisoner and said she had been faced with the task of making bricks without straw, and that the efforts of the children of Israel were nothing as compared with the difficulty she had experienced.[60]
>
> Her manner was quiet and persuasive, and she never ruined a case by over-statement. In argument she was extremely formidable, for she always knew her brief thoroughly, and was prepared to concede a point or two to the other side.[61]

What appeared to matter most to her was not her advancement within the legal profession, but the opportunity it gave her to gain experience and contacts which could then be employed to advance the many causes with which she was actively engaged. This assumption is supported by the following extract from an appreciation by one 'J.S.', printed in *The Scotsman* following her death in 1937:

> I first saw Miss Macmillan at the Bar of the Court of Session, pleading the cause of women graduates. It was an arresting experience which stamped itself on my memory. Years later, I met her at a public debate in Edinburgh, when she and I championed different points of view on some women's question. It was in this way I first came to appreciate Miss Macmillan's worth, and her shining and consistent advocacy of women's rights. I am sure it is by this advocacy she would like best to be remembered. She gained an international reputation for it, and was well known in most capitals of Europe among all progressive leaders of women. While she recognised the good work that is done in broadening women's spheres of activity by numerous women's agencies, Miss Macmillan directed her whole energies to the much more important questions of securing women's statutory, social and economic equality with men. She believed that it was there that the real matters of moment for women must be fought out, and her extraordinary abilities had been of immense help for many years to this side of women's questions. Her legal training, her keen logical brain and her wide experience of affairs fitted her for such work.[62]

Specific examples of some of the ways in which Chrystal Macmillan used her legal training are given here, in an obituary by her colleague, Elizabeth Abbott:

> [she] took an active part in framing and promoting the Public Places (Order) Bill: a measure both to promote order and to rescue from injustice and bullying the woman of the streets. None who heard it will ever forget her evidence before the Street Offences Committee, in 1928, and her calm, relentless, ever recurring reminder to those who sought to rebut her plans for legal changes and substitute their own, that they could only do so if they were seeking to set up a 'Court of Morals': a course which the Committee had that very day explicitly rejected . . . She was actively interested in the Association . . . and gave legal knowledge and aid most generously whenever it was required . . . Many a Parliamentary Bill affecting women, or amendments to them, were drafted on her advice.[63]

There are many other examples of her giving this kind of legal assistance to women's organisations: for instance, in 1935 she presented the case to the Lord Chancellor on behalf of a deputation comprising the ODC and other groups, regarding the report of the law revision committee on married women and the law. She was also approached by and advised women needing assistance in personal legal matters, as for example in a slander case, when a Mrs Cooper wrote to her in 1932 for advice and information. In her letter of reply, Chrystal Macmillan said, 'I had to do a good deal of looking up before I was in a position to be able to set down anything that might be useful to you', and goes on to provide detailed information and guidance.[64]

CONCLUSION

Looking back on Chrystal Macmillan's adult life, it is clear that she was aware from very early on, when she appeared in the House of Lords in 1908, that knowledge of the workings of the law, and the skill of advocacy, were crucial attributes for anyone seeking to advance the causes of justice, equality and peace, all of which she was dedicated to pursuing.

Her part in the campaign to enable women to enter the legal professions was probably as much to do with her general desire for equality as it was to enable her to become a member of the profession herself. By qualifying as a barrister, she not only gained experience and a wider knowledge of the law, she also acquired the respect and status that meant it was more likely that she would be heard when advancing arguments in favour of whatever cause she was promoting. She was also of particular value as a legal expert on committees, particularly in relation to the business of analysing and drafting legislation, and giving evidence to Parliamentary and other committees.

Once qualified as a barrister, she was active in the courts, and clearly dedicated to her work, but it was not her first priority. Indeed, as her colleague Ivy Williams put it, 'She [Chrystal Macmillan] still puts the principle of equality first, whereas I have been saying that we should consider ourselves first as lawyers who would help forward international agreement and only secondarily as women.'[65] Nevertheless, she was clearly highly regarded within legal circles, and especially for her knowledge of the law, particularly as it affected justice for women. This is reflected in the fact that she was invited to speak in place of the Lord Advocate for Scotland at the dinner held to celebrate the passing of The Sex Disqualification (Removal) Act 1919, and that she was chosen to contribute an article on the legal position of women to the fourteenth edition of the *Encyclopaedia Britannica*.[66] It is also reflected in the considerable efforts to which her colleagues went to have her life memorialised in some way at Middle Temple, the Honourable Society of which she was a proud member (see Chapter 9).

Notes

1. *Manchester Courier and Lancashire General Advertiser*, 7 Mar. 1913.
2. The Act begins with the words, 'A person shall not be disqualified by sex or marriage from the exercise of any public function, or from being appointed to or holding any civil or judicial post, or from entering or assuming, or carrying on any civil profession or vocation.' Cited in Mari Takayanagi, 'Sex Disqualification (Removal) Act 1919', in Erika Rackley and Rosemary Auchmuty (eds), *Women's Legal Landmarks* (Oxford: Hart, 2019), pp. 133–8.
3. *The Scotsman*, 9 Mar. 1920.
4. Laura Noakes, 'Chrystal MacMillan and Elsie Bowerman: First Women Barristers' Negotiation of Professional and Political Identities' (PhD thesis, Open University, 2021).
5. Hall v. *The Incorporated Society of Law Agents* 1901, 3 F 1059, and Alison Lindsay, 'First Woman Law Agent, Madge Easton Anderson, 1920', in Rackley and Auchmuty, *Women's Legal Landmarks*, p. 163.
6. Rosemary Auchmuty, 'Whatever Happened to Miss Bebb? Bebb v. The Law Society and Women's Legal History', *Legal Studies* 31.2 (June 2011), pp. 199–230.
7. *London Evening Standard*, 11 Mar. 1919.
8. See Judith Bourne, 'The Vanishing Act of Miss Bertha Cave', *Graya* 133 (2020), pp. 29–38.
9. Mary J. Mossman, *The First Women Lawyers: A Comparative Study of Gender, Law and the Legal Professions* (London: Hart Publishing, 2006), p. 115.
10. Hector MacQueen, 'Scotland's First Women Law Graduates: An Edinburgh Centenary', *Stair Society* 54 (2009), miscellany VI.
11. Ibid.
12. M. Stenton and S. Lees, *Who's Who of British Members of Parliament* (Atlantic Highlands, NJ: Harvester Press, 1979), vol. III, p. 200.
13. Auchmuty, 'Whatever Happened to Miss Bebb?', p. 217.
14. Bar Council Minute Books, Vol. 15 (London: Institute of Advanced Legal Studies).
15. *Journal of the Church League for Women's Suffrage*, 1 Feb. 1917.
16. Auchmuty, 'Whatever Happened to Miss Bebb?', p. 215.
17. *Yorkshire Post and Leeds Intelligencer*, 9 Oct. 1913.
18. Petition sent by Lucy Frances Nettlefold, COLPW secretary on 19 April 1917 Girton Archive GCPP Davies 15/1/15/4a EDXVII/Misc 4.
19. Hansard, Solicitors (Qualification of Women) Bill, House of Lords Debates, 19 Mar. 1918 Vol. 29 cc460–70.
20. Takayanagi, 'Sex Disqualification (Removal) Act 1919', pp. 113–18.
21. Helena Normanton (1882–1957) became the second woman to be called to the Bar, and the first female barrister in England. See Judith Bourne, *Helena Normanton and the Opening of the Bar to Women* (Hook, Hampshire:

Waterside Press, 2016); Ren Pepitone, 'Gender Space and Ritual: Women Barristers, the Inns of Court and the Interwar Press', *Journal of Women's History* 28.1 (Spring 2016), pp. 60–83.
22. Hansard, House of Lords Debates, 11 Mar. 1919, Vol. 33, c591.
23. Ibid.
24. Letter from Ray Strachey to Bonar Law, 21 Jan. 1919. Parliamentary Archives. Bonar Law Papers BL/103/6/1.
25. *The Vote*, 9 May 1919.
26. Ibid.
27. Mari Takayanagi, 'Sacred Year or Broken Reed? The Sex Disqualification (Removal) Act 1919', *Women's History Review* 29.4 (2020), p. 576.
28. *The Woman's Leader*, 12 Mar. 1920.
29. Catriona Cairns, 'First Woman Member of the Faculty of Advocates, Margaret Kidd, 1923', in Rackley and Auchmuty, *Women's Legal Landmarks*, pp. 195–8.
30. Rose Pipes, 'Chrystal Macmillan (1872–1937): A Scotswoman at the Inn', *The Middle Templar* 54 (Michaelmas 2014), pp. 44–6.
31. Dorothy Scott Stokes, 'A Woman Barrister's Views', *Graya* 8 (Easter Term 1931), pp. 29–31.
32. H. Newton Walker, 'Women and the Bar', *The Englishwoman* 42 (April–June 1919), pp. 129–34.
33. *The New Statesman*, 5 May 1917.
34. John Macmillan left each of his children £4,000, to be paid when they reached the age of 24, plus equal shares from the residue of his estate.
35. Walker, 'Women and the Bar'.
36. Patrick Polden, 'Portia's Progress: Women at the Bar in England, 1919–1939', *International Journal of the Legal Profession* 12.3 (Nov. 2005), p. 300.
37. Ibid.
38. Walker, 'Women and the Bar'.
39. Richard O'Havery (ed.), *History of the Middle Temple* (London: Hart Publishing, 2011).
40. Pepitone, 'Gender Space and Ritual', p. 62.
41. Institute of Advanced Legal Studies, London, CLE 11/11.
42. *The Common Cause*, 18 Jan. 1924.
43. Polden says elsewhere that 'It is notoriously hard to establish whether a barrister ever had much of a practice. The published law reports are a poor indicator, but they do give glimpses of some of them at work' ('Portia's Progress', p. 323).
44. A mess was rather like a social club, providing food, company and, for circuit messes, lodgings for barristers away from home.
45. Minute Books of the Western Circuit (Winchester: Hampshire Archives).
46. Minute Book 2, Western Circuit (Winchester: Hampshire Archives).
47. See Bourne for a detailed account: *Helena Normanton*, pp. 112–24.

48. Anthony Harwood, *Circuit Ghosts* (Winchester: The Western Circuit, 1980), p. 169.
49. Central Criminal Court Bar Mess Register, 7 Mar. 1933. London Metropolitan Archives, CLA/040/04/020.
50. Chrystal Macmillan and Helena Normanton, Correspondence, 1933 (London: Women's Library, LSE, 7HLN/A/17).
51. Polden, 'Portia's Progress', p. 333.
52. Ibid., p. 259.
53. Western Circuit records: Kew: National Record Office, Ref. ASSI.
54. Harwood, *Circuit Ghosts*, p. 169.
55. Polden, 'Portia's Progress', p. 311.
56. Ibid., p. 325.
57. Records of County of London Sessions Courts: London Metropolitan Archives, Ref. ILS/B/03/023.
58. Marshall Freeman, *The Times* (obit.), 23 Sept. 1937.
59. Polden, 'Portia's Progress', p. 319.
60. *The Vote*, 23 Jan. 1931.
61. Pendennis, *The Observer*, 26 Sept. 1937.
62. *The Scotsman*, 27 Sept. 1937.
63. Elizabeth Abbot, 'Obituary', *The Shield* 5.3, Dec. 1937, pp. 134–5.
64. Letter Chrystal Macmillan to Mrs Selina Cooper, 14 Nov. 1932. Kew: National Archives DDX1137/3/196.
65. Letter Ivy Wiliams to Sybil Campbell, Mar. 1930 (London: Women's Library, LSE, 5BFW/03/08).
66. *Encyclopaedia Britannica* (1929), Vol. 23.

8

The Nationality of Married Women

Chrystal Macmillan perceived the issue of married women's nationality as an integral part of women's struggle to be acknowledged as full citizens with associated rights. Under the British Nationality and Status of Aliens Act 1914, women, on marriage to a foreign man, automatically lost their British nationality and all rights as British citizens, irrespective of whether they continued to live in Britain after getting married.

She argued that 'there is no reason why the rights of a woman in connection with nationality should be curtailed because of marriage any more than are those of a man . . . The right to nationality in one's own person is the most fundamental political right.'[1] Nowhere was 'the patriarchal form of reasoning more apparent than in the long-running legal debate about married women's nationality'.[2] But it took more than Chrystal Macmillan's considerable endeavours for the law on nationality to be accepted as discriminatory.

The debates on the 'nationality of married women' in the 1920s and 1930s were often impassioned, both at the national and international levels, as women's organisations struggled to show how the law was biased toward men. The variation between nations in their nationality legislation had important consequences, and, for British women who married foreigners, it led to the loss of their civic, economic and political rights.

Although the issue affected only a small number of women, for Chrystal Macmillan, the question of the lack of security in nationality for women signified a woman's lack of autonomy as a citizen, and was therefore a denial of a woman's right to equal citizenship: under British law, married women were under a disability in nationality, their status defined alongside infants, lunatics and idiots. She campaigned at the national and Imperial levels in Britain, and internationally at the

League for a woman to have the independent and indisputable right to her nationality, and continued to do so until close to her death in 1937.

She used her membership of the NUWW and the IWSA committees to raise and review the issue, and to organise lobbying of MPs and Ministers in the British government and at Imperial Conferences. In 1923 she gave evidence, as the sole female witness, before the Select Committee of the House of Lords and House of Commons on Nationality. She also worked internationally as a member of the Women's Representative Committee on Nationality, at the League, where her insistence on the woman's right to 'independent nationality' led to conflict with other members of the committee and in particular with the American lawyer, Alice Paul,[3] who thought that a legal requirement for 'equal nationality' would be sufficient.

Chrystal Macmillan's experience of scrutinising and understanding the implications of legislation, particularly where it concerned women, meant she was well placed to address the complex legal and practical issues surrounding the nationality of married women, and her work earned the respect of lawyers throughout the years of her campaigning on the matter.[4]

PRACTICAL IMPLICATIONS OF THE BRITISH NATIONALITY AND STATUS OF ALIENS ACT, 1914

When she was appointed as the IWSA organiser of relief work with women in London at the start of the First World War, Chrystal Macmillan became aware of the practical implications of the British Nationality and Status of Aliens Act. This Act confirmed that 'the wife of a British subject shall be deemed to be a British subject and the wife of an alien shall be deemed to be an alien': it passed into law in August 1914, just as war was breaking out.[5]

This Act had a far-reaching effect on British women married to foreign men, especially those men, mainly German and Austrian, who were classified as 'enemy aliens', even when they had been resident in Britain for many years and were parents of adult sons serving in the British Army. These women were probably unaware that, due to their husbands' foreign status, they themselves had ceased to be British citizens on marriage, being deemed to have taken the same nationality as their husbands.

With the start of international hostilities in 1914, the question of national identity became one of critical importance for those women and children who, due to the Act, acquired enemy status, resulting in discrimination and, not unusually, their destitution.[6] It has been argued that anti-German feeling had been growing in Britain in the immediate pre-war period.[7] Not only did people in Britain fear Germany's growing ambition as a trading nation, and were apprehensive about their expanding ship-building capacity, many believed that there was a German spy network in Britain. The popular press encouraged a vigilance against the 'hidden hand' of the enemy and the authorities did nothing to assuage the fears. In London, this led to anti-German riots in 1915 when several mobs ransacked not only family shops but also homes belonging to families with foreign-sounding names.[8]

The government rushed through the Aliens Restriction Act 1914 restricting the movement of enemy aliens throughout Britain. This included the British-born wives who were required to:

- register at their local police station;
- notify police of any change of address;
- restrict their travel to within 5 miles of residence unless with police permission;
- reside outwith prohibited areas (on the coast or near to an important military site);
- keep their married name (i.e. they were not allowed to change their foreign name).[9]

In September 1914, Chrystal Macmillan reported to the NUWW EC on the destitution of British-born wives whose husbands, as enemy aliens, had been interned. She pointed out that these wives were now also regarded as enemy aliens and, as such, were being sacked from their employment: some were evicted from their accommodation when the landlord feared attacks on the property, should it become known that Germans lived there. Neither the wives nor their children were eligible for public relief, nor relief from the German government. The Committee duly passed a resolution urging 'the Government to instruct the local Distress Committees, in making regulations to reduce unemployment and in administering relief, to treat British-born wives of aliens as British subjects'.[10]

Writing on the subject for *Jus Suffragii*[11] in October 1916, Chrystal Macmillan laid out the issues for readers and noted that

> The war has brought home to all women, perhaps more especially to those in the warring countries, the need for some drastic alteration in those laws of nationality which decree that a married woman shall have no independent personality with respect to nationality, but shall be 'deemed to be' of the nationality of her husband.

She goes on to note that

> The argument used by those who believe that the nationality of a woman should automatically follow that of her husband is that it is so much simpler. No explanation is ever given why simplicity should be introduced at the expense of the woman . . .

And in a foretaste of the future struggle, she adds,

> That a woman is a separate personality from her husband must come to be recognised with reference to her political rights, nationally and internationally, as it is beginning to be recognised with respect to her civil rights in the more developed countries.[12]

At a special IWSA meeting chaired by Millicent Fawcett in April 1917, to discuss the nationality of married women, Chrystal Macmillan reported that, 'as a result of the special hardships suffered by women married to alien enemies in a number of the warring countries, women's societies all over the world had been taking up the question and urging the need for an alteration of the nationality laws with respect to married women'.[13]

This was an important meeting for two reasons. Firstly, it led to the IWSA setting up a committee on nationality, chaired by Chrystal Macmillan. Secondly, the MP Willoughby Dickinson, who was present at the meeting, took on the task of asking a question in the House of Commons to ascertain the position of the British Empire. Chrystal Macmillan was to work consistently with Willoughby Dickinson MP over many years, to reform British law on nationality. In a debate in the House of Commons in 1918, Willoughby Dickinson argued that 'sooner or later, I believe we shall get to a point where you will treat women on an exact equality with men and allow a British-born woman to retain her nationality in all circumstances',[14] but, as we shall see, 'the women's cause in nationality between 1914 and 1933 was solidly defeated at Westminster by the Imperial cause'.[15]

In July 1917 *Jus Suffragii* printed a further article by Chrystal Macmillan in which she discussed the variations in nationality law across different countries and set out a proposal to undertake a survey of nationality issues as they affected women. She based the questionnaire on previous IWSA surveys of women lawyers and women doctors and took further advice from a meeting of expert women, one of whom, Dr Maria Ogilvie Gordon of ICW, advised that Lady Aberdeen had initiated an ICW international survey in 1905, on the legal position of women, including nationality.[16]

A summary of the 1905 ICW survey, which highlighted the complexities of nationality legislation with respect to women, was written by

Marie Stritt[17] and published in October 1917. Written alongside this summary was a note from Chrystal Macmillan drawing attention to the fact that the British section of ICW had again taken up the subject of nationality as it affected women and men in the British Empire: the ICW were organising a petition to present to the next Imperial Conference, to be signed by women's organisations throughout the Empire, urging that a British woman should have the right to retain her nationality on marriage with a foreigner and that women should be given the same choice of nationality as men.[18]

A Government Amending Bill on the British Nationality and Status of Aliens legislation was introduced to the House of Commons in 1917 and the NUWW intensified their campaign to have the Bill further amended to give married women the same nationality rights as men. Willoughby Dickinson MP was willing to move an amendment but gave way when the Home Secretary promised to set up a subcommittee of experts to deal with the question of nationality. Despite this set-back, the women felt that some progress had been made, as their campaign 'was doubtless partly responsible for the fact that the question of married women's nationality was discussed more thoroughly than ever before'.[19]

When the Home Secretary's promise had still not been honoured in 1921, the NUWW asked Chrystal Macmillan to prepare a draft Bill and they appointed a subcommittee of women and sympathetic MPs to do the work of preparing it and lobbying MPs. The Bill, entitled the Nationality of Married Women Bill (1922), was introduced in the House of Commons by Sir John Butcher MP, but its passage was brought to an end due to the dissolution of Parliament.

CASES OF HARDSHIP EXPERIENCED BY WOMEN MARRIED TO FOREIGN MEN

Many British-born women wrote to Chrystal Macmillan, telling her of their difficulties arising from their status as 'aliens' because of their marriage to a foreign man.[20] As we have seen, during the First World War these difficulties were more severe if their husband was an 'enemy alien', that is German, Austrian or Hungarian.

After the war had ended the situation for these women did not always improve, as the British government had regulations in place to claim reparations from assets belonging to German people. In 1921, one woman wrote to Chrystal Macmillan asking for advice as her German husband refused to support her or her children unless they moved to Germany. She did not want to leave Britain: she had been financially independent as her adoptive mother had left her money. However, this inheritance had been seized from the bank by the British government as part of reparations as she was deemed to be German. As she had borrowed from the bank against these securities to pay living expenses during the war, she now owed the bank a large amount which she could not repay. Moreover, she was unable to obtain employment because her married name, which she was unable to change, was German.

It was not only women married to men from enemy nations that suffered: women whose foreign husbands were from friendly countries were also penalised[21] – the following letter was written to Chrystal Macmillan in September 1922:

> I am a teacher with already 22 years' service, and shall, if my health permits, probably have over 30 years' service before I give up teaching. Ordinarily I should at 60 be entitled to a lump sum of about £340 and a pension of £170 a year till my death.
>
> I forfeit all this because I am married to a Frenchman who has all his life worked for the Entente Cordiale. As editor for many years of a French paper in London, as Chief French Lecturer in our most important London Polytechnic, as Directeur de l'Office National des Universitaires Francaises, his aim has always been to secure a better understanding between the French and English nations. He served during the whole of the War chiefly as Interpreter in the British Army and for his work in this capacity (often in positions of great danger) he received the British Military Medal.
>
> During the War I was treated exactly as if I had married a German, and of course much worse than German women who had married Englishmen, and who were not obliged to go to Police Stations, give notice every time they changed their residence (like a convict on ticket of leave!) nor forbidden to go to certain 'restricted areas' under dire penalties.
>
> I might mention that I had three small children and received no 'Separation allowance' but kept them all on my earnings as a teacher.
>
> I love France but I love my own country also, and feel that I have quite as much right as my husband to retain my own nationality.

Women who married Americans faced becoming stateless, either when they lost their British nationality but did not automatically acquire their husband's nationality or, as in this case, personal reasons, as explained by Mrs L.:

> I am the British wife of an American. I am of British birth, parentage and descent, and I was brought up and educated in England. However, according to the law, I am now an American citizen and am obliged to apply to the American authorities to get a passport. The United States upon issuing a passport requires each recipient to take an oath of allegiance to America.

This I have declined to do, the result being that I am without a passport and cannot visit my native land. We live in Paris, our home is here: but . . . I long to visit England sometimes. All round me this summer, I have seen Poles, Italians, French people etc. going over to England for their holidays, while I, an honest loyal British woman am forced to remain in France.

Another case was brought to Chrystal Macmillan's attention by the MP Willoughby Dickinson who informed her of the difficulties faced by a married British woman who wished to retain her British nationality when her British husband became a naturalised American in October 1924. Willoughby Dickinson had advised the woman to approach the Home Office; he knew that he had succeeded in introducing a clause into Section 12 of British Nationality Act of 1914 which made provision for British women to retain their British nationality when their British husbands subsequently changed their nationality. After much negotiation with the Home Office, the woman was able to retain her British nationality.

Eight years later, in 1932, Chrystal Macmillan took up the case of a woman in similar circumstances. The wife returned to Britain where the police and court system did not acknowledge her legal right to make a declaration to retain her British nationality, fining her for her refusal to register as an alien. She stated in court that she had been 'a ratepayer since 1911, and have never taken out papers as an American citizen, or taken the oath of allegiance to America. If I register as an alien, I will really become a woman without a country.'[22] Chrystal Macmillan took up the case, providing support to the woman, lobbying the Home Office and woman's MP until the claim to British citizenship was recognised as legitimate.

In 1933, British-born women married to foreign men were still regarded as aliens although their situation was slightly improved, as Chrystal Macmillan advised in a letter to Mrs H.:

> . . . by a new order a British woman with a foreign husband can go anywhere without registering with the Police. But she needs to register as an alien if she is staying in a hotel. The new order does not make her a British subject. It only exempts her from registering with the police.

Over the years, Chrystal Macmillan corresponded with many individual British-born women married to foreign men. Most of her correspondents not only listed their difficulties caused by legislation that made them aliens in their own country, they also declared their love for their country and expressed the desire to retain their British nationality.

Chrystal Macmillan worked through personal contacts and government departments, persisting in the campaign for change in nationality laws.

In July 1924, Sir John Pedder,[23] Home office civil servant, chided Chrystal Macmillan:

> I can't help adding that I am disappointed, though it is an experience to which I ought by now to be accustomed, to be charged by you of cherishing a 'down' on women, more particularly since I had taken considerable trouble with this case, both in my letter to Mr W. and my previous arrangements facilitating compliance by Miss W. with the law of Registration, to save her, so far at all events as it lay in my power, from any immediate inconvenient consequence of her unlucky position in regard to nationality.

Chrystal Macmillan made her position clear in her gracious reply in August 1924:

> I am sorry you took my remarks about the principles that underlay the English law and its administration as directed personally to yourself. I had no such intention and, in so far as I created the impression that it was so, I apologise. I saw in your correspondence with Miss S. how very much personal attention you had given to her case. In saying this however, I do not retract what I said about the principles of the law and its administration. I was not referring to its down on women in general but on married women, and you must know from your experience in the Nationality question how very hard the present law is on British women who marry foreigners. You are bound up in the principles and cannot escape any more than anybody else till they are altered; that is one of the handicaps which especially restrict the Civil servant. It's the job of those of us who are outside and free to do political propaganda to see that they are changed.

THE JOINT SELECT COMMITTEE OF THE HOUSE OF COMMONS AND THE HOUSE OF LORDS

In 1923, a Joint Select Committee of the House of Commons and the House of Lords were appointed 'to examine the British Law as to the Nationality of Married Women; to consider in their legal and practical aspects the questions involved in the possession by husband and wife of the same or of different Nationalities'. The Select Committee, comprising ten men and one woman, took evidence from ten people, of whom only one, Chrystal Macmillan, was a woman: the majority of witnesses were male senior civil servants. Although most of the committee members were sympathetic to the women's claim for independent nationality, they were swayed by the view of the male witnesses who emphasised the importance of having unity of nationality within the family unit and of maintaining the British character of a man's family.[24]

Several witnesses to the committee suggested that British women who married foreign men were bringing hardship upon themselves: the claim was made that 'there is no obligation on her to marry a foreigner: it is a deliberate act'. Chrystal Macmillan responded with the observation that 'It is a deliberate act but a woman who marries a foreigner is deprived of her nationality, whereas a man who marries a foreigner is not deprived of his nationality. They both marry foreigners, but the law deals differently with them.'[25] Later in the session she added, 'It is only by a comprehensive Bill that you can get over this feeling of indignity thrust upon a woman, as many of them feel, of having to register as an alien in their own country. It is enormously resented.'[26]

The British legal position was stated firmly in the Select Committee hearing by Sir Cecil Hurst, Legal Adviser to the Foreign Office: 'Our law in this country . . . is founded on the principle that husband and wife are one, and that one is the husband.'[27] That principle, under the law of coverture discriminated against married women in many ways, including their right to nationality.[28]

In giving her testimony to the Select Committee, Chrystal Macmillan restated her conviction that 'a woman is as attached to her nationality as a man is': she argued that depriving a British woman of her nationality or imposing British nationality on an alien woman because of the nationality of her chosen husband, was not treating the woman or her nationality with respect.[29]

In the end, members of the Select Committee were unable to reach consensus: the Members from the House of Commons voted for change while the four Lords voted for the status quo with the result that no further action was taken by the government.

ANNUAL CONFERENCE OF THE INTERNATIONAL LAW ASSOCIATION

Later that year, in October 1923, Chrystal Macmillan attended the Annual Conference of the International Law Association (ILA) in London, at which one of the subjects discussed was married women's nationality. When the chairman failed to invite her to take part in the discussion and prematurely closed the meeting, she politely insisted on being heard and proceeded to urge the assembled lawyers to endorse the legal principle that women should have the same right as men in choosing their nationality. Although she had no formal qualifications in law at that time, she displayed a complete grasp of the international implications caused by the variation in national laws on women's nationalities and challenged the men to consider the issue from a woman's perspective. She 'was perhaps the closest thing to a prominent feminist international lawyer of the time'.[30]

The following year, in a report on the ILA's conference in Stockholm, Margery Corbett Ashby, president of the IWSA, welcomed its resolutions on nationality and naturalisation as being in accord with the policy of the Alliance, and she gave full credit for this to Chrystal Macmillan:

> We should like to congratulate her on this decision of an important body to which we cannot doubt that her work for so many years has helped to contribute . . . Both nationally and internationally . . . Miss Macmillan has been closely identified with the progress of this reform. The Alliance is well aware of its good fortune in having as chairman of the Committee on Nationality a worker so able, so admirably qualified and so indefatigable as Miss Macmillan.[31]

BRITISH GOVERNMENT'S CHANGING ATTITUDES

For Chrystal Macmillan, a constant source of frustration was the failure of lawmakers to understand the woman's perspective: 'The mental outlook of the law-maker did not include any conception that those most concerned might have other views, or that these other views should be taken into account.'[32] She may well have been remembering the comment of the Colonial Secretary, Leo Amery, who in 1914 warned against endangering the common citizenship of the whole of the British Empire merely 'for the sake of removing some small local grievance'.[33]

The argument against women's right to independent nationality presented by Home Office officials was moving from warnings that such legislation would damage the unity of the family to statements that it would threaten the 'common status' legislation on nationality which was necessary throughout the British Empire: any new legislation on nationality would require the agreement of all the Dominions. In 1923 Chrystal Macmillan pointed out the anomaly of 'the agreement' made at Imperial Conference without the issue first being debated in each Parliament of the Empire, as she explained:

> The treatment of [women's nationality] through the Imperial Conference illustrates the danger to the parliamentary control of legislation if the present method of procedure is allowed to crystallise. The matter is serious. The Empire policy on any imperial legislation of this kind should not be produced

in a so-called agreed shape before the different Empire parliaments have themselves had an opportunity of expressing their opinion on the matter. Without such a discussion the individual representatives at the Imperial Conference are not in a position to express the views of their respective countries.[34]

This meant that the delegates to the Imperial Conference might be expressing personal opinions without any debate in the democratically elected Parliaments of the Dominions. She nevertheless remained hopeful that there would be legislative change in Britain when, in 1925, a resolution sponsored by the NUSEC was passed by the House of Commons without opposition: 'that, in the opinion of this House, a British woman shall not lose or be deemed to lose her nationality by the mere act of marriage with an alien, but that it shall be open to her to make a declaration of alienage'.[35] However, British government officials continued to claim that it was not possible for the UK Government to pass legislation on nationality without the agreement of all the nations of the Empire. The women were again disappointed when the Nationality Committee of the Imperial Conference 1928 decided to postpone making a decision, noting that

> On this matter some divergence of view was disclosed, and the Committee were unable to arrive at a unanimous conclusion. Since however, they attach great importance to the maintenance of uniformity throughout the various parts of the Empire in the law relating to British nationality they decided to recommend to the Conference that further consideration of the question should be postponed pending the Report of the Committee of Experts.[36]

Although the debates in the British Parliament from 1925 to 1933 showed a majority in favour of independent nationality for women, the British government continued to promote the principle of 'common status' in nationality and insisted that agreement was needed from all countries represented at the Imperial Conferences in 1926 and 1930. Regrettably, both South Africa and the Irish Free State vetoed all suggestions that husband and wife could have separate nationalities.

British law remained unchanged despite several Private Members' Bills, introduced in 1928, 1929 and 1930, seeking to reform legislation on women's nationality. Each Bill failed to gain government sponsorship and ran out of Parliamentary time. Frustrated by the lack of progress in getting a Bill through Parliament, the NCW decided in 1930 to form a new committee, the Nationality of Married Women Pass the Bill Committee (NMWPBC), with Chrystal Macmillan as chair and coordinator: the aim was to consolidate the planning of the campaign to change British and Commonwealth law to give women equal nationality rights with men, so that a married woman's nationality would be independent of her husband's nationality.

The NMWPBC, made up of representatives from women's organisations (including the NUSEC, IWC, IAWSEC and ERI) and sympathetic MPs, met regularly from 1930 till December 1936, and was well attended.[37] This committee allowed Chrystal Macmillan to discuss and gain support not only for the British campaign but also for her work on nationality at the League.

The archived papers of the NMWPBC attest to the enormous amount of work undertaken by Chrystal Macmillan on the issue of women's nationality: she resolutely organised committee members' efforts, adapting the campaigns in various attempts to influence Parliament and undertook casework with individual women. By 1933 she was known as an expert on the difficulties experienced by women married to foreigners: she brought to the attention of MPs those women who suffered from maladministration or misinterpretation of the complex nationality law,[38] and she directed other women to lawyers specialising in taking nationality cases through the courts. She also supplied memos, under such headings as 'The Hague Convention', 'Conflicts of law', 'Women's support' and 'The Dominions', to MPs who were participating in House of Commons debates.[39]

WOMEN PREPARE FOR THE FIRST LEAGUE OF NATIONS CODIFICATION CONFERENCE ON INTERNATIONAL LAW, 1930

When British women's organisations heard that the subject of nationality was to be on the agenda of the first Conference on the Codification of International Law, to be held under the auspices of the League at The Hague in 1930, they lobbied to have a woman member on the British delegation. The committees of the women's organisations (NCW, IAWSEC, British Federation of University Women (BFUW)) considered that Chrystal Macmillan had the most comprehensive knowledge of the laws on nationality and would be best able to represent their views. However, given the government proviso that the woman delegate must take government instruction, the women realised that this would not be acceptable to Chrystal Macmillan, as she did not agree with the government position. They therefore had to find an alternative delegate with experience of the law, and chose Dr Ivy Williams, the first woman to be called to the English Bar, in May 1922.[40]

After some hesitation, but with encouragement from fellow lawyers Sybil Campbell and Lucy Nettlefold,[41] Ivy Williams accepted the nomination. The British civil servants found her easy to work with and reported that she had spoken with 'brevity and dignity' in favour of equality of nationality at the Conference: she also spoke in French in acknowledgement of most delegates' language skills.

It took some time for the two women to reach a working relationship. Chrystal Macmillan had been working on the nationality issue under the auspices of the ICW and the IFUW, and had presented a paper on nationality to the IFUW Conference in 1929.[42] She was therefore working with international organisations, and was well known to the international committee of university women, the IFUW, while Dr Ivy Williams had been chairing a subcommittee on nationality for the BFUW.

While both women were highly competent lawyers and each had the support of a committee, Chrystal Macmillan was working for the senior international group, IFUW, and this increased the tension between the women on how best to proceed. Ivy Williams wrote to her friend Sybil Campbell:

> Miss Macmillan feels that any woman's organisation should state their full belief in the principle accepted by the International Federation but if this is not possible, she thinks that this resolution [of the British Committee] is at least not opposed to the International Federation declaration.[43]

Ivy Williams appreciated Chrystal Macmillan's legal work on the issue but found her commitment to women's independent nationality too idealistic:

> Liberty of choice advocated by Miss Macmillan and adopted by the Federation as a principle is certainly a controversial matter and as such seems outside the scope of the Codification Conference as a general statement of principle.[44]

She argued that it was much better to attempt to amend the law step by step, and that the Codification Conference would provide an opportunity to improve the lot of women married to foreign men by supporting the resolution: 'That a woman national who marries an alien shall retain her nationality as long as she makes her permanent home in the country of that nationality, unless by a formal and voluntary act she renounces that nationality.'[45] As Ivy Williams saw it, the difference in outlook between herself and Chrystal Macmillan was essentially due to a difference in their priorities. She said of Chrystal Macmillan, 'She still puts the principle of equality first, whereas I have been saying that we should consider ourselves first as lawyers who would help forward international agreement and only secondarily as women.'[46]

At the suggestion of Sybil Campbell, Chrystal Macmillan joined the BFUW Committee meeting, chaired by Ivy Williams, in the hope that their differences of opinion could be explored and conciliated. Over a period of time, after articulating their opinions in long and detailed memos, the two women were able to find a compromise by October 1931 and proposed to the BFUW that it should

> ... declare its support of the policy of the British Government as enunciated by its representative, Dame Edith Lyttelton, in the First Committee of the Assembly of the League on 21 September, 1931, as follows: 'The British Government considers that it is right that all disabilities of married women in matters of Nationality should be removed, and that in so far as nationality is concerned, a married woman should be in the same position as any man – married or unmarried – or any single woman.'[47]

THE FIRST LEAGUE OF NATIONS CODIFICATION CONFERENCE ON INTERNATIONAL LAW, 1930

In the lead-up to the Codification Conference, the ICW and IAWSEC (formerly known as IWSA) coordinated a campaign for complete equality in the standardisation of international nationality laws. This culminated in a Joint Demonstration on the Nationality of Married Women, organised by Chrystal Macmillan, to take place on the evening of the opening of the Codification Conference in The Hague in March 1930. The demonstration included speeches which drew attention to women's claims, as expressed in the resolution passed by the WIOs: 'That a woman, whether married or unmarried, should have the same right as a man to retain or to change her Nationality.'

To illustrate the variations in the nationality laws of different countries, and the different degrees of equality for men and women, a parade of young women wore colours to represent the stage at which a country's laws had reached. The colours ranged from white to black, with different bright colours in between; black was for those countries where women were still subject to their husband's nationality, and the other colours represented different levels of equality. Miss Mathieson, reporting to the NUWW committee, noted that the GB representative was dressed in black, with two tiny white dots representing very small concessions.[48]

The Codification Conference itself was organised by the League, supported by around ninety paid staff from the Secretariat based in Geneva. The women, who funded themselves or were funded by the women's organisations, lobbied delegates to allow a deputation from the WIOs.

Figure 8.1 Joint Demonstration on the Nationality of Married Women, The Hague, 1930
Front row from left: Emmy Belinfante, Maud Wood Park, Betsy Bakker-Nort, Chrystal Macmillan, Margery Corbett Ashby, Emilie Gourd, Lily Van Der Schalk-Schuster. Back row from left: Kathleen Bompass, Allen, Rosa Manus, Söhngen, Sterling, Koechlin-James, Van Beresteyn-Tromp, Ruby Rich (courtesy Collection IAV-Atria, Institute on Gender Equality and Women's History, Amsterdam)

The chairman of the Conference, former Dutch Prime Minister Theodorus Heemskerk, agreed to admit a small group of women, led by Chrystal Macmillan, who presented the case for the independent nationality of women to what was a mostly somewhat hostile audience. They argued that many of the articles proposed by the Conference discriminated against women, either directly as in Articles 8–11, or in other Articles that had indirect effects on women's nationality.

The women's case failed to change the minds of the Conference lawyers who decided against making any amendments. They argued that Articles 8–11 of the Treaty were designed merely to alleviate some of the difficulties arising from the conflict of national laws in different countries which led to statelessness, or double nationality, experienced by women on marriage to a foreigner.

When the Conference finished, the European women returned home to continue their efforts. Back in London, Chrystal Macmillan organised a campaign to send telegrams to League delegates, pointing out that this, the first Treaty of the League, had effectively written the subjection of women into international law, and that they as delegates should urge their national governments not to ratify such a discriminatory measure. In contrast, the American women travelled to Geneva, to set up an office there and to make direct personal approaches to delegates and members of the League Secretariat, with the aim of forming personal networks of political relationships.[49]

In December 1930, Chrystal Macmillan reported to members of NMWPBC that an International Committee for Action on Nationality of Married Women had been formed with herself as chair and Mrs van der Schalk Schuster as honorary secretary. Its objects were to press for recognition of the right of the married woman to an independent nationality; to urge that in determining the nationality of children the nationality of one parent should have no preference over the other; to bring the equality resolution of the Codification Conference to the attention of governments; and to postpone ratification of The Hague Convention until after the League had considered the question again. Four international organisations had agreed to cooperate with the new committee – the ICW, Inter-American Commission of Women (IACW), IAWSEC and ERI.

WOMEN'S CONSULTATIVE COMMITTEE ON NATIONALITY (WCCN)

In recognition of the dissatisfaction with the Articles in the Codification Convention expressed by the WIOs, the Secretary General of the League asked nine WIOs to form a Committee of Representatives of Women's International Organisations to advise the League on women's perspective on the reform of international nationality law.[50] Eight organisations agreed to form the committee – ICW, IAWSEC, IACW, ERI, IFUW, All-Asian Conference of Women (AACW), WILPF and WUWIC. Maria Verone, the French lawyer representing ICW, was elected chair and Dorothy Evans, a British activist representing ERI, was elected secretary.

In contravention of the League's suggestion, the women on the newly formed committee chose to call themselves the Women's Consultative Committee on Nationality (WCCN), much to the annoyance of the League Secretariat who felt that the new title suggested, incorrectly, that this was an 'official' committee of the League. In fact, the WCCN was not funded by the League – all committee expenses, travel, accommodation and clerical support were to be met by individual women or through fundraising by the women's organisations. Given this need to raise money to fund their activities, and to negotiate with the Secretariat to obtain a suitable room for meeting, it took time for the women to set up meetings, and these delays often led to tensions between them.

Chrystal Macmillan and the Belgian lawyer Mme Nelly Schreiber-Favre were chosen by the IFUW as its two representatives to the WCCN, which, inevitably, comprised women with different outlooks and attitudes. For example, several women, including Chrystal Macmillan, had their roots in the constitutional women's suffrage movement, whereas others had worked for radical and more militant suffrage organisations such as the WSPU. Moreover, as noted above, American and European women generally took different approaches to the ongoing campaign, as did individual women. For example, the American lawyer, Alice Paul, who had worked intensively on the nationality issue in the USA and South America, placed particular value on personal negotiations with League delegates, whereas Chrystal Macmillan, by now an experienced barrister, focused her attention on the interpretation of the law.

First responses at the League of Nations to the Codification Conference

On 6 July 1931, the WCCN presented their report to the Secretary General: the women's committee declared 'that it is opposed to The Hague Nationality Convention inasmuch as it differentiates between men and women as regards nationality', and noted their support for the Chilean proposal, namely that 'The contracting States agree that, from the going into effect of this Convention there shall be no distinction based on sex in their law and practice relating to nationality.' The WCCN report also urged the League of Nations Assembly 'to bring about the reconsideration of The Hague Nationality Convention; and to submit to Governments for ratification a new Convention founded on the principle of equality between men and women with regard to nationality'.[51]

The full report was signed by six organisations but the representatives of two of them, Chrystal Macmillan and Nelly Schreiber-Favre of IFUW, and Margery Corbett Ashby and Dr Bakker-Nort of IAWSEC, signed with the proviso that they were doing so 'on the understanding that the **equality** asked for includes the right of a married woman to her **independent** nationality and that the nationality of a woman will not be changed by reason only of marriage or a change during marriage in the nationality of her husband'.[52] Given their experience of dealing with government officials, Chrystal Macmillan and Margery Corbett Ashby were concerned that some governments might interpret 'equal nationality rights for husband and wife' to mean that husband and wife must have the same nationality – and as they saw it, husbands were usually

Figure 8.2 Women's Consultative Committee on Nationality of Married Women at the League of Nations, 1931 (photographer: Photographie Bacchetta, Geneva. Courtesy Schlesinger Library, Harvard Radcliffe Institute)

the more dominant partner in marriage, and therefore the wife would be induced to take her husband's nationality: both were committed to women having sole control over their decision on whether to retain or change their nationality.

On 27 July 1931, the Secretary General presented his report, to be circulated to members of the League, the Assembly and the Council, outlining the discussions and decisions made at The Hague Codification Conference, and attaching the report of the WCCN. He suggested the main question for consideration was whether the League of Nations Assembly should resume an examination of the nationality of women in the light of the WCCN report, or whether the results of The Hague Conference represented the maximum that could secure international agreement at that time. He noted that the next step was to present the reports to governments and request that they submit their observations in time for the next Assembly.

At the First Committee meeting of the Assembly on 21 September 1931, the British delegate to the League, Dame Edith Lyttelton, proposed that the League follow procedure, thereby requiring government observations to be ready for discussion at the next Assembly. Calling for the WCCN to continue its work, she surprised many when she stated that

> The British Government considers that it is right that all disabilities of married women in matters of nationality should be removed, and that, in so far as nationality is concerned, a married woman should be in the same position as any man – married or unmarried – or any single woman.[53]

Dame Edith added that women had a right to ask for this 'elementary measure of equity and justice [as] they had proved that they loved their countries quite as much as men'. She went even further a few days later when the League Assembly met on 26 September, stating, 'We women see no reason why we should not be equals with men in this matter of nationality ... We do not want our nationality to be treated as a coat or garment which a man can cut or alter or dye or throw away just as he likes.'[54]

Following the passionate pleas of Dame Edith and several other speakers, the Assembly resolved to request governments, and the WCCN, to submit their observations on the issue for reconsideration by the thirteenth Assembly, due to be held in 1932.

Divisions within the WCCN

Most governments submitted their diverse views on women's nationality and The Hague Convention between July and November 1932 and WCCN submitted their reports in September the same year. The request by the League for a second report from the women had led to the exposure of divisions of opinion within the WCCN, with Chrystal Macmillan's views differing from those of some of her colleagues.[55] She had become convinced that the proposal from Chile (see above) would not lead to women holding their own full right to their nationality, and thereby would fail to acknowledge women as full citizens.

Chrystal Macmillan and Margery Corbett Ashby were also concerned that the Propaganda Sub-committee of the WCCN, encouraged by Alice Paul, was undertaking work that had not been authorised by the WCCN membership. In April 1932, the *International Women's News* published an article drawing the attention of readers to a move by the Propaganda Sub-committee to lobby for the WCCN to become an official committee of the League and to extend its remit to include all matters in the codification of international law that related to the status of women.[56] This move had not been endorsed by the full committee and was actively opposed by Chrystal Macmillan and Margery Corbett Ashby.

These differences of view, and a general increase in tensions within the committee, proved too great for the women to reach a consensus concerning international law on the nationality of women, so two separate WCCN reports were presented to the Assembly in September 1932. One report, signed by representatives of AACW, ERI, IACW and WILPF, placed an emphasis on the need for international law to be free of inequalities based on sex, and recommended that all future codification projects affecting the *status of women* should consider women's points of view.

The other report, signed by representatives of IAWSEC, ICW, IFUW and WUWIC, concentrated on legal arguments for women's objection to The Hague Convention and concluded that, as the League had established the principle of equality between the sexes, the organisation should apply that principle in international legislation. On the surface, there seemed little difference between the two reports, but the divisions became somewhat clearer following the publication of two opposing articles: one by WILPF representative Eugenie Meller defined the argument in terms of 'equality *or* independence' and the other by Chrystal Macmillan argued for 'equality *and* independence'.[57]

The divisions between the WCCN members on matters of principle continued to grow,[58] leading to personal animosities which in turn led to such a deep split that Chrystal Macmillan, representing IFUW, and her colleague Margery Corbett Ashby, representing IAWSEC, withdrew from the WCCN. They were encouraged in this action by Princess Gabrielle

Radziwill, the officer employed by the League to liaise with WCCN, who felt that the actions of the Propaganda Sub-committee were both unhelpful and damaging to the women's cause:

> I think it would be extremely useful if the Women's Organisations decided to keep a closer watch on the action of this Consultative Committee . . . I want to make it quite clear that the action of the Women's Consultative Committee on Nationality is not feared by the Secretariat, and I am not urging you to take up this question for the sake of the Secretariat, but there is not the slightest doubt in my mind that this activity of the Women's Consultative Committee is doing the Women's Organisations a great deal of harm.[59]

After reviewing the submissions from governments and the WCCN reports, the Secretary General presented his report to the League's Council on 24 January 1933. He noted that 'The Hague Codification did not intend to embody in the Convention any principle in contradiction with the independence of the nationality of married women but rather to put an end to certain difficulties which arise from existing divergences between the law governing the matter in different countries', adding that a 'large number of Governments had expressed the opinion that Articles 8–11 of The Hague Convention represented the degree of progress which could be obtained by way of general international agreement' at that time.

With the support of Princess Radziwill, Chrystal Macmillan and Margery Corbett Ashby wrote to the Secretary General informing him of their withdrawal and suggesting that, as they considered that the work of the WCCN was complete, the WCCN should be closed. However, the six other member organisations of WCCN disagreed with the suggestion for closure, and the WCCN continued its work under the leadership of Alice Paul, opening out the debate with the League on its future role. They asked for the WCCN to be recognised as an official Committee of the League and urged the Assembly to undertake an investigation into the status of women worldwide.

Despite the lack of support from the Secretariat, members of WCCN continued to meet and to lobby government delegates. On 21 September 1934, fifteen government delegations[60] wrote to the Secretary General:

> In view of the worldwide restrictions upon the rights of women – the right to earn a living, the right to an education, to hold public office, to enter the professions – and in view of the interdependence of nationality and the right to work, the following delegations request that there be brought before the First Committee the Convention for Equality for Women in Nationality entered into at the recent Conference of American Republics at Montevideo.[61]

This letter was followed a few days later, on 26 September 1934, by a letter signed by ten South American delegates asking

> That there be included on the agenda, not only the subject of women's nationality, but also the entire status of women, giving particular attention to the Treaty signed by four Governments at Montevideo (December 1933) to remove all legal distinctions based on sex.[62]

Thereafter the Council of the League approved the proposal to place the questions of nationality and the status of women on the agenda of the 1935 Assembly. The women's organisations, including IAWSEC and IFUW who had previously withdrawn from WCCN, welcomed the invitation from the Secretary General to present their views on 'nationality and the status of women'. Perhaps surprisingly, Chrystal Macmillan did not contribute a statement on nationality, but signed the statement from ODI urging equal rights for women in the workplace.

ORGANISATIONAL TENSIONS AND PERSONALITY DIFFERENCES AT THE LEAGUE OF NATIONS

Underlying the formal negotiations and the intergovernmental politics at the League of Nations,[63] the relationships between individual officials in the Secretariat and the members of the WCCN committee were not always supportive; neither were they always cooperative between women in the International Women's Organisations. At times, the women disagreed on matters of political or legal principle[64] but there is also evidence that some disagreements were due to an anxiety to protect the standing of their own nation or organisation,[65] whereas on other occasions it was due to a clash of personality.

Chrystal Macmillan was a member of several international organisations and did not feel the need to protect the interests of any one of them, unlike Lady Aberdeen, president of ICW, who was mindful of the organisation's standing. Writing in 1931, she noted that

> ... the decision of the Council of the League of Nations ... on nationality of married women is a great triumph and we have every reason to offer our thanks and congratulations to Chrystal Macmillan who watched over our common interests at Geneva on this subject.[66]

An organisation represented on WCCN, ERI, was not formed until 1930. The Chair of ERI, Helen Archdale (who like Chrystal Macmillan was a former pupil at St Leonards School – see Chapter 1) was based in Geneva where she worked to promote an Equal Rights Treaty at the League.

In April 1931, she received a letter from Lily van der Schalk Schuster, a member of ERI and secretary of the International Committee for Action on Nationality of Married Women, which made her aware that feelings were running high among the women lobbying the League on the nationality of women:

> I feel really ashamed of all these women and quite agree with you, that faults are on both sides. It would have been better if the League had decided who was to go on that committee and the League would perhaps have been willing to do so, if Alice Paul had not prevented it from the very beginning, as she wanted to have control of the committee.[67]

And one month later, Lily van der Schalk Schuster was voicing her anxieties about Alice Paul's behaviour in relation to the ERI:

> Alice Paul can only lead! All through the Suffrage movement and later on her vision has been remarkable. Only she cannot cooperate with other people... But it gives you a very queer impression, if in the middle of an organisation, there all of a sudden, is one woman, claiming to work independently and not even informing the Executive what is going on.[68]

After the Secretary General issued the formal invitation in July 1931 to form a committee to advise the League, the women's organisations struggled to form the advisory committee and arrange meetings – with no support from the League.

Flora Drummond noted the troubled relations within the WCC:

> ... this Commission has turned out a real battle of wits mainly between McMillan [sic] and Corbett Ashby on one side and Paul on the other. And when I arrived, feeling was at its height, Paul having gradually won the majority on her side. D Evans was elected secretary and did magnificently against terrible odds and what do you think, daily, MacMillan [sic] and Ashby made attacks on the ERI saying we were not international, we had no branches and not even a constitution and that we were not qualified for this Commission; and it seems to me they are determined to get us off. They, McMillan [sic] and Ashby fought hard to close the Commission after this job was finished but failed again.[69]

The tensions and struggles within the advisory committee had an effect on Helen Archdale's relationship with her young colleague Dorothy Evans, ERI representative and secretary of WCCN, whom she accused of falling under the undue influence of Alice Paul:

> [Y]ou allow Miss Paul's influence over you to govern your actions to the extinction of your responsibility as Secretary to the other Member

Organisations of WCCN and your responsibility to the organisation which you represent.[70]

Relationships between European members of WCCN and the American, Alice Paul, were increasingly strained, and by the end of June, Helen Archdale was even more concerned that members of WCCN were unhappy with WCCN arrangements: she wrote again to Dorothy Evans, as her 'Chairman and friend, personally and confidentially':

> I have heard complaints that no meetings have happened. There was always some unexplained postponement or meetings proposed that did not take place, nobody knowing why . . . You were accused of never answering letters of anyone without first consulting Miss Paul, a proceeding leading to delay and naturally annoying other representatives.[71]

The relationship between Chrystal Macmillan and the American women on WCCN had started off reasonably well, as witnessed by a letter sent by Chrystal Macmillan to Doris Stevens of the IACW. In it, she expressed her pleasure that 'the Pan American Women's Committee is going to help us in this matter', although, by the tone of her letter, she seemed unaware that the American women had been working on the issue of women's nationality for some time and they also considered themselves experts on the subject.[72] The following year, Mrs Alva Belmont, a wealthy American donor to the American suffrage organisation, the National Women's Party, expressed her antagonism to the British women in a letter to Alice Paul on 16 September 1929: 'I do not believe that we will get any assistance from England. They take the position that they are friendly to us but they are very jealous of our powers and will not in any way assist us to increase it.'[73]

There are very few letters that provide evidence of how Chrystal Macmillan herself felt during the course of discussions at WCCN from 1931 till she resigned from the committee in June 1933. However, it is unlikely, given that she and Alice Paul both considered themselves to be experts on the issue of nationality, that the two women could work together in harmony. As the above letters show, Alice Paul was not a person who found it easy to cooperate with others.

Writing to Dorothy Evans, WCCN secretary, in March 1934, Alice Paul quotes from a letter written by Chrystal Macmillan to an officer of the ERI:

> I think that any international agreement should provide for the independent nationality of each spouse as well as for equality. The particular form of

treaty quoted in Equal Rights as adopted at Montevideo is weak in that it omits this essential, and is consequently open to dangerous application.[74]

And in response to this note, Alice Paul suggests that WCCN should not encourage Chrystal Macmillan to rejoin the WCCN, as her withdrawal from the committee

> ... Is a very great blessing ... I should think we ought to accept their resignations and go forward without further communication with them concerning their membership on the Committee. It seems to me wise not to send them further notices of Committee meetings. We have a wonderful opportunity to make some headway this coming Assembly ... It would be impossible to get them to join in a recommendation of the Treaty adopted at Montevideo and a failure by our committee to unite on such a recommendation would certainly enfeeble us in our campaign with the Assembly.[75]

But as the correspondence between members of ERI demonstrates, the women's organisations were given an impossible task by the League. They were expected to work together, without any League support, financial or clerical, to produce one joint view with recommendations on the complex issues of international law on the nationality of women, all in a matter of months. They had previous experience of working internationally on campaigns within their own organisations or within their own country, but little experience of managing the task across organisations and across nations. Also, unlike government delegates, who were paid a salary and had their accommodation in Geneva paid by their governments, and who were given time, rooms and clerical support by the League to meet in committee, the members of WCCN were expected to organise and to fund themselves.

As to the relationship between Chrystal Macmillan and Alice Paul, both strong-minded women and both lawyers, the only evidence to go on are the few surviving letters between them. One of them, a long letter written to Alice Paul by Chrystal Macmillan in 1934, discussed the implications of the American Equal Nationality Act of 1934, and it suggests an attempt at reconciliation between the two women:

> I have for some weeks been intending to write to you to congratulate you on the passage of the nationality bill which gives the married woman her own independent nationality on the same terms as a man and makes nationality transmissible from the mother in the same way as it is from the father. I am sure that its adoption will be a great help to those in other countries who are working for the same reforms ... I appreciate what a prodigious amount of work you must have done to secure this enactment, knowing how hard a parliament is to move.[76]

CONCLUSION

Did Chrystal Macmillan recognise that international legislators were not going to be willing to admit women to independent rights of nationality in her lifetime, and if so, was that why she withdrew her efforts from the WCCN campaign? Whatever her reasons, what in fact happened was that the reform of international law on the nationality of married women did not take place until 1957, twenty years after her death. However, reform of British law, giving women the right to their nationality independent of their marital status, happened a few years earlier, in 1948.

A dinner was held in London on 25 January 1949 to celebrate the restoration of the right to independent nationality to British women:

> Lord Pethick-Lawrence, friend and fellow worker in the equality cause, spoke of the fine lead given by Chrystal Macmillan who, when consulted in 1925, refused to accept a watering down of the demand. He congratulated those who had worked for this reform on their splendid achievement – it was both a surprise and a pleasure to him that the Government had gone all the way in the matter of restoration by making it retrospective . . . Miss Florence Barry, Hon. Secretary of the Nationality of Married Women Committee in replying to the toast of the Committee, paid tribute to that brilliant lawyer, Miss Chrystal Macmillan who, having a wide knowledge of national and international law, had planned the campaign.[77]

Even though it took many more years to bring about change in international law on the nationality of women, it has been acknowledged that the negotiations around the Nationality Resolution at the League of Nations in 1931 did have a stimulating effect on the international women's movement and consolidated their presence at the League:

> The Resolution constituted an important stepping stone in the evolution of women's international human rights, since the UN Commission on the Status of Women relied on the Resolution and the work of the international women's organisations when it drafted the UN Convention on the Nationality of Married Women which went into effect on August 11, 1958.[78]

Notes

1. Chrystal Macmillan, *The Nationality of Married Women* (London: Nationality of Married Women Pass the Bill Committee, 1931; Women's Library, LSE), p. 197.
2. Lucinda M. Finley, 'Breaking Women's Silence in Law: The Dilemma of the Gendered Nature of Legal Reasoning', *Notre Dame Law Review* 64 (1989), p. 886.

3. Alice Paul (1885–1977) was a brilliant American feminist lawyer who had worked for the WSPU in Britain and served three prison sentences before returning to the USA where she became leader of the National Women's Party.
4. Karen Knop and Christine Chinkin, 'Remembering Chrystal Macmillan: Women's Equality and Nationality in International Law', *Michigan Journal of International Law* 22.4 (2001).
5. Helen Kay and Rose Pipes, 'British Nationality Act 1948', in Erika Rackley and Rosemary Auchmuty (eds), *Women's Legal Landmarks* (Oxford: Hart Publishing, 2019), pp. 233–9.
6. *Daily Mirror*, 'Police Powerless to stop', 13 May 1915, p. 6; Katherine Storr, *Excluded from the Record: Women, Refugees and Relief 1914–1929* (Bern: Peter Lang, 2010); Anna Braithwaite Thomas, *St Stephen's House: Friends Emergency Work in England 1914 to 1920* (London: Friends Emergency Committee for the Assistance of Germans, Austrians and Hungarians in Distress, n.d.).
7. John Clement Bird, 'Control of Enemy Alien Civilians in Great Britain 1914–1918' (PhD thesis, LSE, 1981).
8. Panikos Panayi, *The Enemy in Our Midst: Germans in Britain during the First World War* (Oxford: Berg Publishers, 1991).
9. For examples see Laura Tabili, 'Outsiders in the Land of Their Birth: Exogamy, Citizenship, and Identity in War and Peace', *Journal of British Studies* 44.4 (October 2005), pp. 796–815.
10. NUWW Minutes, 8 Sept. 1914.
11. *Jus Suffragii* was the journal of the IWSA.
12. *Jus Suffragii* 11.1, 1 Oct. 1916, p. 2.
13. Minutes IWSA Special Meeting 17 April 1917. Manchester Public Archive M50/2/22/215.
14. House of Commons debate 17 July 1918, Vol. 108, c1179.
15. Dorothy Page, 'A Married Woman, or a Minor, Lunatic or Idiot: The Struggle of British Women against Disability in Nationality 1914–33' (PhD thesis, University of Otago, 1984).
16. *Jus Suffragii* 11.10, July 1917, p. 146.
17. Marie Stritt (1855–1928), German feminist and one of the founders of IWSA.
18. *Jus Suffragii* 12.1, Oct. 1917, pp. 2–3.
19. *Jus Suffragii* 12.11, Aug. 1918, p. 179.
20. All the quotations in this section are based on Chrystal Macmillan's correspondence file of 'Hard Cases' in the Nationality of Married Women files 5NMW/B/01 Women's Library, LSE.
21. This was still the case in 1943, when the Scottish mother-in-law of one of the authors, Helen Kay, was expected to register as an alien and visit the police station every week in her home town after she married a Polish

officer stationed in Scotland: like all British-born wives, she did not have the right to her own independent nationality until 1948.

22. Press cutting in Correspondence file of Hard Cases (London: Women's Library, LSE 5NMWB01) *Reynold's Illustrated News*, 27 Nov. 1932, pp. 1 & 7.
23. Sir John Pedder was Principal Assistant Secretary at the Home Office, 1904–32.
24. Select Committee of House of Commons and House of Lords, *Report on the Nationality of Married Women*, 1923. HMSO.
25. Ibid., p. 136.
26. Ibid., p. 139.
27. Ibid., p. 38.
28. Coverture is widely discussed in Rackley and Auchmuty, *Women's Legal Landmarks*; Tim Stretton and Krista Kesselring (eds), *Married Women and The Law: Coverture in England and the Common Law* (Montreal: McGill-Queen's University Press, 2015), *passim*.
29. Ibid., p. 127.
30. Knop and Chinkin, 'Remembering Chrystal Macmillan', p. 524.
31. *Jus Suffragii* 19.1, Oct. 1924.
32. Chrystal Macmillan, 'Nationality of Married Women: Present Tendencies', *Journal of Comparative Legislation and International Law*, 3rd ser., 7 (1925), p. 142. For full discussion of the effects of Parliamentary change and the influence of senior civil servants, see Page, 'A Married Woman, or a Minor, Lunatic or Idiot'.
33. House of Commons debate 29 July 1914, Vol. 65, cc1500.
34. Chrystal Macmillan, 'The Coming Imperial Conference and the Nationality of Married Women', *Time and Tide*, 4 May 1923, quoted in Page, 'A Married Woman, or a Minor, Lunatic or Idiot', p. 173.
35. Parliamentary Debates, 18 Feb. 1925, p. 1188, and later referred to by Sir John Sandeman Allen, House of Commons Debate, Vol. 279, col. 1335, 27 June 1933.
36. Cabinet Memo 398(28), p. 22.
37. Minutes of the Nationality of Married Women Pass the Bill Committee (London: Women's Library, LSE, 5NMW/A/01).
38. Tabili, 'Outsiders in the Land of Their Birth', p. 796.
39. Quoted in Page, 'A Married Woman, or a Minor, Lunatic or Idiot', p. 351.
40. Caroline Morris, 'Dr Ivy Williams: Inside yet Outside', *Women's History Review* (2020), pp. 583–614, https://doi.org/10.1080/09612025.2019.1702783.
41. Correspondence between Williams, Campbell and Nettlefold. British Federation University Women (London: Women's Library, LSE, 5BFW/05/54).
42. Macmillan, 'The Nationality of Married Women'.
43. Letter Ivy Williams to Sybil Campbell, Dec. 1929 (London: Women's Library, LSE, 5BFW/03/08).

44. Memorandum Ivy Williams, Dec. 1929, BFUW papers (London: Women's Library, LSE, 5BFW/05/54).
45. Letter BFUW secretary to Rt Hon. Sir John Anderson, Home Office, 25 Jan. 1930. (London: Women's Library, LSE, BFW/03/08).
46. Letter Ivy Williams to Sybil Campbell, 11 Jan. 1930 (London: Women's Library, LSE, 5BFW/03/08).
47. Minute BFUW subcommittee on Nationality, 17 Oct. 1931 (London: Women's library, LSE, 5BFW/05/54).
48. NUWW Minutes Executive Committee 11 April 1930, p. 41.
49. Ellen Carol Dubois, 'Internationalizing Married Women's Nationality: The Hague Campaign of 1930', in Karen Offen (ed.), *Globalizing Feminisms 1789–1945* (London: Routledge, 2010), pp. 208–9.
50. *Report by the Secretary General on Nationality of Women*. League of Nations, 27 July 1931, A.19.1931.V, p. 1.
51. Ibid., pp. 7–14.
52. 'Statement by the Women's Consultative Committee on Nationality with regard to the Hague Nationality Convention', in Report of Secretary-General to League of Nations Members and the Assembly and the Council, Geneva 27 July 1931, p. 11.
53. Minutes of First Committee of 12th Assembly, 21 Sept. 1931. *Official Journal of League of Nations: Special Supplement* No. 94, p. 49.
54. Verbatim record 15th Plenary Meeting of 12th Assembly. League of Nations, 26 Sept. 1931.
55. Nationality of Women Observations by Women's International Organisations. League of Nations, 7 Sept. 1932, A.23.1932.V.
56. *The International Women's News* 26.7, April 1932, pp. 71–2.
57. *Women's International News* 28.6, Mar. 1934, p. 42 and 28.8, p. 59.
58. Carol Miller, 'Lobbying the League: Women's International Organisations and the League of Nations' (DPhil thesis, University of Oxford, 1992), https://ora.ox.ac.uk/objects/uuid:f517ac72-18b3-42b2-9728-31129462bf4a/files/m8a9dc648f42c02edbce251148cef4f41.
59. Letter Gabrielle Radziwill to Maria Ogilvie Gordon, president of the Women's Council for Representation of Women in the League of Nations, 23 Jan. 1933. League of Nations Archive, R3585-50-9105-9105, p. 3.
60. USSR, Czechoslovakia, Turkey, Mexico, Chile, Colombia, China, Panama, Siam, Dominican Republic, New Zealand, Latvia, Argentine, Haiti and Yugoslavia.
61. Nationality of Women 15 May 1935. Note by Secretary General. League of Nations, A.7.1936.V.
62. Status of Women, 15 May 1935. League of Nations, A.8.1935.V.2.
63. Page, 'A Married Woman, or a Minor, Lunatic or Idiot', *passim*.
64. Ibid., p. 323.
65. Catherine Jacques, 'Tracking Feminist Intervention in International Law Issues at The League of Nations: From the Nationality of Married Women

to Legal Equality in the Family 1919–1970', in Sara Kimble and Marion Röwekamp (eds), *New Perspectives on European Women's Legal History* (London: Routledge, 2017), p. 328.
66. Letter Lady Aberdeen ICW to Mrs Bompass, IAWSEC 3 Feb. 1931 (London: Women's Library, LSE).
67. Letter Lily van der Schalk Schuster to Helen Archdale, 11 April 1931. ERI papers 5ERI/1A (London: Women's Library, LSE).
68. Letter Lily van der Schalk Schuster to Helen Archdale, 4 May 1931. ERI papers 5ERI/1A (London: Women's Library, LSE).
69. Letter Flora Drummond to Helen Archdale, 1 Aug. 1931. ERI papers 5ERI/1A (London: Women's Library, LSE).
70. Letter Helen Archdale to Dorothy Evans, 27 June 1932. ERI papers 5ERI/1A (London: Women's Library, LSE).
71. Ibid.
72. Letter Chrystal Macmillan to Doris Stevens, 18 July 1928. Doris Stevens Archive, Schlesinger Library.
73. Letter Alva Belmont to Alice Paul. Alice Paul Archive, 491962229, Schlesinger Library.
74. Letter Alice Paul to Dorothy Evans, quoting Chrystal Macmillan, 12 Mar. 1934. Alice Paul Archive, Schlesinger Library.
75. Letter Alice Paul to Dorothy Evans, 12 Mar. 1934. Alice Paul Archive, Schlesinger Library.
76. Letter Chrystal Macmillan to Alice Paul, 11 July 1934 (London: Women's Library, LSE, 5NMW/A/02).
77. *The Woman Teacher* 30.9, 18 Feb. 1949.
78. Carol Lockwood, Daniel Magraw, Margaret Spring and S. I. Strong (eds), *The International Human Rights of Women: Instruments of Change* (Washington, DC: American Bar Association, Section of International Law and Practice, 1998), p. 125.

9

Death, Memorials and Recollections

DEATH

Chrystal Macmillan had been suffering from a heart condition for some months before her death, which was registered as being due to tubular disease of the heart, chronic nephritis (inflammation of the kidneys) and uraemia. According to her niece Ialeen, she had developed a clot in her leg that had remained undetected for some time and resulted in her having an amputation. Her disablement, and continuing ill health, must have prompted the move back to her home city of Edinburgh, presumably to be close to those members of her family who were still living there. She died in a nursing home at 8 Chalmers Crescent on 21 September 1937.

At her death, her estate was valued at £14,439, and in her will she left significant sums of money to the organisations with which she was most closely involved at the time: ODI, of which she was president from 1929 until her death; the ODC, and the AMSH (£500 left to each one). Her funeral, held in an Edinburgh crematorium, was attended by family members, friends and colleagues. Among them were Cicely Hamilton, Elizabeth Abbott, Countess Rhondda, Frances Melville and Isobel Donzé.

Wreaths for the funeral were sent by most of the organisations with which she had had a long relationship, and representatives of these, and many other organisations, attended her memorial service. This was held on 1 October 1937 at St Clement Danes church in the Strand – the church, close to the Temple district, where she had lived and worked as a barrister. Over one hundred people attended the service, including leading figures from the suffrage movement, the legal world and politics.

Obituaries

In the absence of written memoirs and other personal material, obituaries and tributes are the main sources for insights into Chrystal Macmillan's character and activities. Inevitably, obituaries tend to be more hymns of praise than rounded character studies, but in this case, there is a consistency in the tributes which suggests that she was universally admired and respected by those she worked alongside and who witnessed her in action. Lord Alness was one such: as a junior counsel at the Scottish Bar, he had appeared for the Scottish graduates in their action against the universities in the Court of Session in Edinburgh (see Chapter 2), and recalled Chrystal in his 'appreciation' in *The Scotsman*:

> Association with Miss Macmillan throughout this uphill fight revealed her to me as a brave and gifted woman, as the pivotal personality and mainspring of any enterprise to which she set her hand, as one who refused to acknowledge defeat so long as the avenue of appeal was open to her. She continued to be the pioneer and protagonist of her sex in the many advance movements with which she was subsequently associated. It is not too much to say that Miss Macmillan dedicated her life to the emancipation of women, and that, in that regard, she has made the women of this country her debtors for all time. Though she is dead, her work will never die.[1]

In another, unattributed, appreciation in *The Scotsman*, the writer recalled meeting Chrystal Macmillan

> . . . at a public debate in Edinburgh, when she and I championed different points of view on some women's question. It was in this way I first came to appreciate Miss Macmillan's worth, and her shining and consistent advocacy of women's rights. I am sure it is by this advocacy she would like best to be remembered. She gained an international reputation for it, and was well known in most capitals of Europe among all progressive leaders of women. While she recognised the good work that is done in broadening women's spheres of activity by numerous women's agencies, Miss Macmillan directed her whole energies to the much more important questions of securing women's statutory, social and economic equality with men. She believed that it was there that the real matters of moment for women must be fought out, and her extraordinary abilities had been of immense help for many years to this side of women's questions. Her legal training, her keen logical brain and her wide experience of affairs fitted her for such work.[2]

The above quote appears in the biographical sketch of Chrystal Macmillan that was, until 2021, presented to the winner of the eponymous prize awarded by the Honourable Society of the Middle Temple to an outstanding woman law student.³ Another part of the sketch refers more to her personal qualities:

> Chrystal Macmillan was utterly without the spirit of enmity, even towards those most bitterly opposed to her. Her dislikes were for policies, not persons, of whom her judgement erred on the side of charity. If there was enmity towards herself she did not resent it, she did not even perceive it; and this for the very good reason that she never thought of herself. Her interest was only and always in the work to be done, in the thousands of women throughout the world who needed redress from injustice. There were for her no 'classes' of women; all who suffered injustice had a claim upon her.⁴

Of all the many tributes to her, perhaps the most revealing about her character and personal qualities is the one that appeared in *Open Door*, the newsletter of ODI:

> It is impossible to close without mention of the sterling quality of her character. Loyalty was its keynote – loyalty to her friends, to the cause she served. Her integrity, steady courage, inflexible determination, and utter lack of self-seeking won the esteem of all who came in contact with her. The stimulus of her personality was felt by all who had the privilege of working with her. It was characteristic, too, that with all her great gifts she was truly humble.
>
> To those who knew her in private life a wealth of kindliness, understanding and ready help was revealed. Her conversational powers over a wide range of subjects, her wit, and love of anecdote made her a delightful companion . . . by her death the world is made poorer.⁵

As a last word on her life and character, the following extract from *The Women Teacher* is particularly apposite:

> Her [Chrystal Macmillan's] life is ended but her work must go on and it behoves the NUWT [National Union of Women Teachers], as part of the woman's movement, to help to place on permanent record some of the outstanding achievements of this truly remarkable woman. We must often feel profoundly thankful that it has been given to us to live in an age which produced women such as Chrystal Macmillan and proud, too, that our lives and work have touched those of great pioneers for women's freedom.
>
> She might have planned her life for great personal aggrandisement. Instead, she gave herself for more than forty years to help the poor and the weak. Her passion was to give to women of every class and kind and nation the one and only protection: Justice. She was herself a great and a very just human being. Let us help to PASS ON THE SACRED FLAME.⁶

Memorials

Soon after her death in 1937, Chrystal Macmillan's friends and colleagues made great efforts to raise funds for a suitable memorial 'to record her association with the Bar of England – as a member of the Middle Temple and of the Western Circuit'.[7] A small group of people, including Elizabeth Abbott, Marshall Freeman, Lord and Lady Balfour of Burleigh, Cicely Hamilton, Isobel Donzé and Chrystal Macmillan's Scottish friends, Frances Melville, Eunice and Sylvia Murray, met to discuss plans for a memorial and planned to approach a number of distinguished individuals from both the UK and elsewhere to donate to a memorial fund. Among those they contacted were The Duchess of Atholl, Viscountess Astor, Lord Cecil, Carrie Chapman Catt (USA), Viscountess Rhondda, Vera Brittain and Charlotte Despard.

One early suggestion was for a plaque to be placed on the wall of Chrystal's home at 4 Pump Court, and another was for her flat to be retained as a library. An appeal for funds was launched in the press in February 1938, by which time the proposal was to use the sum raised to fund an annual prize for women law students. Donations were received, but the intervention of the war meant that the project had to be shelved and was not revived again until 1946. There was still hope that the Inn would agree to mount a plaque on 4 Pump Court, which had miraculously survived the bombing, but the Inn turned the idea down. Instead, they agreed to establish a Chrystal Macmillan prize, to be awarded each year to the highest performing female student of the Honourable Society of the Middle Temple in the Bar Final exams of the previous year. The prize was originally in the form of books selected by the prize-winner, according to the income available from time to time from the fund, and to be accompanied by a short biography of Chrystal Macmillan.

The plan to mount a memorial plaque in the Temple was never revived, but, fittingly, it is as an alumna of the University of Edinburgh that Chrystal Macmillan is now commemorated, both in the form of a plaque, and the name of a building, the first of the university's buildings to be named after a woman (see Introduction).

Recollections: Life on the hill

In his obituary for Chrystal Macmillan, her colleague and friend Marshall Freeman wrote that she undoubtedly lived a 'life of serious purpose', but

> ... was not without a keen sense of Scottish humour. She had many friends in the Temple and her tall, distinguished figure will long be missed from among

us . . . She had a great love for flowers, and on the roof of her flat in Pump Court maintained a model garden, frequently replenished from her bungalow at Boxhill.[8]

This is a rare and tantalising glimpse into her private life, revealing as it does her less serious side, as well as her interest in gardening. In another obituary, reference is again made to Chrystal Macmillan's love of nature: '[she delighted] specially in the beauty of the ever-changing landscape seen from her country retreat'.[9]

The country retreat referred to here, and by Marshall Freeman, was Box Hill, also known as Betchworth Fort or Hill, on the North Downs in Surrey. From written accounts by some of the women who spent weekends there,[10] it appears that a group of them owned what were mostly primitive dwellings on the hill, including caravans, a one-room shack and a converted tram, but in Chrystal Macmillan's case, a bungalow with a veranda. Of the women who spent time there, as well as Chrystal there was her friend Cicely Hamilton, a playwright and active member of the ODC; Lilian Baylis, owner of the Old Vic Theatre; and Edith Picton-Turbervill, a suffragist and Labour MP.

It is not clear how or when the hut community was first established, but it must have been before 1925 since that was the year when Cicely Hamilton first invited her close friend Lilian Baylis to join her there for a weekend retreat.[11] Three years later, Lilian Baylis acquired her own tiny one-roomed hut with a veranda overlooking the South Downs, and often invited women friends, including Elizabeth Abbott, to join her there. The fourth member of the clique, Edith Picton-Turbervill, also owned a hut on Box Hill, measuring 12 feet by 8,

> . . . which was sarcastically named 'Chatsworth'. Here I spent many, many happy weekends. We were a little colony of friends who all possessed habitations on the opposite side of Box Hill to that part of it which is vested in the National Trust. We were close to a farmhouse from where we got milk, butter, eggs and other necessities.[12]

In her autobiography, Edith Picton-Turbervill vividly describes 'life on the Hill', and makes particular mention of Chrystal Macmillan:

> Lilian Baylis, Cicely Hamilton, Chrystal Macmillan (barrister-at-law), and myself composed our clique. Chrystal possessed a great brain and was a brilliant pleader . . . [she] was the plutocrat of the party for she had a real bungalow with several rooms, a kitchen and a tap from which water flowed! She even brought her housekeeper with her very often who cooked the most delicious dishes. We others lived very simply.

> ... Chrystal Macmillan, Cicely Hamilton and I generally 'messed' together on Chrystal's broad balcony each bringing our own contribution, and we had many a delightful meal together. We used to call ourselves 'the fellowship of the Hill'. We had great fun. There was a swimming-pool nearby with a loudspeaker. I can now see Lilian Baylis learning to swim accompanied by the strains of Beethoven's Fifth Symphony![13]

According to her niece, Ialeen Gibson Cowan, who visited Chrystal's 'hut', it may not have been quite as luxurious as recalled by her friends on the Hill:

> Although reputed to have been a much less primitive 'hut' than those of her friends nearby, I have to say that it wasn't exactly my cup of tea and I was quite relieved to get back to London. I have no idea whether or not I ever went there again but the 'hut' stuck in my mind as somewhere dank and drear. Yet I know that Aunt Chrys loved the place so it could be that I only saw it in damp weather and, as Picton relates, all the huts were set in the midst of bushes and trees.[14]

The account in the Picton-Turbervill autobiography includes a description of a moment of frivolity on 'the Hill' which reveals Chrystal Macmillan's 'keen sense of Scottish humour', and the relaxed conviviality she enjoyed with her group of close friends when off-duty:

> Extract from current issue of the *Boxhill Bolshevist* (with which is incorporated the *Chatsworth Red Flag*)
> On Sunday April 24, a touching ceremony took place on the summit of Boxhill: the interment of a humble victim of the capitalist system – a sardine, whose ashes lie far from his native ocean. In accordance with the wishes of Comrade Picton-Turbervill – the legal representative of the deceased – the funeral took place with full military honours and the corpse lay in state for nearly a week before it was placed in the grave ... Miss Chrystal Macmillan, barrister-at-law (representing the English Bar, the minority movement in the Socialist Party, the Earl of Birkenhead and the Amalgamated Society of Aberdeen Fish Curers) laid a wreath on the bier and made a suitably moving oration.
> It is hoped to erect a permanent memorial to the blameless personality who has passed beyond the reach of capitalist oppression; but even if funds should not be forthcoming for this worthy object, those who know Comrade Picton-Turbervill will be well assured that the humble grave beneath her window will never lack its flowers or its tear! C.H.[15]

The bonds between the women may have been forged on the Hill, or more probably before they met there. For example, Cicely Hamilton and Chrystal Macmillan may have encountered one another as early as

1912, when Chrystal was delegated by the NUWSS to attend a meeting of the Actresses Franchise League (AFL) to discuss possible ways of using drama as propaganda for the suffrage cause.[16] Cicely Hamilton was a member of the AFL, and produced skits and plays, such as *A Pageant of Great Women*, which were performed by the League. She was also a member of the ODC, so would certainly have met Chrystal Macmillan in that context, as well as through the suffrage movement.

All three women were feminists, suffragists and social reformers, and were clearly very close friends: it was Cicely Hamilton who, along with Elizabeth Abbott and others, formed a group to fund a memorial to Chrystal after her death (see above), and Edith Picton-Turbervill accompanied Chrystal on the evening she was called to the Bar. As she said in her autobiography, 'women's strong attachments can be . . . as deep, as beautiful, and as exhilarating as any human relationship',[17] and from the little evidence we have, it would appear that these women certainly did care deeply about one another, as well as sharing a good deal in common.

MEMORIES OF AUNT CHRYS

One of Chrystal Macmillan's family visitors to her home in Pump Court was her niece Ialeen, the daughter of Norman, one of Chrystal's younger brothers. Looking back on her visits many years later, in 2010, Ialeen recalled her aunt as being 'rather intimidating', though she warmed to her later on and 'grew to have a high regard for her achievement' when she 'learned of her [Chrystal's] herculean strivings for peace during World War I'. Tellingly, Ialeen goes on to observe 'how strange that this most interesting phase of her career appears never to have been discussed within the family'.

Chrystal Macmillan apparently did her best to entertain her young niece, taking her to the National Gallery, helping her to make paper chains for Christmas decorations, and travelling with her in a cousin's chauffeur-driven limo to a Christmas luncheon in his enormous country mansion. When work prevented her aunt from spending time with her, Ialeen was left in the care of Mrs Edith Jones, the 'kindly housekeeper', who on one occasion indirectly precipitated a crisis:

> What I do remember is that although Mrs Jones offered to take me to Mass on Christmas Day this was *not* allowed. Instead, it was conveyed to me that I would be welcome to accompany Aunt Chrys to her church. When I declined Mrs Jones again had to act as intermediary and not a word ever passed between aunt and niece! Clearly our characters were more alike than one might have suspected![18]

Ialeen Gibson Cowan's last memory of her aunt was when Chrystal was in the London Clinic, recovering from having a leg amputated. The 12-year-old Ialeen was thoroughly intimidated by the visit, not least because she had been told by her mother to show Chrystal her school report, which included a 'quite uncharacteristically' poor result for RE, namely 0/100. Apparently, Chrystal was on good form and warmly congratulated her niece on the result, which, as Ialeen surmised, must have been because her aunt mistook the 0/100 for 100/100! Later, in a touching letter she wrote to her niece after moving to Edinburgh to convalesce, Chrystal reported that she was exercising her 'little leg', and making good progress. She died a few weeks later, in September 1937.[19]

CONCLUSION

In an observation 'by a woman journalist' in *The Scotsman*, regarding the forthcoming elections in November 1935, the point was made that election time was one of considerable strain for all candidates, but that

> It is not quite so bad for the man who has a sensible wife, who understands just how to follow the poor man up and administer nourishing food, insisting on short periods of rest and relaxation, fencing him off from interruption. For the bachelor candidates, the moral is obvious. But what of the women?[20]

In Chrystal Macmillan's case, having a housekeeper, private income and no husband certainly made the tasks she undertook, including standing for Parliament (see Chapter 3), much easier than for many women. Although she experienced the same frustrations, prejudices and setbacks encountered by most women in her world, she was fortunate in that she belonged to and was supported by a network of highly committed individuals with whom she shared similar aspirations and ambitions. She also had many close and constant friends with whom she obviously enjoyed escaping the rigours of working life to delight in moments of levity, often at her country retreat in Surrey.

Notes

1. *The Scotsman*, 24 Sept. 1937.
2. Ibid.
3. The prize was established from funds raised by family, friends and colleagues in her memory.
4. Middle Temple, *Chrystal Macmillan Memorial Prize. Chrystal Macmillan: Biographical Sketch* (London: Middle Temple, 1937), p. 7.

5. *Open Door* No. 21, Dec. 1937, p. 1.
6. *The Woman Teacher*, 1938.
7. The story of their efforts over the years is recorded in correspondence, most of which was between Elizabeth Abbott and William Macmillan, one of Chrystal's eight brothers. Letters held by Hugh Macmillan.
8. Marshall Freeman, *The Times* (obit.), 23 Sept. 1937.
9. *Open Door* No. 21, Dec. 1937, p. 1.
10. See Elizabeth Shafer, *Lilian Baylis: A Biography* (Hatfield: University of Hertfordshire Press and The Society for Theatre Research, 2006); Edith Picton-Turbervill, *Life Is Good: An Autobiography* (London: Frederick Muller, 1939); Lis Whitelaw, *The Life and Rebellious Times of Cicely Hamilton* (London: The Women's Press, 1990).
11. Shafer, *Lilian Baylis*.
12. Picton-Turbervill, *Life Is Good*.
13. Ibid.
14. Ialeen Gibson Cowan, personal recollections (2010).
15. Ibid.
16. Whitelaw, *The Life and Rebellious Times of Cicely Hamilton*.
17. Picton-Turbervill, *Life Is Good*.
18. Gibson Cowan, personal recollections.
19. Ibid.
20. *The Scotsman*, Nov. 1935.

10

Review and Conclusion

The young Chrystal Macmillan who stood at the Bar of the House of Lords in 1908 to address the Lord Chancellor, and accompanying Law Lords, was to become famous overnight. Perhaps surprisingly, that early experience of fame did not lead her to seek further public acclaim: rather, the experience inspired her to work for the rest of her life to challenge and seek change in the laws and circumstances that discriminated against women and denied them equality with men in so many spheres of activity.

On her appearance in the House of Lords, when she argued the claim of the Scottish women graduates to vote for the university candidate in Parliamentary elections, she gave evidence of being intellectually interested in the interpretation of laws. She learned from the judgement of the Lords that the law discriminated against women because laws were written by men for men's benefit, and that it was of no interest or concern to them that women had a different perspective. Once she had experienced the male bias in the administration of the law, this remarkable woman spent the rest of her life trying to redraft and reform legislation that discriminated against women, both nationally and internationally. Some campaigns resulted in a change in the law during her lifetime, notably women's right to vote in Parliamentary elections, but other campaigns, like the struggle to gain a married woman's right to independent nationality, took many more years to achieve: indeed, British legislation granting that right was not passed into law until 1948[1] and the International Convention on the Nationality of Married Women was not agreed until 1957, twenty years after her death.

REPRESENTATION OF WOMEN

Chrystal Macmillan was a long-serving member of the constitutional women's suffrage movement and believed in the power of reasoned argument to bring about change. She became aware that 'Extending the right to vote had never been simply a matter of weighing the arguments of principle; politicians were often much more concerned about the practical implications for their parties or for them as individual MPs.'[2] She realised that to bring about change to franchise legislation it was necessary to be persistent in keeping the issue at the forefront of people's minds, and to keep up the pressure on government and all the political parties until the governing party judged that the reform would not be disadvantageous to their party. That time came in 1928, with the passing of the Representation of the People (Equal Franchise) Act 1928, which finally gave all women over the age of 21 the right to vote in Parliamentary elections, with the same voting rights as men. Chrystal Macmillan joined with the women who attended the House of Lords in 1928 to hear the passing of the Act – an occasion which must have given them a great deal of pleasure.

All her life Chrystal Macmillan was concerned with the representation of women at the national and international levels. Unsurprisingly, statements of intent to end discrimination against women did not and still do not always lead to affirmative action. Chrystal Macmillan was alert to injustices arising from inaction, and took whatever steps she could to correct them. On the international front, an instance of this arose in connection with the constitution of the League of Nations. This stated that women were eligible for posts at all levels in the organisation, yet it remained difficult for women to gain proper representation:

> Our request for the appointment of another woman on the Permanent Mandates Commission has so far been unsuccessful. When ... this question was raised three years ago [we] were informed that the request could not be granted without altering the Constitution, which laid down the number of members as nine. Yet last year when the Mandates Commission was anxious to retain the services of their retiring Director, Dr. Rappard, the obstacle of numbers was not allowed to stand in the way, and Dr. Rappard joined the Committee as additional member with full voting powers.[3]

Chrystal Macmillan could not let this injustice go unremarked as she had a very clear vision that women should be equally involved in the international work of the League and that the women should not be allocated a role subservient to that of men. In response to a request from the Secretary General of the League of Nations for more cooperation from the women's organisations, she wrote that

> Full and equal cooperation means a great deal more than being asked to supply information, or mere doing of propaganda and educational work on a policy framed by bodies in which women are not included, or where they are in a very small minority, or inadequately represented. Full and equal cooperation involves the power of directing effective criticism to policies in course of formation, with an effective voice in determining what these policies shall be. It also involves adequate representation among those who administer these policies.[4]

COMMITTEE WORK FOR NATIONAL AND INTERNATIONAL ORGANISATIONS

Chrystal Macmillan was regularly on the EC of the various organisations and causes that she championed. Occasionally, she acted as an officebearer for a short period of time, as with the Scottish Women's Hospitals for Foreign Service and the Council for Representation of Women in the League of Nations. She supported the organisations until other women joined and took on the work, enabling her to back out and return to her other work.

She rarely took on the role of the leader of an organisation but was often the one who raised resolutions and watched over the organisation's constitutional issues: more importantly, she was the person who advised on how an issue could be tackled through a campaign for legislative reform. She has by some been described critically as a 'committee woman', but she was someone who always worked collaboratively, even when she disagreed with the majority view on the committee.

Chrystal Macmillan was ahead of her time in promoting an awareness of good governance within an organisation but her attention to the constitution and rules of procedure was not always appreciated by other members of the committees:

> The argument as to whether the release to the press sanctioned by the officers and the statement to the NAC approved by the special executive had in fact modified National Union policy and were therefore ultra vires, continued to rumble away, characteristically troubling Chrystal Macmillan, in her valuable if irritating role of constitutional watchdog, more than it did anyone else.[5]

Although she worked mainly with organisations in Britain, some of her work combined local campaigning with committee work for their international counterparts. For example, she worked with both the NUWW and the ICW; the NUWSS and the IWSA; the Women's International League and the WILPF; the ODC and the ODI; the NMWPBC and the League of Nations Consultative Committee on the Nationality of Married Women. She was unusual in being a committee member of all three main WIOs, the ICW, the IWSA and the WILPF, at times working for all three organisations simultaneously, which illustrates her commitment to the overarching principle of seeking justice and equality for women wherever they might live, rather than to loyalty to one particular organisation to the exclusion of others.[6]

Figure 10.1 Portrait, Chrystal Macmillan, ODI Conference, Prague, 1933 (courtesy John Herdman)

Her work in Britain for the NUWSS was surpassed by her commitment to work for the IWSA. She was an active member of IWSA from 1908 to 1937 and was appreciated as 'among its ablest and most single-minded leaders'.[7] This sustained commitment over a period of nearly thirty years of working for an international women's committee was unusual: her interest may be explained by the fellowship and the challenges she enjoyed when working with women from many countries.

The following tribute to her from the IWSA shows both their respect for her character and her propensity for hard work but also an awareness of her weaknesses:

> Her activities in the women's movement were so varied, that it might almost be said that she took part in every effort made to improve women's status, and there can hardly be a woman's society which has not at some time or other had the benefit of her advice and help, which was also given freely to individuals, especially in connection with the heart-rending personal problems with which so many women married to other nationalities are faced. Her single-mindedness, her undeviating adherence to principle, her inability to understand mere compromise were sometimes misunderstood and occasionally led her colleagues to fail to recognise her very real desire to see the other point of view. But in the end, everyone who had the privilege of working with her, learnt to place their entire confidence in her.[8]

Chrystal Macmillan was always a committed internationalist. During the First World War, she displayed none of the patriotic nationalism of some of her colleagues in the suffrage movement, especially evident in statements by her NUWSS colleague Millicent Fawcett. As secretary of WILPF, she was the first woman to encourage Japanese women to join the organisation, and toward the end of the War in 1918, she surprised her friend Eunice Murray by declaring her commitment to immediate self-determination for the people of India.

WORKING FOR INTERNATIONAL PEACE

In the first decade of the twentieth century, the WIOs supported committees working for international friendship and peace. Chrystal Macmillan was one of those women who held an internationalist perspective.

In 1915 she was one of the main organisers of the International Women's Congress held at The Hague, which attracted 1,200 women from twelve countries. The women travelled across war-torn Europe, or journeyed across the Atlantic from the USA and Canada, despite submarine activity, to join with other women to study ways to avoid war. Both in 1915 and 1919, Chrystal Macmillan acted as chair of the committee which managed the proposed resolutions from women in different countries and wrote the final report of 1915 Congress, which included the twenty resolutions passed by the Congress (Appendix 2).

Throughout the summer of 1915, she and her five colleagues displayed much bravery and considerable diplomatic skill as they travelled to every European country, and the USA, meeting with political leaders in an effort to establish a mediated settlement of the conflict. On her return to Britain, she displayed none of the patriotic nationalism of some of her colleagues in the women's international organisations, especially evident in statements by her NUWSS president, Millicent Fawcett.

As secretary and organiser of their early Congresses, Chrystal Macmillan made a significant contribution to the establishment of the WILPF, the oldest active women's peace organisation. She helped establish a sound constitution for the organisation, which continues to campaign today for the peaceful settlement of international disputes and works to encourage the development of systems of government which promote peaceful international relations.

WOMEN'S CITIZENSHIP

The concept underpinning all of Chrystal Macmillan's work was the right of a woman to claim full rights as a citizen of her country.[9] Many of the campaigns she worked on focused on the right to be treated fairly as an acknowledged citizen under the law, whether that was a woman's right to vote or the right of a married woman to her own nationality, independent of her husband.

When Chrystal Macmillan had the vision to draft a Women's Charter in 1919 (see Chapter 6), women had none of the rights demanded in the document, but she was able to outline a path to a future in which women would be equal and active citizens in political and public life. Undoubtedly, she would have taken great pleasure in the fact that many of the rights denied to women in 1919 have since been achieved through women's campaigning over the years.

On the international front, she sought to achieve greater engagement of women in international affairs, recommending the establishment of an International Women's Office which, although it took many years to achieve, does now exist within the United Nations. Nevertheless, her vision of equality has yet to be realised and will take some more years to achieve, as has been acknowledged in a recent UN statement:

> Women's equal participation and leadership in political and public life are essential to achieving the Sustainable Development Goals by 2030. However, data show that women are underrepresented at all levels of decision-making worldwide and that achieving gender parity in political life is far off.[10]

CONCLUSION

Chrystal Macmillan was a remarkable Scotswoman who was in the forefront of women's struggle for equality in the first half of the twentieth century. She campaigned throughout Scotland for women's suffrage and worked on several British and international committees committed to women's equality. Her understanding of legal argument allowed her to negotiate with men of influence in law and politics, in Britain and internationally, including the administrative and political leaders at the League.

Chrystal Macmillan not only challenged the gendered inequities in laws but showed the reasons why they should be reformed and often gave examples of how the law could be made more equitable. Her work on British and international law contributed to the reform of legislation to take account of women's lives and women's work, leading to her being assessed as 'perhaps the closest thing to a prominent feminist international lawyer of the time'.[11]

Notes

1. Kay and Pipes, 'British Nationality Act 1948', pp. 233–9.
2. Pugh, *Votes for Women in Britain 1867–1928*, p. 16.
3. 'Representation of Women in League of Nations', *Annual Report*. Council for Representation of Women in the League of Nations (London: Women's Library, LSE, 1926).
4. 'League of Nations and Women's Cooperation'. Memorandum by ODI in *The Open Door 9*, Aug. 1932, p. 30.
5. Vellacott, *From Liberal to Labour with Women's Suffrage*.
6. Leila Rupp and Verta Taylor, 'Forging a Feminist Identity in an International Movement: A Collective Identity Approach to Twentieth Century Feminism', *Signs* 24.2 (Winter 1999), p. 370.
7. *International Women's News* 32.1, Oct. 1937, p. 2.
8. Ibid.

9. A study of citizenship which discusses Chrystal Macmillan's work on the nationality of married women: Helen Irving, *Citizenship, Alienage and the Modern Constitutional State: A Gendered History* (Cambridge: Cambridge University Press, 2016).
10. 'Facts and figures: Women's Leadership and Political Participation', 2023 UN Women, https://www.unwomen.org/en/what-we-do/leadership-and-political-participation/facts-and-figures#:~:text=Women%27s%20equal%20participation%20and%20leadership,political%20life%20is%20far%20off (underline in original).
11. Knop and Chinkin, 'Remembering Chrystal Macmillan'.

Appendix 1
Chrystal Macmillan's Membership of Committees, and Select Committees to which she gave evidence

NATIONAL AND INTERNATIONAL COMMITTEES

Association of Moral and Social Hygiene
   Executive Committee January 1917–March 1923
   Sub-committee: Police Court Rota 1917–19
   Sub-committee for Foreign Affairs 1921
Committee for the Opening of the Legal Profession to Women 1916–19
Committee of Women Graduates of Scottish Universities
   Secretary and Treasurer 1906–8
Consultative Committee of Constitutional Women's Suffrage Societies 1916–18
Council for Representation of Women in the League of Nations
   Vice-president 1921–2
Edinburgh National Women's Suffrage Union
   Member
   Honorary Vice-president 1915
International Committee for Action on Nationality of Married Women
   Chair 1930–1
International Council of Women
   British Representative ICW Standing Committee Legal Position of Women 1915
   National Council of Women formerly known as National Union of Women Workers
      Hon. Sec. Standing Committee of Scottish Federation 1904–16
      Executive Committee Member 1917–21
International Labour Organisation
   Correspondence Committee on Women's Work 1932
   Panel of Experts 1933
International Women Suffrage Alliance
   Recording Secretary 1913–20

    Chairman of the Headquarters Committee 1914–18
    Coordinator International Women's Relief Committee 1914–15
    Organiser of Geneva Congress 1921
        Vice-president (1921–3)
    Chair British Overseas Committee 1923
    Chair Standing Committee on Nationality of Married Women 1920–37
League of Nations: Women's Consultative Committee on Nationality 1931–4
National Council for Unmarried Mother and Her Child
    Legal Sub-committee 1918–24
        Chair of Legal Subcommittee was Robert Newton Crane – who sponsored her Middle Temple Application
    CM worked with Clarke Hall on amendments to Guardianship of Children Bill
National Union of Societies for Equal Citizenship
    Executive Committee 1919–24
        NUSEC Economic Independence of Women Subcommittee 1919–21
        NUSEC Equal Franchise Special Committee 1922
        NUSEC Equal Moral Standard Committee 1919–21
        NUSEC Married Women (Parliamentary Bills) Committee 1924–6: Chair
            Married Women (Torts) Bill 1924
            Coverture Disabilities (Abolition) Bill 1925
            Women Jurors Bill 1926
        NUSEC Status of Wives and Mothers Committee 1921–4
        NUSEC Widows Pensions and Equal Guardianship Committee 1919–21
National Union of Women's Suffrage Societies
    Executive Committee 1910–18
Nationality of Married Women Pass the Bill Committee
    Chair and Coordinator 1930–7
Open Door Council
    Member of Executive Committee 1923–9
Open Door International
    President 1929–37
Scottish Churches League for Woman Suffrage
    Member of General Council 1913
Scottish Federation of Women's Suffrage Societies
    Member 1909
    Chair 1914–15
Scottish University Women's Suffrage Union
    Secretary 1913
Scottish Women's Hospitals for Foreign Service
    Chair October 1914
Women's International League for Peace and Freedom (formerly known as International Committee of Women for Permanent Peace)
    Secretary 1915–20

Chair Resolutions Committee 1915–19
CM resigned WILPF EC to organise IWSA Congress in Geneva 1921
Member Women's International League (UK WILPF) 1922–6
Member of British Council of Women's International League (UK WILPF) 1925–8

GAVE EVIDENCE TO

Select Committee on the Guardianship of Infants 1922
Joint Select Committee on the Nationality of Married Women 1923
Street Offences Committee 1928
Committee on the Powers of Ministers and Delegated Legislation 1929
  Royal Commission on Unemployment Insurance 1932

Appendix 2
Twenty Resolutions from the International Women's Congress 1915

RESOLUTIONS ADOPTED BY THE INTERNATIONAL CONGRESS OF WOMEN
THE HAGUE, HOLLAND APRIL 28-29-30, 1915

I. WOMEN AND WAR

1. PROTEST

We women, in International congress assembled, protest against the madness and the horror of war, involving as it does a reckless sacrifice of human life and the destruction of so much that humanity has laboured through centuries to build up.

2. WOMEN'S SUFFERINGS IN WAR

This International Congress of Women opposes the assumption that women can be protected under the conditions of modern warfare. It protests vehemently against the odious wrongs of which women are the victims in time of war, and especially against the horrible violation of women which attends all war.

II. TOWARDS PEACE

3. THE PEACE SETTLEMENT

This International Congress of Women of different nations, classes, creeds and parties is united in expressing sympathy with the suffering of all, whatever their nationality, who are fighting for their country or laboring under the burden of **war**.

Since the mass of the people in each of the countries now at war believe themselves to be fighting, not as aggressors but in self-defense and for their national existence, there can be no irreconcilable differences between them, and their common ideals afford a basis upon which a magnanimous and honourable peace might be established. The congress therefore urges the governments of the world to put an end to this bloodshed, and to begin peace negotiations. It demands that the peace which follows shall be permanent and therefore based on principles of justice, including those laid down in the resolutions[1] adopted by this congress, namely:

That no territory should be transferred without the consent of the men and women in it, and that the right of conquest should not be recognized.

That autonomy and a democratic parliament should not be refused to any people.

That the governments of all nations should come to an agreement to refer future international disputes to arbitration or conciliation and to bring social, moral and economic pressure to bear upon any country which resorts to arms.

That foreign politics should be subject to democratic control.

That women should be granted equal political rights with men.

4. CONTINUOUS MEDIATION

This International Congress of Women resolves to ask the neutral countries to take immediate steps to create a conference of neutral nations which shall without delay offer continuous mediation. The conference shall invite suggestions for settlement from each of the belligerent nations and in any case shall submit to all of them simultaneously reasonable proposals as a basis of peace.

III. PRINCIPLES OF A PERMANENT PEACE

5. RESPECT FOR NATIONALITY

This International Congress of Women, recognizing the right of the people to self-government, affirms that there should be no[2] transference of territory without the consent of the men and women residing therein, and urges that autonomy and a democratic parliament should not be refused to any people.

6. ARBITRATION AND CONCILIATION

This International Congress of Women, believing that war is the negation of progress and civilization, urges the governments of all nations to come to an agreement to refer future international disputes to arbitration and conciliation.

7. INTERNATIONAL PRESSURE

This International Congress of Women urges the governments of all nations to come to an agreement to unite in bringing social, moral and economic pressure to bear upon any country, which resorts to arms instead of referring its case to arbitration or conciliation.

8. DEMOCRATIC CONTROL OF FOREIGN POLICY

Since war is commonly brought about not by the mass of the people, who do not desire it, but by groups representing particular interests, this International Congress of Women urges that foreign politics shall be subject to democratic control; and declares that it can only recognize as democratic a system which includes the equal representation of men and women.

9. THE ENFRANCHISEMENT OF WOMEN

Since the combined influence of the women of all countries is one of the strongest forces for the prevention of war, and since women can only have full responsibility and effective influence when they have equal political rights with men, this International Congress of Women demands their political enfranchisement.

IV. INTERNATIONAL CO-OPERATION

10. THIRD HAGUE CONFERENCE

This International Congress of Women urges that a third Hague Conference be convened immediately after the war.

11. INTERNATIONAL ORGANIZATION

This International Congress of Women urges that the organization of the Society of Nations should be further developed on the basis of a constructive peace, and that it should include:

a. As a development of the Hague Court of Arbitration, a permanent International Court of Justice to settle questions or differences of a justiciable character such as arise on the interpretation of treaty rights or of the law of nations.

b. As a development of the constructive work of the Hague Conference, a permanent International Conference holding regular meetings in which women should take part, to deal not with the rules of warfare but with practical proposals for further international co-operation among the states.

This conference should be so constituted that it could formulate and enforce those principles of justice, equity and good will in accordance with which the struggles of subject communities could be more fully recognized and the interests and rights not only of the great powers and small nations but also those of weaker countries and primitive peoples gradually adjusted under an en lightened international public opinion. This International Conference shall appoint:

A permanent Council of Conciliation and Investigation for the settlement of international differences arising from economic competition, expanding commerce, increasing population and changes in social and political standards.

12. GENERAL DISARMAMENT

The International Congress of Women, advocating universal disarmament and realizing that it can only be secured by international agreement, urges, as a step to this end, that all countries should, by such an international agreement, take over the manufacture of arms and munitions of war and should control all international traffic in the same. It sees in the private profits accruing from the great armament factories a powerful hindrance to the abolition of war.

13. COMMERCE AND INVESTMENTS

a. The International Congress of Women urges that in all countries there shall be liberty of commerce, that the seas shall be free and the trade routes open on equal terms to the shipping of all nations.

b. Inasmuch as the investment by capitalists of one country in the resources of another and the claims arising there from are a fertile source of international complications, this International Congress of Women urges the widest possible acceptance of the principle that such investments shall be made at the risk of the investor, without claim to the official protection of his government.

14. NATIONAL FOREIGN POLICY

a. This International Congress of Women demands that all secret treaties shall be void and that for the ratification of future treaties, the participation of at least the legislature of every government shall be necessary.

b. This International Congress of Women recommends that National Commissions be created and International Conferences convened for the scientific study and elaboration of the principles and conditions of permanent peace, which might contribute to the development of an International Federation.

These commissions and conferences should be recognized by the governments and should include women in their deliberations.

15. WOMEN IN NATIONAL AND INTERNATIONAL POLITICS

This International Congress of Women declares it to be essential, both nationally and internationally, to put into practice the principle that women should share all civil and political rights and responsibilities on the same terms as men.

V. THE EDUCATION OF CHILDREN

16. This International Congress of Women urges the necessity of so directing the education of children that their thoughts and desires may be directed towards the ideal of constructive peace.

VI. WOMEN AND THE PEACE SETTLEMENT

17. This International Congress of Women urges that in the interests of lasting peace and civilization the conference which shall frame the peace settlement after the war should pass a resolution affirming the need in all countries of extending the parliamentary franchise to women.

18. This International Congress of Women urges that representatives of the people should take part in the conference that shall frame the peace settlement after the war, and claims that amongst them women should be included.

VII. ACTION TO BE TAKEN

19. WOMEN'S VOICE IN THE PEACE SETTLEMENT

This International Congress of Women resolves that an international meeting of women shall be held in the same place and at the same time as the Conference of the Powers which shall frame the terms of the peace settlement after the war for the purpose of presenting practical proposals to that **conference.**

20. ENVOYS TO THE GOVERNMENTS

In order to urge the governments of the world to put an end to this bloodshed and to establish a just and lasting peace, this International Congress of Women delegates envoys to carry the message expressed in the congress resolutions to the rulers of the belligerent and neutral nations of Europe and to the President of the United States.

These envoys shall be women of both neutral and belligerent nations, appointed by the International Committee of this congress. They shall report the result of their missions to the International Women's Committee for Constructive Peace as a basis for further action.

---

[1] NOTE. The resolutions in full are Nos. 5, 6, 7, 8, 9.

[2] NOTE. The congress declared by vote that it interpreted no transference of territory without the consent of the men and women in it to imply that the right of conquest was not to be recognized.

Appendix 3
List of visits undertaken by Women Envoys in 1915

Date	Place	Minister	Name of Minister	WILPF Women
1915				
		Belligerent Countries		
7 May	The Hague	PM	Cort van der Linden	JA, AJ, RG, CM, RS
13 May	London	FM	Sir Edward Grey	JA, AJ, RG
14 May	London	PM	Asquith	JA, AJ, RG
21 May	Berlin	FM	Von Jagow	JA, AJ
22 May	Berlin	Reichskanzler (Imperial Chancellor)	Von Bethmann Hollweg	JA
26 May	Vienna	PM	von Sturgkh	JA, AJ
27 May	Vienna	FM	von Burian	JA, AJ
30 May	Buda Pesth	PM	von Tisza	JA
2 June	Berne	FM	Hoffmann	JA, AJ
4 June	Rome	FM	Sonnino	JA, AJ
5 June	Rome	PM	Salandra	JA, AJ
8 June	Rome	The pope		JA, AJ
12 June	Paris	FM	Delcasse	JA, AJ
14 June	Paris	PM	Viviani	JA, AJ
16 June	Havre	FM (Belgium)	D'Avignon	JA, AJ
		Neutral Countries		
28 May	Copenhagen	PM	Zahle	EB, CM, C R-H, RS
		FM	Scavenius	
31 May	Christiana	King	Haakon	EB, CM, C R-H, RS
		FM	Ihlen	

Date	Place	Minister	Name of Minister	WILPF Women
1 June	Christiana	PM	Knudsen	EB, CM, C R-H, RS
2 June	Stockholm	FM	Wallenberg	EB, CM, C R-H, RS
16 June	Petrograd	FM	Sazonoff	EB, CM, BEP, C R-H
26 June	Stockholm	FM	Wallenberg	EB, CM, BEP, C R-H
30 June	Christiana	FM	Ihlen	CM
30 June	The Hague	PM	Cort van der Linden	AJ, RS
7 July	The Hague	PM	Cort van der Linden	AJ, EB, CM, C R-H, RS
8 July	The Hague	FM	Loudon	AJ, EB, CM, C R-H, RS
August	USA	President	Wilson	JA, AJ

Note: Nine prime ministers (PM), fourteen foreign ministers (FM), two presidents, one king, one pope. AJ = Aletta Jacobs; BEP = Baroness Ellen Palmstierna; CM = Chrystal Macmillan; C R-H = Cor Ramondt-Hirschman; EB = Emily Balch; JA = Jane Addams; RG = Rosa Genoni; RS = Rosika Schwimmer.

Bibliography

PRIMARY SOURCES: ARCHIVES, NEWSPAPERS, JOURNALS AND PERIODICALS

Archival sources

Aletta Jacobs papers: Atria Institute on Gender Equality and Women's History: Amsterdam
Alice Paul papers: Schlesinger Library, Harvard University
Association of Moral and Social Hygiene papers: Women's Library, LSE
Bar Council Minute Books: Institute of Advanced Legal Studies
Bonar Law papers: Parliamentary Archive, House of Lords
British Federation of University Women papers: Women's Library, LSE
British Newspaper Archive
Catherine Marshall Papers, Cumbria Archive: Carlisle
Central Criminal Court Bar Mess register: London Metropolitan Archive
Company of Merchants Archive: Edinburgh
Consultative Committee of Constitutional Women's Suffrage Societies Papers: Women's Library, LSE
Doris Stevens papers: Schlesinger Library: Harvard University
Edinburgh University Court Minutes: Special Collections, Edinburgh University Library
Elizabeth Wolstenholme Elmy papers: British Library
Equal Rights International papers: Women's Library, LSE
Girton Archive: Cambridge
Gude Cause Archive: National Library of Scotland, Edinburgh
Helena Normanton papers: Women's Library, LSE
Institute of Advanced Legal Studies Archive: London
International Labour Organisation Archive: Geneva
International Woman Suffrage Alliance papers: Manchester Public Archive
International Woman Suffrage Alliance papers: Rylands Library, University of Manchester

League of Nations Archive: Geneva
Macmillan Family papers
Minute Books of the Western Circuit: Hampshire Archive
National Council for the Unmarried Mother and Her Child papers: Women's Library, LSE
National Union of Societies for Equal Citizenship papers: Women's Library, LSE
National Union of Women's Suffrage Societies papers: Women's Library, LSE
National Union of Women Workers papers: City of Edinburgh Archive
National Union of Women Workers papers: London Metropolitan Archive
Nationality of Married Women Pass the Bill Committee papers: Women's Library, LSE
Open Door International papers: British Library, London
Parliamentary Archives: House of Lords, London
Records of County of London Sessions Courts: London Metropolitan Archive
Scottish Federation of Women's Suffrage Societies papers: Mitchell Library, Glasgow
Scottish Women's Liberal Federation papers: National Library of Scotland, Edinburgh
TUC Library Archive: Metropolitan University, London
Western Circuit Records: National Record Office, Kew
Women's International League for Peace and Freedom Archive: University of Colorado, Boulder
Women's International League for Peace and Freedom papers: Women's Library, LSE

Newspapers

Aberdeen Press & Journal
Bath Chronicle & Weekly Gazette
Birmingham Daily Gazette
Daily Chronicle
Daily Mirror
Dumfries & Galloway Standard
Dundee Courier
Dundee Evening Telegraph
Edinburgh Evening News
Greenock Telegraph & Clyde Shipping Gazette
Linlithgowshire Gazette
Liverpool Echo
London Evening Standard
Manchester Courier and Lancashire General Advertiser
Midlothian Journal
Northern Whig
Nottingham Evening Post

Orkney Herald & Weekly Advertiser
Shetland News
Shetland Times
St Andrews Citizen
The Observer
The Orcadian
The Queen
The Scotsman
The Times
Western Times
Yorkshire Post and Leeds Intelligencer

Journals

Graya
Internationaal
International Journal of the Legal Profession
International Labour Review
International Organization
International Woman Suffrage News (formerly *Jus Suffragii*)
Journal of British Studies
Journal of Comparative Legislation and International Law
Journal of International Women's Studies
Journal of the Church League for Women's Suffrage
Journal of Women's History
Juridical Review
Jus Suffragii (renamed *International Woman Suffrage News* 1 January 1917)
Legal Studies
Michigan Journal of International Law
Notre Dame Law Review
Official Journal of the League of Nations
The Common Cause
The Englishwoman
The Middle Templar
The New Statesman
The Open Door
The Shield
The Spectator
The Survey
The Vote
The Woman Teacher
The Women's Leader
Time & Tide
Toward Permanent Peace

Votes for Women
Women's Franchise
Women's History Review
Women's Suffrage Record

PUBLISHED BOOKS AND ARTICLES

Note: Ewan et al., *The New Biographical Dictionary of Scottish Women* (see below) contains entries on many of the women referred to in this book, including Chrystal Macmillan.

Abbott, Elizabeth. 'Obituary'. *The Shield* 5.3 (December 1937), pp. 134–5.

Addams, Jane, Balch, Emily and Hamilton, Alice. *Women at The Hague: The International Peace Congress of 1915*. New York: Humanity Books, 1915, repr. 2003.

Auchmuty, Rosemary. 'Whatever Happened to Miss Bebb? Bebb v. The Law Society and Women's Legal History'. *Legal Studies* 31.2 (June 2011), pp. 199–230.

Baldwin, M. P. 'Subject to Empire: Married Women and the British Nationality and Status of Aliens Act'. *Journal of British Studies* 40.4 (2001), pp. 522–56.

Bates, Victoria. *Sexual Forensics in Victorian and Edwardian England: Age, Crime and Consent in Courts*. London: Palgrave Macmillan, 2016.

Beale, Dorothea, Soulsby, Lucy H. M. and Dove, Jane Frances (eds). *Work & Play in Girls' Schools by Three Headmistresses*. London: Longmans Green, 1898.

Bean, Mary Jean Woodward. *Julia Grace Wales: Canada's Hidden Heroine and the Quest for Peace 1914–1918*. Nepean, ON: Borealis Press, 2005.

Berry, P. and Bishop, A. (eds). *Testament of a Generation: The Journalism of Vera Brittain and Winifred Holtby*. London: Virago, 1985.

Bird, John Clement. 'Control of Enemy Alien Civilians in Great Britian 1914–1918'. PhD thesis, LSE, 1981.

Bourne, Judith. *Helena Normanton and the Opening of the Bar to Women*. Hook, Hampshire: Waterside Press, 2016.

Bourne, Judith. 'The Vanishing Act of Miss Bertha Cave'. *Graya* 133 (2020), pp. 29–38.

Boussahba-Bravard, M. (ed.). *Suffrage outside Suffragism: Women's Vote in Britain 1880–1914*. Basingstoke: Palgrave Macmillan, 2007.

Breitenbach, Esther. 'Edinburgh Suffragists: Exercising the Franchise at Local Level'. *Book of the Old Edinburgh Club New Series* 15 (2019), pp. 63–80.

Breitenbach, E. and Thane, P. (eds). *Women and Citizenship in Britain and Ireland in the Twentieth Century*. London: Continuum International Publishing Group, 2021.

Brittain, Vera. 'Committees versus Professions' (1929). In Paul Berry and Alan Bishop (eds), *Testament of a Generation: The Journalism of Vera Brittain and Winifred Holtby*, pp. 105–8. London: Virago, 1985.

Brown, Heloise. *The Truest Form of Patriotism: Pacifist Feminism in Britain, 1870–1902*. Manchester: Manchester University Press, 2003.

Burness, Catriona. 'Count up to Twenty-one: Scottish Women in Formal Politics, 1918–1990'. In Esther Breitenbach and Pat Thane (eds), *Women and Citizenship in Britain and Ireland in the Twentieth Century*, pp. 151–73. London: Continuum International Publishing Group, 2010.

Burton, Antoinette. *Burdens of History: British Feminists, Indian Women & Imperial Culture 1865–1915*. Chapel Hill and London: University of North Carolina Press, 1994.

Bush, Julia. 'The National Union of Women Workers and Women's Suffrage'. In M. Boussahba-Bravard (ed.), *Suffrage outside Suffragism: Women's Vote in Britain 1880–1914*, pp. 105–31. Basingstoke: Palgrave Macmillan, 2007.

Bussey, Gertrude and Tims, Margaret. *Women's International League for Peace & Freedom 1915–1965: A Record of Fifty Years' Work*. London: Allen & Unwin, 1965.

Cairns, Catriona. 'First Woman Member of the Faculty of Advocates, Margaret Kidd, 1923'. In Erika Rackley and Rosemary Auchmuty (eds), *Women's Legal Landmarks: Celebrating the History of Women and Law in the UK and Ireland*, pp. 195–9. Oxford: Hart Publishing, 2019.

Cooley, Winifred Harper. 'The Internationalism of the International'. *Jus Suffragii*, 15 July 1913, p. 6.

Cooper, Sandi. 'Women's Participation in European Peace Movements: The Struggle to Prevent Wold War I'. In R. R. Pierson (ed.), *Women and Peace: Theoretical, Historical and Practical Perspectives*, pp. 51–75. Beckenham: Croom Helm, 1987.

Cowan, D. *St Leonards School Gazette* (obit.), November, 1937.

Crawford, Elizabeth. *Enterprising Women: The Garretts and Their Circle*. London: Francis Boutle, 2002.

Crawford, Elizabeth. 'Scotland'. In *The Women's Suffrage Movement in Britain and Ireland: A Regional Survey*, pp. 225–51. Abingdon: Routledge, 2006.

Crozier-De Rosa, Sharon. 'Emotions and Empire in Suffrage and Anti-suffrage Politics: Britain, Ireland and Australia in the Early Twentieth Century'. In Alexandra Hughes-Johnson and Lyndsey Jenkins (eds), *The Politics of Women's Suffrage: Local, National and International Dimensions*, pp. 309–30. London: Royal Historical Society, Institute of Historical Research, University of London Press, 2021.

DiCenzo, Maria. 'Unity and Dissent: Official Organs of the Suffrage Campaign'. In Maria DiCenzo, Lucy Delap and Leila Ryan (eds), *Feminist Media History Suffrage, Periodicals and the Public Sphere*, pp. 76–119. London: Palgrave Macmillan, 2011.

Donaldson, G. (ed.). *Four Centuries: Edinburgh University Life, 1583–1983.* Edinburgh: Edinburgh University Press, 1983.

Dove, Jane Frances. 'Cultivation of the Body'. In Dorothea Beale, Lucy H. M. Soulsby and Jane Frances Dove (eds), *Work & Play in Girls' Schools by Three Headmistresses*, pp. 369–423. London: Longmans Green, 1898.

Dubois, Ellen Carol. 'Internationalizing Married Women's Nationality: The Hague Campaign of 1930'. In Karen Offen (ed.), *Globalizing Feminisms 1789–1945*, pp. 204–16. London: Routledge, 2010.

Ewan, E., Innes, S., Pipes, R. and Reynolds, S. *The Biographical Dictionary of Scottish Women.* Edinburgh: Edinburgh University Press, 2006.

Ewan, E., Pipes, R., Rendall, J. and Reynolds, S. *The New Biographical Dictionary of Scottish Women.* Edinburgh: Edinburgh University Press, 2018.

Finley, Lucinda M. 'Breaking Women's Silence in Law: The Dilemma of the Gendered Nature of Legal Reasoning'. *Notre Dame Law Review* 64 (1989), pp. 886–910.

Gates, G. E. (ed.) *The Woman's Year Book 1923–1924.* London: Women Publishers, n.d.

Gillespie, T. H. *The Story of Edinburgh Zoo.* Slains, Aberdeenshire: Michael Slains, 1964.

Gilman, Charlotte Perkins. 'The Wonders of an International Congress of Women'. *Jus Suffragii* 7.10, 15 July 1913.

Grant, Julia, McCutcheon, K. and Sanders, E. (eds). *St Leonards School 1877–1927.* London: Oxford University Press, n.d.

Hamilton, Sheila. 'The First Generations of University Women 1869–1930'. In Gordon Donaldson (ed.), *Four Centuries: Edinburgh University Life, 1583–1983*, pp. 99–115. Edinburgh: Edinburgh University Press, 1983.

Harwood, Anthony. *Circuit Ghosts: A Western Circuit Miscellany.* Winchester: The Western Circuit, 1980.

Holton, Sandra Stanley. *Feminism and Democracy: Women's Suffrage and Reform Politics in Britain, 1900–1918.* Cambridge: Cambridge University Press, 2002.

Hughes-Johnson, A. and Jenkins, L. (eds). *The Politics of Women's Suffrage: Local, National & International Dimensions.* London: Royal Historical Society, Institute of Historical Research, University of London Press, 2021.

Hume, Leslie Parker. *The National Union of Women's Suffrage Societies.* New York and London: Garland Publishing, 1982.

International Women's Committee for Permanent Peace. *Report of International Congress of Women The Hague April 1915.* Amsterdam: ICWPP, 1915.

Irving, Helen. *Citizenship, Alienage, and the Modern Constitutional State: A Gendered History.* Cambridge: Cambridge University Press, 2016.

Jacques, Catherine. 'Tracking Feminist Intervention in International Law Issues at the League of Nations: From the Nationality of Married Women to Legal Equality in the Family 1919–1970'. In Sara Kimble and Marion Röwekamp (eds), *New Perspectives on European Women's Legal History*, pp. 321–48. London: Routledge, 2017.

Kay, Helen. 'Chrystal Macmillan: From Edinburgh Woman to Global Citizen'. *DEP*. https://www.unive.it/pag/fileadmin/user_upload/dipartimenti/DSLCC/documenti/DEP/numeri/n18-19/09_18e19_-Kay.pdf.

Kay, Helen. Fifteen Questions about Chrystal Macmillan. https://www.sps.ed.ac.uk/sites/default/files/assets/pdf/Fifteen_questions_about_Chrystal_Macmillan_ILW.pdf. 2012.

Kay, Helen. 'Remembering Chrystal Macmillan: Challenging Authority, Championing Equality'. https://dangerouswomenproject.org/2016/03/24/chrystal-macmillan/. 2016.

Kay, Helen and Pipes, Rose. 'British Nationality Act 1948'. In Erika Rackley and Rosemary Auchmuty (eds), *Women's Legal Landmarks: Celebrating the History of Women and Law in the UK and Ireland*, pp. 233–41. Oxford: Hart Publishing, 2019.

Kay, Helen and Pipes, Rose. 'Chrystal Macmillan, Scottish Campaigner for Women's Equality through Law Reform'. *Women's History Review* 29.4 (2020), pp. 716–36.

Kimble, Sara and Röwekamp, Marion (eds). *New Perspectives on European Women's Legal History*. London: Routledge, 2017.

King, Elspeth. 'The Scottish Women's Suffrage Movement'. In Esther Breitenbach and Eleanor Gordon (eds), *Out of Bounds: Women in Scottish Society 1800–1945*, pp. 121–50. Edinburgh: Edinburgh University Press, 1992.

Knight, H. *Journal of the Church League for Women's Suffrage*. London: The Church League, 1917.

Knop, Karen and Chinkin, Christine. 'Remembering Chrystal Macmillan: Women's Equality and Nationality in International Law'. *Michigan Journal of International Law* 22.4 (2001), pp. 523–85.

Laite, Julia Ann. 'The Association for Moral and Social Hygiene: Abolitionism and Prostitution Law in Britain, 1915–1959'. *Women's History Review* 17.2 (2008), pp. 207–23.

Lammasniemi, Leah. 'Regulation 40D: Punishing Promiscuity on the Home Front during the First World War'. *Women's History Review* 26.4 (2017), pp. 584–96.

Laqua, D. (ed.). *Internationalism Reconfigured: Transnational Ideas and Movements between the World Wars*. London: I. B. Tauris, 2011.

Law, Cheryl. *Suffrage and Power: The Women's Movement 1918–1928*. London: I. B. Tauris, 2000.

Leneman, Leah. *A Guid Cause: The Women's Suffrage Movement in Scotland*. Aberdeen: Aberdeen University Press, 1991.

Leneman, Leah. 'When Women Were Not "Persons": The Scottish Women Graduates' Case, 1906–8'. *Juridical Review* (1991), pp. 109–18.

Lindsay, Alison. 'First Woman Law Agent, Madge Easton Anderson, 1920'. In Erika Rackley and Rosemary Auchmuty (eds), *Women's Legal Landmarks: Celebrating the History of Women and Law in the UK and Ireland*, pp. 161–7. Oxford: Hart Publishing, 2019.

Lockwood, Carol, Magraw, Daniel, Spring, Margaret and Strong, S. I. (eds). *The International Human Rights of Women: Instruments of Change*. Washington, DC: American Bar Association, Section of International Law and Practice, 1998.

Lumsden, Louisa. *On Higher Education of Women in Great Britain and Ireland*. Aberdeen: J. & J. P. Edmond & Spark, 1884.

Macmillan, Chrystal. *The Struggle for Political Liberty*. London: WSPU, 1909.

Macmillan, Chrystal. *Facts versus Fancies on Woman Suffrage*. London: NUWSS & King, 1914.

Macmillan, Chrystal. 'Nationality of Married Women'. *Jus Suffragii* 11.1, October 1916.

Macmillan, Chrystal. *And Shall I Have a Parliamentary Vote?* London: NUWSS, 1918.

Macmillan, Chrystal. *A New Danger: Departmental Orders versus Legislation for Venereal Disease*. London: Association for Moral and Social Hygiene, 1919.

Macmillan, Chrystal. 'The Feminist Movement in Spain'. *Jus Suffragii* 14.4, 1920, p. 50.

Macmillan, Chrystal. 'The Future of the International Woman Suffrage Alliance'. *Jus Suffragii* 14.5, 1920, pp. 65–7.

Macmillan, Chrystal. *Disabilities of the Married Woman and Inequalities in the Law between Husband and Wife*. London: NUSEC, 1922.

Macmillan, Chrystal. 'The Present Position of Women Internationally' (1923). In Evelyn Gates (ed.), *Women's Year Book 1923–1924*, pp. 21–9. London: Women's Publishers, n.d.

Macmillan, Chrystal. *The Coverture Disabilities (Abolition) Bill*. London: NUSEC, 1925.

Macmillan, Chrystal. 'Nationality of Married Women: Present Tendencies'. *Journal of Comparative Legislation and International Law*, 3rd ser., 7 (1925), pp. 142–54.

Macmillan, Chrystal. 'Legal Position of Women'. *Encyclopaedia Britannica* 14th edition, 1929, s.v.

Macmillan, Chrystal. 'The Nationality of Married Women'. Paper presented at 5th Conference of the International Federation of University Women, Geneva 13 August 1929.

Macmillan, Chrystal. *The Nationality of Married Women*. London: The Nationality of Married Women Pass the Bill Committee, 1931.

Macmillan, Chrystal. *Weightlifting and the Heavy Trades, Including Mining*. London: ODI, 1931.

Macmillan, Chrystal. 'Married Women'. *New Statesman and Nation* 9 (1935), p. 10.

Macmillan, Chrystal. *The Nationality of Married Women*. London: The Nationality of Married Women Pass the Bill Committee, 1938.

Macmillan, Chrystal. *Weightlifting, the Heavy Trades and the Woman Earner*. London: ODI, n.d.

Macmillan, Chrystal, Stritt, Marie and Verone, Maria. *Woman Suffrage in Practice*. London and New York: IWSA, NUWSS, NAWSA, 1913.
MacQueen, Hector. 'Scotland's First Women Law Graduates: An Edinburgh Centenary'. *Stair Society* 54 (2009), miscellany VI.
Marlow, Joyce (ed.). *Virago Book of Women and the Great War*. London: Virago, 1999.
Middle Temple. *Chrystal Macmillan Memorial Prize. Chrystal Macmillan: Biographical Sketch*. London: Middle Temple, 1937.
Miller, Carol. 'Lobbying the League: Women's International Organisations and the League of Nations'. DPhil thesis, University of Oxford, 1992. https://ora.ox.ac.uk/objects/uuid:f517ac72-18b3-42b2-9728-31129462bf4a/files/m8a9dc648f42c02edbce251148cef4f41.
Molinari, Véronique. 'Educating and Mobilizing the New Voter: Interwar Handbooks and Female Citizenship in Great Britain, 1918–1931'. *Journal of International Women's Studies* 15.1 (2014). http://vc.bridgew.edu/jiws/vol15/iss1/2.
Moore, Lindy. *Bajanellas and Semilinas: Aberdeen University and the Education of Women 1860–1920*. Aberdeen: Aberdeen University Press, 1991.
Morris, Caroline. 'Dr Ivy Williams: Inside yet Outside'. *Women's History Review* 29.4 (2020), pp. 583–614. https://doi.org/10.1080/09612025.2019.1702783.
Mossman, Mary J. *The First Women Lawyers: A Comparative Study of Gender, Law and the Legal Professions*. London: Hart Publishing, 2006.
Noakes, Laura. 'Chrystal MacMillan and Elsie Bowerman: First Women Barristers' Negotiation of Professional and Political Identities'. PhD thesis, Open University, 2021.
Offen, K. (ed.). *Globalizing Feminisms 1789–1945*. London: Routledge, 2010.
Ogilvie Gordon, Maria. *A Handbook of Employments Specially Prepared for the Use of Boys and Girls on Entering the Trades, Industries, and Professions*. Aberdeen: Rosemount Press, 1908.
O'Havery, Richard (ed.). *History of the Middle Temple*. London: Hart Publishing, 2011.
Oldfield, Sybil. *Spinsters of This Parish*. London: Virago, 1984.
Oldfield, Sybil. *Women Humanitarians: A Biographical Dictionary of British Women Active between 1900 and 1950*. London: Continuum, 2001.
Page, Dorothy. 'A Married Woman, or a Minor, Lunatic or Idiot: The Struggle of British Women against Disability in Nationality 1914–33'. PhD thesis, University of Otago, 1984.
Panayi, Panikos. *The Enemy in Our Midst: Germans in Britain during the First World War*. Oxford: Berg Publishers, 1991.
Pankhurst, Sylvia. *The Home Front: A Mirror to Life in England during the First World War*. London: Hutchinson, 1987; first pub. 1932.
Patterson, David S. *The Search for Negotiated Peace: Women's Activism and Citizen Diplomacy in World War One*. New York: Routledge, 2008.

Pedersen, Susan. *Eleanor Rathbone and the Politics of Conscience.* New Haven and London: Yale University Press, 2004.

Pepitone, Ren. 'Gender Space and Ritual: Women Barristers, the Inns of Court and the Interwar Press'. *Journal of Women's History* (Spring 2016), pp. 60–83.

Picton-Turbervill, Edith. *Life Is Good: An Autobiography.* Frederick Muller, 1939.

Pierson, Ruth Roach (ed.). *Women and Peace: Theoretical, Historical and Practical Perspectives.* Beckenham: Croom Helm, 1987.

Pipes, Rose. 'Chrystal Macmillan (1872–1937): A Scotswoman at the Inn'. *The Middle Templar* (Michaelmas 2014), pp. 44–6.

Polden, Patrick. 'Portia's Progress: Women at the Bar in England, 1919–1939'. *International Journal of the Legal Profession* 12.3 (Nov. 2005), pp. 293–338.

Pugh, Martin. *The March of the Women: A Revisionist Analysis of the Campaign for Women's Suffrage 1866–1914.* Oxford: Oxford University Press, 1994.

Pugh, Martin. *Votes for Women in Britain 1867–1928.* London: Historical Association, 1994.

Putnam, Robert. 'Diplomacy and Domestic Politics: The Logic of Two-level Games'. *International Organization* 42 (1988), pp. 427–60.

Rackley, Erika and Auchmuty, Rosemary (eds). *Women's Legal Landmarks: Celebrating the History of Women and Law in the UK and Ireland.* London: Hart Publishing, 2019.

Rae, Lettice Milne. *Ladies in Debate: Being a History of the Ladies Edinburgh Debating Society.* Edinburgh: Oliver & Boyd, 1936.

Ramsay, G. M. N. 'Foundation and Government'. In Julia Grant, J. McCutcheon and E. Saunders (eds), *St Leonards School 1877–1927*, pp. 3–23. London: Oxford University Press, 1927.

Rennes, J. 'Legal Distinctions or Discriminations? Political Strategies and Epistemological Challenges'. *Politix* (2011), translation. http://www.cairn-int.info/journal-politix-2011-2-page-35.htm.

Rupp, Leila. *Worlds of Women: The Making of an International Women's Movement.* Princeton: Princeton University Press, 1997.

Rupp, Leila and Taylor, Verta. 'Forging a Feminist Identity in an International Movement: A Collective Identity Approach to Twentieth Century Feminism'. *Signs* 24.2 (Winter 1999), pp. 363–86.

Sandell, Marie. '"A Real Meeting of the Women of the East and the West": Women and Internationalism in the Interwar Period'. In Daniel Laqua (ed.), *Internationalism Reconfigured: Transnational Ideas and Movements between the World Wars*, pp. 161–85. London: I. B. Tauris, 2011.

Schwimmer, R. and Macmillan, Chrystal. *Memorandum*, August. Boulder Archive, 1915.

Shafer, Elizabeth. *Lilian Baylis: A Biography.* Hatfield: University of Hertfordshire Press and The Society for Theatre Research, 2006.

Sharp, Evelyn. 'The Congress and the Press'. In *Toward Permanent Peace: A Record of the Women's International Congress.* London: British Committee of the Women's International Congress, 1915.

Staff, Michelle. 'Women's Rights on the World Stage: Feminism and Internationalism in the Life of Chrystal Macmillan (1972–1937)'. *Journal of Women's History* 32.3 (Fall 2020), pp. 38–63. https://doi.org/10.1353/jowh.2020.0026.

Stansfeld Trust. 'Origins'. London: Women's Library, LSE, 1896.

Stanton, Theodore (ed.). *The Woman Question in Europe: A Series of Original Essays*. London: Sampson Low, Marston Searle & Rivington, 2015.

Stenton, M. and Lees, S. *Who's Who of British Members of Parliament*. Vol. III. Atlantic Highlands, NJ: Harvester Press, 1979.

Stokes, Dorothy Scott. 'A Woman Barrister's Views'. *Graya* 8 (1931), p. 29.

Storr, Katherine. *Excluded from the Record: Women, Refugees and Relief 1914–1929*. Bern: Peter Lang, 2010.

Stretton, Tim and Kesselring, Krista (eds). *Married Women and the Law: Coverture in England and the Common Law*. Montreal: McGill–Queen's University Press, 2015.

Tabili, Laura. 'Outsiders in the Land of Their Birth: Exogamy, Citizenship and Identity in War and Peace'. *Journal of British Studies* 44.4 (Oct. 2005), pp. 796–815. https://www.jstor.org/stable/10.1086/431942.

Takayangi, Mari. 'Parliament and Women, c.1900–1945'. PhD thesis, Kings College London, 2012.

Takayanagi, Mari. 'Sex Disqualification (Removal) Act 1919'. In Erika Rackley and Rosemary Auchmuty (eds), *Women's Legal Landmarks: Celebrating the History of Women and Law in the UK and Ireland*, pp. 133–9. Oxford: Hart Publishing, 2019.

Takayanagi, Mari. 'Sacred Year or Broken Reed? The Sex Disqualification (Removal) Act 1919'. *Women's History Review* 29.4 (2020), pp. 563–82. https://doi.org/10.1080/09612025.2019.1702782.

Taylor, Marsali. *Women's Suffrage in Shetland*. Self-published, 2010. https://www.lulu.com/shop/marsali-taylor/womens-suffrage-in-shetland/ebook/product-1j9g25mv.html?q=Marsali+Taylor&page=1&pageSize=4.

Thomas, Anna Braithwaite. *St Stephen's House: Friends Emergency Work in England 1914 to 1920*. London: Friends Emergency Committee for the Assistance of Germans, Austrians and Hungarians in Distress, n.d.

UN Women. 'Facts and Figures: Women's Leadership and Political Participation'. 2023. https://www.unwomen.org/en/what-we-do/leadership-and-political-participation/facts-and-figures#:~:text=Women%27s%20equal%20participation%20and%20leadership,political%20life%20is%20far%20off.

Vellacott, Jo. 'Feminist Consciousness and the First World War'. In Ruth Roach Pierson (ed.), *Women and Peace: Theoretical, Historical and Practical Perspectives*, pp. 114–36. Beckenham: Croom Helm, 1987.

Vellacott, Jo. *From Liberal to Labour with Women's Suffrage: The Story of Catherine Marshall*. Montreal and Kingston: McGill–Queen's University Press, 1993.

Vellacott, Jo. *Pacifists, Patriots and the Vote: The Erosion of Democratic Suffragism in Britain during the First World War*. Basingstoke: Palgrave Macmillan, 2007.

Wales, Julia G. *The International Plan for Continuous Mediation without Armistice*. Chicago: Women's Peace Party, 1915.
Walker, H. Newton. 'Women and the Bar'. *The Englishwoman* 42 (April–June 1919), pp. 129–34.
Whitelaw, Lis. *The Life and Rebellious Times of Cicely Hamilton*. London: The Women's Press, 1990.
Wilson, Francesca. *In the Margins of Chaos*. New York: Macmillan, 1945.
Wiltsher, Anne. *Most Dangerous Women: Feminist Peace Campaigners of the Great War*. London: Pandora Press, 1985.
Zimmerman, Susan. 'Equality of Women's Economic Status? A Major Bone of Contention in the International Gender Politics Emerging during the Interwar Period'. *International History Review* 41.1 (2017), pp. 200–27. http://dx.doi.org/10.1080/07075332.2017.1395761.

Index

Note: page numbers in **bold** refer to figures

Abbott, Elizabeth, **115**, 142, 177, 180, 181, 183
Aberdeen, Lady, 47, 66, 102, 103, 120, 150, 168
Aberdeen University Women's Suffrage Association, 45
Aberdeen Women's Suffrage Society, 10
Actresses Franchise League (AFL), 183
Addams, Jane, **72**, 75, 78, 79, **80**, 200
AFL *see* Actresses Franchise League (AFL)
Aliens Restriction Act 1914, 149
Allen, Archibald, 96
Alness, Lord, 178
Amery, Leo, 156
AMSH *see* Association for Moral and Social Hygiene (AMSH)
Amtsberg, Alwine (second wife of John Macmillan), 14, 17
Archdale, Helen, 9, 168–9, 170
Ashby, Margery Corbett, 48, 111, 120, 156, **161**, 163, 166, 166–7, 169
Asquith, Herbert, 42–3, 45, 46, 54, 73, 127
Association for Moral and Social Hygiene (AMSH), 3, 87, 94–8, 134, 177
  Police Court Rota Committee, 95, 97, 194
Atkinson, Evelyn, 49
Auchmuty, Rosemary, 128

Bakker-Nort, Betsy, 161, 163
Balch, Emily, 74, **76**, 78, 200
Balfour, Lord and Lady, 180
Ballantyne, Andrew, 50, **51**
Barristers and Solicitors (Qualification of Women) Bill, 130
Barry, Florence, 172
Baylis, Lilian, 181–2
Bebb, Gwynedd, 126, 129
Belmont, Alva, 170
Benes, Edvard, 121
Bethune-Baker, Edith, 88
BFUW *see* British Federation of University Women (BFUW)
Box Hill, 181–3
British Empire, 42, 101, 135, 150, 151, 156
British Federation of University Women (BFUW), 158, 159, 160
British Nationality and Status of Aliens Act 1914, 92, 147, 148–51, 153
Brittain, Vera, 2, 98, 180
Buckmaster, Lord, 129–30
Bush, Julia, 90–1

Cadbury, Elizabeth, 103
Campbell, Sybil, 158, 159, 160
Catt, Carrie Chapman, 57, 68, 105, **105**, **110**, 180
Cave, Bertha, 127
Cecil, Lord Robert, 69, 82, 127

Church League for Women's Suffrage, 128
Coit, Adela Stanton, 57, 105, **105**, 106, 108, **110**
Committee for the Opening of the Legal Profession to Women (COLPW), 3, 129, 130, 131, 194
Committee of Women Graduates of the Scottish Universities, 23, 26–7, 33, 193
The Common Cause, 38, 44–5, 136
Conciliation Bills, 43, 46
Conference on Women's Representation in the League of Nations, 1919, 108–9
Consultative Committee of Constitutional Women's Suffrage Societies *see* Women's Consultative Committee (WCC)
Cooley, Winifred Harper, 104
Cooper, Sandi, 83
Corstorphine Hill House, 6–7, 13, 14, 16–17, 18, 19n
Costello, Karin, 126, 129
Council for the Representation of Women at the League of Nations, 109, 119–20, 188
Courtney, Katherine, 49, 70
Cowan, Ialeen Gibson, 182, 183–4
Crane, Robert Newton, 98, 134, 136
Crewe, Lord, 78
Crofts, Maud, 126
Crowdy, Rachel, 97

Davy, Beatrice Honour, 137
Defence of the Realm Act (DORA), 92–3, 95
Dickinson, Sir Willoughby, 96–7, 150, 151, 153
disarmament, 60, 198
Divorce Law Amendment Bill, 94
Donzé, Isobel, 177, 180
Dove, Frances, 10–11, **12**
Drummond, Flora, 1, 169
  Drummond-Pankhurst combination, 44
Drummond, Sir Eric, 78, 97, 109, 111

Edinburgh Association for the University Education of Women (EAUEW), 13
Edinburgh Ladies Education Association (ELEA), 13, 21
Edinburgh National Society for Women's Suffrage (ENSWS), 33, 37, 39, 42, 50, 52, 104
Edinburgh Town Council, 42–3
Edinburgh University
  Chrystal Macmillan Building, 4, **4**
  electorate voting rights, 22–4
  and secondary education for girls, 21
  women students, 13–14, 21, 22
Edinburgh University Women's Suffrage Society (EUWSS), 37, 42
ELEA *see* Edinburgh Ladies Education Association (ELEA)
Elmy, Elizabeth Wolstenholme, 24
Encyclopaedia Britannica, 1, 94, 143
ENSWS *see* Edinburgh National Society for Women's Suffrage (ENSWS)
Equal Franchise Act 1928, 56, 61
Equal Rights International (ERI), 113, 162, 166, 168–9, 170, 171
EUWSS *see* Edinburgh University Women's Suffrage Society (EUWSS)
Evans, Dorothy, 162, 169–71

Facts versus Fancies on Woman Suffrage (Macmillan), 104
Fawcett, Millicent, 24, 32, 37, 48, 49, 50, **51**, 52, 53, 54, 55, 67, 73–4, **105**, 111, 150, 191
  relationship with Chrystal Macmillan, 57, 104–5, 106, 107–8, 190
  and world peace, 65, 68, 69–70
Freeman, Marshall, 141, 180–1

gender equality, 60–1
General Councils of the Universities, 22, 25, 28
  Register of General Council, 23
Gilman, Charlotte Perkins, 102
Glasgow and West of Scotland Association for Women's Suffrage (GWSAWS), 50

Gordon, Maria Ogilvie, 91, 102, 119, 120, 150
Gray, Frances, 127
Guardianship of Infants Bill, 88
GWSAWS *see* Glasgow and West of Scotland Association for Women's Suffrage (GWSAWS)

Hall, Margaret, 126
Hamilton, Cicely, 180, 181–3
Hansen, Ingeborg, 113
Henderson, Mary, **51**, 53
Hills, John, 127, 129, 131
Hooper, Edith, 27, 31, 35n
House of Lords Scottish graduates case *see* Scottish women graduates' case
How-Martin, Edith, 130–1
Hubback, Eva, 88–9
Hurst, Sir Cecil, 155

ICW *see* International Council of Women (ICW)
ICWPP *see* International Committee of Women for Permanent Peace (ICWPP)
IFUW *see* International Federation of University Women (IFUW)
ILO *see* International Labour Organisation (ILO)
Inglis, Elsie, 22, 33, 40, 50, **51**, 53
Ingram, Maud, 127
International Alliance of Women for Suffrage and Equal Citizenship (IAWSEC), 112, 160, 168
International Committee of Women for Permanent Peace (ICWPP), 79
Zurich Congress 1919, 81–2, 83
International Confederation of Christian Trade Unions, 117
International Council of Women (ICW), 3, 82, 101, 102–3, 104, 113, 120, 121, 159, 160, 162, 166, 189
peace work, 66–7
Quinquennial Congress, Toronto 1909, 18, 102
Rome Congress 1914, 102
survey of nationality issues, 150–1

International Federation of University Women (IFUW), 101, 113–14, 122, 163, 168
International Inquiry Bureau, 107
International Labour Organisation (ILO), 114–19, 122
Committee of Experts on Women's Work, 117, 118
International Law Association, 155–6
International Standing Committee on the Legal Position of Women, 94, 133–4
International Woman Suffrage Alliance (IWSA), 3, 18, 32, 49, 50, 65–6, 67–8, 73, 82, 83, 101, 103–13, 121, 148, 150, 189, 190
British Overseas Committee, 111
Budapest Congress, 57, 104, 105, **105**
cancellation of IWSA Berlin congress, 68–70
Committee on the Nationality of Married Women, 111, 112
Geneva Congress, 1920, 110–11, **110**
International Manifesto of Women, 67, 106
Istanbul Congress, 1935, 112
IWSA Board, 1913, **105**, 112
and links with the press, 105
and peace work, 67–8
planning an alternative congress, 70–1
relief work, 106–7
Rome Congress, 1923, 111–12, **112**
Stockholm Congress 1911, 104
wide-ranging agenda and international reach, 103–4
International Women's Congress, 1915, 3, 65, 70, 83, 93, 102–3, 121, 190–1
cancellation and planning an alternative, 68–71
criticism of, 73
at The Hague, 71–4, **72**
resolutions 1915, 71, 73, 79, 198
resolutions 1919, 81–2
visits by envoys to political leaders 1915, 74–9, 199–200

International Women's Relief
  Committee, IWSA, 54, 106–7
IWSA *see* International Woman Suffrage
  Alliance (IWSA)

Jacobs, Aletta, 68, 70, **72**, 75, 78, **110**, 200
Jex-Blake, Sophia, 13
Joint Standing Committee of Women's
  International Organisations for
  Securing the Appointment of
  Women to the International and
  Expert Committees of the League of
  Nations, 120
Jus Suffragii, 67, 68, 69, 71, 105, 107, 149–50
Justices of the Peace (Qualification of
  Women) Bill, 131

Kidd, Margaret, 131
King, Elspeth, 1–2
Knight, Holford, 127, 128, 130

La Fédération Internationale des
  femmes Magistrats et Avocats, 113
Labour Party, 45, 47–8, 59
Law Society, 126, 130
Le Sueur, Winifred, 119
League of Nations, 4, 39, 73, 81, 82, 97, 101
  Codification Conference on
    International Law, 1930, 113, 158–60, 163, 165
  Constitution, 111, 187–8
  Consultative Committee on Women's
    Nationality, 113–14, 120, 122, 148, 162–8, 189
  International Women's Office, 108
  and married women's nationality, 113–14
  organisational tensions and
    personality differences, 168–71
  women and women's organisations, 119–21
  Women's Charter, 109, 191
  women's representation, 108–10, 111, 113, 119–20, 187–8

legal profession, 125–46
  Barristers and Solicitors (Qualification
    of Women) Bill, 130
  Bebb v. the Law Society, 126–7, 129
  costs of qualifying, 134
  court appearances, 139–43
  dock briefs and Poor Prisoner's
    Defence (PPD) cases, 139–41
  Edward Barnicoat rape case, 139–40
  exam results, 135–6
  lavatory facilities for women, 138–9
  Legal Profession (Admission of
    Women) Bill, 127
  Macmillan's call to the Bar, 3–4, 82, 112, 131, 135, 136
  mess memberships, 136–8
  Middle Temple rules affecting women, 135
  seniority among women barristers, 138
  Solicitors (Qualification of Women)
    Bill, 129
  women's efforts to pursue a legal
    career, 126–31
  working within the profession, 131–43, **132**
Leneman, Leah, 1–2
Liaison Committee of Women's
  International Organisations, 113, 120, 121
Liberal Party, 43, 46, 47, 59
Liverpool Suffrage Society, 48
London Society for Women's Suffrage, 53, 57
Lumsden, Louisa, 10
Lyttelton, Dame Edith, 160, 165

McIlquham, Helen, 24
MacLaren, Eveline, 127
McLaren, Lord, 26, 29–30
McLaren, Patricia Bright, 26, 33, 37
Macmillan, Chrystal, **51**, **58**, **72**, **76**, **80**, **105**, **110**, **112**, **115**, **161**, **189**
  appeal to the House of Lords, 27–32, **27**, 33, 186
  aspiration to be an MP, 57–61, 133
  in Berlin, 14
  campaign for women's suffrage, 37–43, **44**

chair of Scottish Federation, 52, 53
committee work for national and
  international organisations,
  188–90, 194–6
criticism of, 57
death, 177
education, 7, 9–13, **12**, 18–19
family background and early life, 4–9,
  8, 9
family recollections of, 183–4
illness, 119, 177, 184
memorials, 180, 183
moves to London, 18
NUWSS Executive Committee
  membership, 46–50
obituaries, 97–8, 141, 142, 178–9,
  180–1
post-university years in Edinburgh,
  16–18
public speaking and lectures, 38–42,
  43, 46, 60–1, **112**, 115–16, 118–19,
  125–6, 129, 131
recollections of, 180–3
referred to as the 'Scottish Portia',
  125–6
relationships within the suffrage
  movement, 56–7, 104–5, 106,
  107–8, 169–71, 190
representation of women, 187–8
reputation, 1, 32, 34, 57, 61
at university, 13–14, **15**, 21
and women's citizenship, 191–2
see also legal profession; married
  women, nationality; world peace
Macmillan, George, 6, 7, **8**
Macmillan, Jessie Chrystal (née
  Finlayson) (mother), 6, 7, **8**, 19n
  death, 12, 13–14
Macmillan, John (father), 6–7, **8**
  death, 14, 16, **16**
Macmillan, Tom, 6, 7
Mair, John, 31
Mair, Sarah Siddons, 13, 17, 33, 50, **51**
Manchester Courier, 125
Manus, Rosa, 79, **161**
married women *see* nationality
Marshall, Catherine, 47, 49, 56, 70
Meller, Eugenie, **115**, 166

Melrose Tea Company, 6, 7
Melville, Frances, 22, **27**, 33, 177, 180
Middle Temple, 3, 18, 19, 98, 130–4
Murray, Dorothy, 9–10, 11
Murray, Eunice, 9–10, 11, 17, 27, 30,
  101, 180, 190
  diary entries, 10, 14, 18, 39–40
Murray, Frances, 18
Murray, Sylvia, 9–10, 11, 32, 180

Nairn, Margaret, 22, 33
National Council for Combatting
  Venereal Diseases (NCCVD), 96, 97
National Council for the Unmarried
  Mother and Her Child (NCUMC),
  98, 134
National Council of Women (NCW),
  67, 90
  Nationality of Married Women Pass
    the Bill Committee (NMWPBC),
    157–8, 162, 189
National Federation of Women
  Workers, 67
National Insurance Bill, 91–2
National Union of Societies for Equal
  Citizenship (NUSEC), 3, 55–6, 61,
  87–90, 157, 158
National Union of Women Workers
  (NUWW) (later National Council
  of Women), 3, 17, 18, 57, 67, 90–4,
  102–3, 125, 128–9, 130, 148, 149,
  151, 160, 189
  Legislation Committee, 92–4, 133
  and the National Insurance Bill, 91–2
National Union of Women's Suffrage
  Societies (NUWSS), 37–8, 39, 43,
  44, 51, 55, 73–4, 83, 104–5, 189,
  190
  Annual Council, 1915, 48–9
  attitude to war, 48–9
  attitude to WSPU violence, 43–5
  deputation to the Lord Advocate, 46
  Electoral Fighting Fund (EFF), 47, 48,
    52–3
  Executive Committee, 46–50
  Organisation Committee, 46–7, 56–7
  Parliamentary Committee, 47
  peace education discussion, 49

politics and tensions between the Scottish Federation and NUWSS Executive, 50, 52–4
Quarterly Council meeting, 1909, 45
summer schools, 57, **58**
support for Labour Party, 47–8
see also National Union of Societies for Equal Citizenship (NUSEC)
nationality, married women, 3–4, 82, 92, 94, 107, 113, 134, 147–76, 186
British Nationality and Status of Aliens Act 1914, 147, 148–51
changing attitudes of the British government, 156–8
demonstrations, 160, **161**
divisions in the WCCN, 165–8
first League of Nations Codification Conference on International Law, 1930, 158–60
first responses at the League of Nations to the Codification Conference, 163, 165
International Committee for Action on Nationality of Married Women, 162
International Law Association Annual Conference 1923, 155–6
Joint Select Committee of the House of Commons and the House of Lords, Macmillan's testimony, 154–5
Macmillan's campaigning, 147–8, 149–50, 155–8, 191–2
Nationality of Married Women Bill (1922), 151
Nationality of Married Women Pass the Bill Committee, 157–8, 189
organisational tensions and personality differences at the League of Nations, 168–71
rights to nationality in British law, 172
survey of nationality issues, 150–1
wives' destitution and hardship cases, 149–50, 151–4
Women's Consultative Committee on Nationality (WCCN), 162–8, **164**

NCCVD *see* National Council for Combatting Venereal Diseases (NCCVD)
NCUMC *see* National Council for the Unmarried Mother and Her Child (NCUMC)
NCW *see* National Council of Women (NCW)
Neilans, Alison, 94–5
Nettlefold, Lucy, 126, 158
Noakes, Laura, 126
Normanton, Helena, 129–30, 135–6, 137, 138, 141
North Edinburgh Liberal Association, 59
Nottingham Evening Post, 31
NUSEC *see* National Union of Societies for Equal Citizenship (NUSEC)
NUWSS *see* National Union of Women's Suffrage Societies (NUWSS)
NUWW *see* National Union of Women Workers (NUWW)

Open Door Council (ODC), 90, 114, 189
Open Door International (ODI), 101, 114–19, **115**, 121, 189
Prague Conference 1933, 117–18
Orcadian Women's Suffrage Association, 41
Orme, Eliza, 127

Pankhurst, Christabel, 1, 38, 127
Pankhurst, Emmeline, 38
Pankhurst, Sylvia, 68
Parliamentary elections, 2, 22, 28, 31, 34, 39, 47, 48, 59–61, 92, 184, 186, 187
Paul, Alice, **115**, 148, 163, 166, 167
relationship with Macmillan, 169–71
Pedder, Sir John, 154
Pethick-Lawrence, Emmeline, 70
Pethick-Lawrence, Lord Frederick, 172
Picton-Turbervill, Edith, 181–2, 183
Polden, Patrick, 134, 136, 141
prostitution, 95–7
public morality, 93, 95–7

Radziwill, Princess Gabrielle, 166–7
Rathbone, Eleanor, 3, 47, 48, 54, 55, 87, 89–90, **110**
refugees, 106–7
relief work, 48, 53, 54, 106–7, 148
Representation of the People Act 1918, 55, 99, 129
Representation of the People (Equal Franchise) Act 1928, 61, 187
Representation of the People (Scotland) Act 1868, 22
Rhondda, Lady, 99, 177
Rupp, Leila, 101

St Andrews University, 9, 17, 22–3
St Leonards School, 7, 9–13, **12**, 18–19
Salvesen, Lord, 24, 25–6, 29
school boards, 28, 29, 36n
Schreiber-Favre, Nelly, 113, 163
Schuster, Lily van der Schalk, **161**, 162, 169
Schwimmer, Rosika, **72**, 74, 75, **76**, 78, **105**, 200
Scottish Federation of Women's Suffrage Societies (SFWSS), 10, 17, 37, 50, **51**, 125
  politics and tensions between the Scottish Federation and NUWSS Executive, 50, 52–4
  Scottish Women's Hospital for Foreign Service, 53, 54, 188
  war relief work, 53
Scottish Home Rule Bill, 50, 52
Scottish National Party (SNP), 60
Scottish University Women's Suffrage Union (SUWSU), 17, 41, 43
Scottish women graduates' case, 2–3, 13, 18, 21–36, 38, 61, 125–6
  appeal to the House of Lords, 27–32, **27**, 186
  Court of Session in Edinburgh, 24–7
  decision to refuse voting papers for women graduates, 23–4
  legal incapacity issue, 22, 25, 29–30
  newspaper reports, 31, 33, 34

suffragists' reaction to the appeal dismissal, 32–3
  university electorate voting rights, 22–3
Scottish Women's Hospital for Foreign Service, 53, 54, 188
Scottish Women's Liberal Federation, 46
Sex Disqualification (Removal) Act 1919, 1, 3, 99, 125, 131, 143
SFWSS *see* Scottish Federation of Women's Suffrage Societies (SFWSS)
Sheepshanks, Mary, 71, 107–8
Simson, Frances, 13, 22, 27, **27**, 30, 32, 33, **44**
SNP *see* Scottish National Party (SNP)
Sorabji, Cornelia, 127
Staff, Michelle, 101
Standing Committee of the Scottish District Unions of Women Workers, 102
Stansfeld Trust, 93
Stevens, Dorothy, 170
Stewart, Eleanor, 59
Strachey, Ray, 129, 130
Stritt, Marie, 104, **110**, 150–1
'The Struggle for Political Liberty' (pamphlet), 38
Stuart, Josephine Gordon, 127
SUWSU *see* Scottish University Women's Suffrage Union (SUWSU)
Swanwick, Helena, 96

Takayangi, Mari, 55

Universities (Scotland) Act 1889, 13, 21, 22, 28, 29

venereal disease, 95–6
Verone, Maria, 104, 162
Versailles, Treaty of, 81–2, 101
Votes for Women, 38

Waddell, Helen, 22–3
Wales, Julia Grace, 74, 75–6
Walkington, Letitia, 127
WCC *see* Women's Consultative Committee (WCC)

WCCN *see* Women's Consultative Committee on Nationality (WCCN)
WFL, *see* Women's Freedom League (WFL)
Williams, Ivy, 143, 158–60
WILPF *see* Women's International League for Peace and Freedom (WILPF)
Wilson, Florence, 111
Wilson, President Woodrow, 78, 200
  Fourteen Points, 79
Wolmer, Lord, 127
Woman Suffrage in Practice (Macmillan), 104
Woman's Yearbook 1924, 94
Women Graduates' Committee, 17–18, 23, 26–7, 28, 33
women workers
  discriminatory insurance schemes, 117, 118
  Night Work Convention, 115, 118
  pregnant women, 116–17
  right to paid employment, 116, 119
  Women Workers' Charter, 114
Women's Charter, 39, 82, 109, 191
Women's Consultative Committee on Nationality (WCCN), 162–8, **164**
  divisions in the WCCN, 165–8
  first responses at the League of Nations to the Codification Conference, 163, 165
  Propaganda Sub-committee, 166–7
  withdrawal of Macmillan and Ashby, 166–7, 170–1
Women's Consultative Committee (WCC), 54–5
Women's Cooperative Guild, 67
Women's Debating Society, 17
Women's Freedom League (WFL), 33, 38, 39, 43, 130
Women's International League for Peace and Freedom (WILPF), 3, 65, 75, 82, 83, 101, 189, 191
Women's Labour League, 67
The Women's Leader, 55, 131
Women's Representative Committee, 14
Women's Social and Political Union (WSPU), 33, 38, 39, 42, 43, 45

women's suffrage, 1–3, 10
  anti-suffrage perspective, 42
  changing public attitudes, 54
  Chrystal Macmillan's campaign in Scotland, 37–43
  Chrystal Macmillan's relationships within the movement, 56–7
  committee work 1919–28, 55–6
  committee work up to 1919, 45–50, 54–5
  demonstrations, 43, **44**
  deputation to Edinburgh Town Council, 42–3
  harmony and discord within the movement, 43–5
  and the local government register, 55
  newspaper reports, 41, 42, 43–5
  non-violent campaign measures, 38
  political progress, lack of, 45–6
  processions, 39, 42
  public meetings and speaking, 38–42, 43
  Scottish Federation, 50–4, **51**
  violence, 42, 43–4, 45
Women's Suffrage Record, 26
'Women's Work and Labour Laws: A Survey of Protective Legislation (ILO), 118
Women's Work (ILO), 116
world peace, 65–86, **76**, 190–1
  1915 Hague Congress, 71–4, **72**
  1919 Zurich Congress, 80, 81–2
  cancellation of 1915 IWSA conference and planning an alternative, 68–71
  envoys from the Hague congress to governments, 74–9, **76**, 77, 83, 199–200
  peace work with the International Council of Women (ICW), 66–7
  peace work with the International Women's Suffrage Alliance (IWSA), 67–8
WSPU *see* Women's Social and Political Union (WSPU)

Zimmerman, Susan, 114

EU representative:
Easy Access System Europe
Mustamäe tee 50, 10621 Tallinn, Estonia
Gpsr.requests@easproject.com

www.ingramcontent.com/pod-product-compliance
Lightning Source LLC
Chambersburg PA
CBHW051123160426
43195CB00014B/2312